The Internet Book

The Series of Internetworking Books
from Douglas Comer and Prentice Hall

Internetworking with TCP/IP, Volume I: Principles, Protocols, and Architecture, 2nd edition, 1991.

Internetworking with TCP/IP, Volume II: Design, Implementation, and Internals (with D. Stevens), 2nd edition, 1994.

Internetworking with TCP/IP, Volume III: Client-Server Programming and Applications (with D. Stevens).

BSD Socket Version, 1992.
AT&T TLI Version, 1993.

The Internet Book: Everything you need to know about computer networking and how the Internet works, 1994.

The Internet Book

Everything you need to know about computer networking and how the Internet works

DOUGLAS E. COMER

Department of Computer Sciences
Purdue University
West Lafayette, IN 47907

PRENTICE HALL
Englewood Cliffs, New Jersey 07632

Library of Congress Cataloging-in-Publication Data

Comer, Douglas
     The Internet book : everything you need to know about computer
networking and how the Internet works / Douglas E. Comer.
          p. cm.
     Includes bibliographical references and index.
     ISBN 0-13-151565-9
     1. Internet (Computer network) I. Title.
TK5105.875.I57C65 1994
004.67--dc20   94-22316
                                       CIP

Acquisitions editor: ALAN APT
Production editor: IRWIN ZUCKER
Buyer: LINDA BEHRENS
Editorial assistant: SHIRLEY MCGUIRE

©1995 by Prentice-Hall, Inc.
A Simon & Schuster Company
Englewood Cliffs, New Jersey 07632

TRADEMARK INFORMATION: UNIX is a registered trademark of Unix System Laboratories, Inc.;
Compuserve is a trademark of Compuserve, Incorporated; Prodigy is a registered trademark of Prodigy
Systems Inc.; America Online is a registered trademark of Quantum Computer Services Inc.

The author and publisher of this book have used their best efforts in preparing this book. These efforts
include the development, research, and testing of the theories and programs to determine their effectiveness.
The author and publisher make no warranty of any kind, expressed or implied, with regard to these programs
or the documentation contained in this book. The author and publisher shall not be liable in any event for
incidental or consequential damages in connection with, or arising out of, the furnishing, performance, or
use of these programs.

The map that appears on the inside cover of this book and on page 79 is copyright 1994 by Larry Landweber
and the Internet Society. Unlimited permission to copy or use is hereby granted subject to inclusion of this
copyright notice. This map may be obtained via anonymous ftp from ftp.cs.wisc.edu, connectivity_table
directory.

Printed in the United States of America

10 9 8 7 6 5 4 3

0-13-151565-9

Prentice-Hall International (UK) Limited, London
Prentice-Hall of Australia Pty. Limited, Sydney
Prentice-Hall Canada Inc., Toronto
Prentice-Hall Hispanoamericana, S.A., Mexico
Prentice-Hall of India Private Limited, New Delhi
Prentice-Hall of Japan, Inc., Tokyo
Simon & Schuster Asia Pte. Ltd., Singapore
Editora Prentice-Hall do Brasil, Ltda., Rio de Janeiro

To Everyone Who
Is Curious

This book was typeset by the author
and sent across the Internet in digital form.
It was then converted to a photographic
form that was used in printing.

About This Book

The Internet Book examines computer networking and the Internet from a nontechnical perspective. It explains how computers communicate, what the Internet is, how the Internet works, and what the Internet can do for you. No background is required because early chapters clearly explain the terminology and concepts.

The book focuses on fundamentals – it describes basic Internet capabilities and shows how they apply to a variety of services. When you finish reading, you will know what the Internet is, how it can be used, and why people find it so exciting. In addition, you will understand the origins of the Internet and why it is growing so rapidly. More important, you will understand the potential ways the Internet can change your life.

About The Author

Douglas Comer is a professor of computer science at Purdue University, where he teaches courses on computer operating systems and internetworking. One of the researchers who contributed to the Internet as it was being formed in the late 1970s and 1980s, he has served as a member of the Internet Architecture Board, the group responsible for guiding the Internet's development. In addition, he has written a popular series of textbooks that describe the technical details of the Internet, and presents lectures on the subject around the world.

Professor Comer has had direct Internet access from his home since 1981, and uses the Internet daily. He wrote this book as a response to everyone who has asked him for an explanation of the Internet that is both technically correct and easily understood by anyone. An Internet enthusiast, Comer displays *INTRNET* on the license plate of his car.

Acknowledgements

The author thanks many people who have contributed to this book. John Lin, Keith Rovell, Rob Slade, Christoph Schuba, and Charlotte Tubis read early drafts and made suggestions. Scott Comer provided a high-school perspective. As always, my wife, Chris, carefully edited the manuscript, solved many problems, and improved the wording.

Contents

Chapter 1   The Internet Has Arrived   **1**

The World Is Changing   1
Numbers Do Not Tell The Story   2
Learning About The Internet   3
Understanding The Big Picture   3
Terminology And Technology   4
Growth And Adaptability   4
The Impact Of The Internet   4
Organization Of The Book   4
A Personal Note   5

PART I   Introduction To Networking

Chapter 2   Telephones Everywhere   **9**

Introduction   9
A New Communication Service   9
Selling Communication   9
Limited Access   10
High Cost   11
The Difficult Transition   11
Ubiquitous Access   12
Relevance To The Internet   12

Chapter 3   The World Was Once Analog   15

Introduction   15
Sound, Vibrations, And Analog Recording   15
Analog Electronic Devices   16
Many Electronic Devices Are Analog   17
The First Analog Communication   17
Analog Is Simple But Inaccurate   17
Sending An Analog Signal Across A Wire   18
Digital Music   19
The Digital Revolution   19
Computers Are Digital   20
Digital Recording   20
Using Digital To Recreate Analog   21
Why Digital?   22
Summary   22

Chapter 4   The Once And Future Digital Network   25

Introduction   25
The World Was Once Digital   25
A Telegraph Is Digital   26
Morse Code   26
Letters And Digits In Morse Code   27
Users Did Not Encounter Morse Code   28
Virtually Instant Communication   28
Speed Is Relative   28
The Telephone Became Digital   29
Relevance To The Internet   29
Binary Encoding Of Data On The Internet   30
Summary   30

Chapter 5   Basic Communication   31

Introduction   31
Communication Using Electricity   31
Signals On Wires   32
Information Coding   32
Modems Allow Two-Way Traffic   33

A Character Code For Digital Information   34
Detecting Errors   36
Summary   37

Chapter 6   The Local Area Network Arrives   39

Introduction   39
Motivation   39
Interchangeable Media   40
A Computer Consists Of Circuit Boards   40
Circuit Boards Plug Into A Computer   40
Connecting One Computer To Another   41
LAN Technologies   42
Connecting A Computer To A LAN   43
The Importance Of LAN Technology   44
Relationship To The Internet   45

PART II   A Brief History Of The Internet

Chapter 7   Internet: The Early Years   49

Many Independent Networks   49
The Proliferation Of LANs   49
Facts About LANs   50
LANs Are Incompatible   51
Wide Area Technologies Exist   51
Few WANs, Many LANs   52
WANs and LANs Are Incompatible   52
The Desirability Of A Single Network   53
The Department Of Defense Had Multiple Networks   54
Connecting Disconnected Machines   54
The Internet Emerges   54
The ARPANET Backbone   55
Internet Software   55
The Name Is TCP/IP   55
The Shock Of An Open System   56
Open Systems Are Necessary   57
TCP/IP Documentation Is Online   57

The Military Adopts TCP/IP   58
Summary   58
A Personal Note   59

Chapter 8   A Decade Of Incredible Growth   **61**

Introduction   61
Disseminating The Software   61
Meanwhile, Back In Computer Science   62
The Internet Meets UNIX   62
The U.S. Military Makes A Commitment   63
The Internet Doubles In Size In One Year   63
Every Computer Science Department   64
Graduate Students Volunteer Their Time   65
The IAB evolves   65
The IETF   66
Doubling Again In A Year   66
The Internet Improves Science   66
NSF Takes A Leadership Role   67
Target: All Of Science And Engineering   67
NSF's Approach   68
The NSFNET Backbone   68
A Major Reorganization   68
The ANS Backbone   69
Exponential Growth   69
A Commercial Assessment   71
The End Of Growth   71

Chapter 9   The Global Internet   **73**

Introduction   73
Early ARPA Networks   73
Electronic Mail Among Computers   73
BITNET   74
Networks In Europe   74
EBONE: A European Backbone   76
EBONE Is The Top Level   76
Internet On Other Continents   77
The World Of Internet   78

A Personal Note   78

Chapter 10   A Global Information Infrastructure   81

Introduction   81
Existing Infrastructure   81
Communication Infrastructure   82
The Current Approach   84
The Internet Was Designed To Be General   85
The Internet Offers Diverse Information Services   85
TCP/IP Provides Communication Facilities   86
A Personal Note   86

PART III   How The Internet Works

Chapter 11   Packet Switching   89

Introduction   89
Sharing Saves Money   89
Sharing Introduces Delays   89
Sharing Wires   90
Selectable Channels   90
Sharing By Taking Turns   91
Packet Switching Avoids Delays   92
Each Packet Must Be Labeled   92
Computers Have Addresses   92
Packets Are Not All The Same Size   93
Packet Transmission Seems Instantaneous   93
Sharing Is Automatic   93
Network Hardware Handles Sharing   94
Many Devices Can Use Packet Switching   94
Relevance To The Internet   94
Summary   95

Chapter 12   Internet: A Network Of Networks   97

Introduction   97
Network Technologies Are Incompatible   97

Coping With Incompatibility   98
Two Fundamental Concepts   98
Using A Computer To Interconnect Networks   100
Interconnecting Computers Pass Packets   101
Interconnecting Computers Are Called Routers   102
Routers Are The Building Blocks Of The Internet   102
Routers Accommodate Multiple Types Of Networks   102
Routers Can Interconnect WANs And LANs   103
Dial-up Access For Personal Computers   104
Interconnecting Networks Was Revolutionary   105
Summary   105

Chapter 13   IP: Software To Create A Virtual Network   107

Introduction   107
Protocol: An Agreement For Communication   107
Basic Functionality: The Internet Protocol   108
IP Software On Every Machine   108
Internet Packets Are Called Datagrams   108
The Illusion Of A Giant Network   109
The Reality Of Internal Structure   110
Datagrams Travel In Packets   111
Every Computer Is Assigned A Unique Address   112
Internet Addresses   112
An Odd IP Address Syntax   112
IP Addresses Are Not Random   113
An Example Trip Through The Internet   113
Summary   114

Chapter 14   TCP: Software For Reliable Communication   115

Introduction   115
A Packet Switching System Can Be Overrun   115
TCP Helps IP Guarantee Delivery   117
TCP Provides A Connection Between Computer Programs   118
The Magic Of Recovering Lost Datagrams   118
TCP Retransmission Is Automatic   119
TCP And IP Work Together   119
Summary   120

Chapter 15   Clients + Servers = Distributed Computing   121

Introduction   121
Large Computers Use Networks For Input And Output   121
Small Computers Use Networks To Interact   122
Distributed Computing On The Internet   122
A Single Paradigm Explains All Distributed Computing   123
Programs Are Clients Or Servers   124
A Server Must Always Run   125
Summary   125

Chapter 16   Names For Computers   127

Introduction   127
People Prefer Names To Numbers   127
Naming A Computer Can Be Difficult Or Fun   128
Computer Names Must Be Unique   128
Suffixes On Computer Names   129
Names With Many Parts   130
Domain Names Outside The US   130
Translating A Name To An Equivalent IP Address   131
Domain Name System Works Like Directory Assistance   131
Computer Name Lookup Is Automatic   132
IP Addresses And Domain Names Are Unrelated   133
Summary   134

Chapter 17   Why The Internet Works Well   135

Introduction   135
The Internet Works Well   135
IP Provides Flexibility   136
TCP Provides Reliability   137
TCP/IP Software Was Engineered For Efficiency   137
TCP/IP Research Emphasized Practical Results   138
The Formula For Success   138
Summary   139

PART IV   Services Available On The Internet

Chapter 18   Electronic Mail   143

Introduction   143
Description Of Functionality   143
The Best Of All Worlds   144
Each User Has A Mailbox For E-mail   144
Sending An E-mail Message   144
Notification That E-mail has Arrived   144
Reading An E-mail Message   145
E-mail Messages Look Like Interoffice Memos   145
E-mail Software Fills In Header Information   146
How E-mail Works   147
Using E-mail From A Personal Computer   148
Mailbox Address Format   148
Abbreviations Make E-mail Friendly   149
Aliases Permit Arbitrary Abbreviations   149
Aliases Shared By All Users Of A Computer System   150
Sending To Multiple Recipients   150
Mailing List: An Alias for Multiple Recipients   151
Public Mailing Lists And Mail Exploders   151
E-mail To And From Non-Internet Sites   152
Access To Services Via E-mail   153
Speed, Reliability, And Expectations   153
Impact And Significance Of Electronic Mail   154
Joining A Mailing List   155

Chapter 19   Bulletin Board Service (Network News)   157

Introduction   157
Description Of Functionality   157
Many Bulletin Boards With Diverse Topics   158
Network News   159
Newsgroup Names   159
Obtaining Network News And The Software To Read Articles   160
How Network News Appears To A User   161
Checking For News Articles   161

Article Expiration 161
Reading Network News 162
Selecting Articles 162
Subscribing And Unsubscribing To Newsgroups 164
Submitting An Article 164
Moderated Newsgroups 164
Size Of Network News 165
How Network News Works 165
Redundant Newsfeeds And Duplicate Elimination 166
Relationship Between Netnews And Electronic Mail 167
Impact And Significance Of Network News And Mailing Lists 167
Hints And Conventions For Participating In Discussions 168
Summary 169

Chapter 20   File Transfer (FTP)   171

Introduction 171
Data Stored In Files 171
Copying A File 172
FTP Is Interactive 172
Example Commands 172
A Client Can Store Or Retrieve A File 173
Commands For Binary And Text File Format 173
Choosing ASCII or Binary Transfer 174
Commands For Authorization And Anonymous FTP 175
Listing The Contents Of A Remote Directory 175
Example Use Of FTP 175
Miscellaneous Commands 178
How FTP Works 179
Impact And Significance Of FTP 179
Summary 180

Chapter 21   Remote Login (TELNET)   181

Introduction 181
Users Access A Timesharing System Through Terminals 181
A Timesharing System Requires Accounting Information 182
Remote Login Resembles Conventional Login 183
Remote Login Provides General Access 183

Generality Makes Remote Login Powerful   184
Remote Login Accommodates Multiple Types Of Computers   184
How Remote Login Works   185
Escaping From Remote Login   186
Displays And Windows   186
Internet Remote Login Is Called TELNET   186
Using TELNET To Access Other Internet Services   187
Assessment Of Remote Login   187
Summary   188

Chapter 22   Information Browsing (Gopher)   189

Introduction   189
Description Of Functionality   189
Searching For Information   190
Tools To Aid Searching   190
Searching The Internet   190
An Example Information Browsing Service   191
Gopher Is Menu-Driven   191
A Menu Item Can Point To Another Computer   192
How Gopher Works   192
Gopher Has Two User Interfaces   193
Gopher's Point-And-Click Interface   193
Gopher's Textual Interface   195
An Example Trip Through Gopher   197
Backing Out Of A Browsing Session   203
Remembering A Menu   204
Gopher Remembers Locations In Bookmarks   204
Summary   205

Chapter 23   Advanced Browsing (WWW, Mosaic)   207

Introduction   207
Description Of Functionality   207
Menus Can Be Embedded In Text   208
The Importance Of Integrated Menus   209
Menus Embedded In Text Are Called Hypertext   210
Some Computers Have Multimedia Capabilities   211
Video And Audio References Can Be Embedded In Text   212

The World Wide Web   213
Mosaic Software Used To Access WWW   213
An Example Hypermedia Display   214
Recording The Location Of Information   216
How The World Wide Web Works   218
A URL Tells Mosaic Which Computer To Contact   219
A URL Tells Mosaic Which Server To Contact   219
Composing A Page Of Multimedia Information   219
Mosaic Provides Access To Multiple Services   219
Hotlists And Private WWW Documents   221
Getting Started With Mosaic   221
Summary   222
An Observation About Hypermedia Browsing   222

Chapter 24   Automated Title Search (Archie, Veronica)   223

Introduction   223
Description Of Functionality   223
Browsing Vs. Automated Searching   224
Automated Searching Proceeds By Name or Description   224
The Archie Directory Service   225
Multiple Archie Servers Handle The Load   225
How Archie Appears To A User   226
Archie Can Be Accessed Using A One-Line Command   227
Archie Can Be Accessed Using E-Mail   228
Archie Can Be Accessed Using TELNET   229
Archie Can Be Accessed With A Mouse   230
How Archie Works   230
A Second Search Tool Example   233
How Veronica Appears To A User   233
Veronica Displays Results As A Menu   234
Complex Search Patterns   234
How Veronica Works   235
Summary   235
A Comic Strip and A Joke   235

Chapter 25   Automated Contents Search (WAIS)   237

Introduction   237
Names Vs. Contents   237
Reading Vs. Scanning   238
Document Scanning Does Not Suffice   239
Automated Document Search Is Not New   239
The Wide Area Information Service   240
How WAIS Appears To A User   241
A Question Can Be Written in English   241
A User Chooses Among Collections Of Documents   242
Using A Mouse To Access WAIS   242
Selecting Among Sources   243
Posing A Question To WAIS   247
Retrieving A Document With WAIS   248
How WAIS Works   249
Special Computers Make WAIS Efficient   249
Summary   250

Chapter 26   Audio And Video Communication   251

Introduction   251
Description Of Functionality   251
Audio And Video Require Special Hardware   252
Radio Programs On The Internet   253
Audio Teleconferencing   253
A Cooperative Document Markup Service   254
Marking A Document   256
The Participants Discuss And Mark A Document   256
Video Teleconferencing   257
Video Teleconference Among Groups Of People   258
A Combined Audio, Video, And Whiteboard Service   258
Summary   259
A Personal Note   259

Chapter 27   The Global Digital Library   261

Introduction   261
A Cornucopia Of Services   261
New Services Appear Regularly   262
Flexibility Permits Change   262
A Digital Library   263
Card Catalogs And Search Tools   263
Internet Services Can Be Integrated   263
Mr. Dewey, Where Are You?   264
Information In The Digital Library   265
What Is The Internet?   265
A Personal Note   266

Appendix 1   Example Netnews Newsgroups   267

Appendix 2   Example Internet Services   277

Introduction   277
InterNIC   277
Astra   278
Finger   278
Internet Relay Chat   278
LISTSERV   279
Mud   279
Netfind   279
NFS   279
Ping   280
Ph or Cso   280
Prospero   280
Talk   280
Traceroute   281
Trickle   281
Whois   281
X Window system   281
X.500   282

Appendix 3   Glossary Of Internet Terms   **283**

Index   **307**

1

The Internet Has Arrived

The World Is Changing

A revolution is taking place. It started quietly and has grown to involve much of the world. On an average day, the following events occur:

- A scientist in Berkeley, California finishes working on an experiment and rushes to a computer to send a message about the results. Within minutes, colleagues around the world learn about the experiment.
- An investment broker in Houston, Texas sits down at a personal computer and runs a program that accesses current prices on the New York Stock Exchange. After looking at the list, the broker purchases two stocks and sells another.
- A class of elementary school children in Chicago, Illinois are learning to use a computer network. They run a computer program that searches libraries for a book by Dr. Seuss.
- A college professor in Lisbon, Portugal uses a computer to send a question about an example in a textbook to the author in Indiana. Later that day, a reply is waiting on the computer.
- A grandparent in Boston, Massachusetts uses a computer to inquire about airline flights, make a reservation, and purchase a ticket for a trip to visit a grandchild.
- A group of company executives hold a meeting. One executive is in New York, another in Florida, and a third is on vacation in Colorado. Each sits in front of a computer that has both a camera and microphone attached. They see pictures of one another on the screen and hear each others' voices.

1

- A computer program runs at 6:00 PM in Atlanta, Georgia to send a copy of a company's daily sales receipts to a branch office in Paris, France.
- A high school student in Taiwan uses a computer to see and hear a tour of the campus at the University of Hawaii. Later, the student uses the computer to send a FAX to a relative who is visiting Australia.

What do all these events have in common? In each, people are using the Internet, a communication system that is revolutionizing the way we work and play.

It may seem that the Internet will not affect you, but it will. In fact, the Internet will affect you soon – it probably has already. Let's look at some statistics:

- The Internet currently reaches millions of people in over 61 countries.

- Over one-half of all 2-year and 4-year U.S. colleges and universities have access to the Internet.

- The U.S. military has been using Internet technology for over a decade; it played a role in military actions such as Operation Desert Storm.

- Scientists have been using the Internet since 1980.

- The U.S. President and the White House are accessible via the Internet as are other government agencies in many countries.

Numbers Do Not Tell The Story

The most common assessment of the Internet's significance measures the number of computers that connect to it. However, conventional computer connections tell only part of the story. The Internet reaches ships at sea, planes in the air, and mobile vehicles on land. Private companies provide access to Internet services through the telephone system, making it possible to reach the Internet from any home or office that has a telephone.

To assess the impact of the Internet, one might ask, ''What has it affected?'' The answer is, ''Almost everything.''

So, the question becomes:

The Internet has arrived; are you ready for it?

Learning About The Internet

This book answers the question "What is the Internet?" in the broadest sense. It examines the origins of computer networking and its application to everyday problems. It focuses on the services that the Internet provides and helps the reader understand their importance.

Learning about the Internet is not something one can complete in an afternoon – learning never stops because the Internet keeps changing. The Internet is similar to a newsstand – when new information appears, it replaces older information. Each time you visit the newsstand or the Internet, you can find something new.

Of course, information on the Internet changes much more rapidly than information in a conventional newsstand. In fact, because information on the Internet comes from computers and automated systems, it can change instantly. For example, if one accesses weather information twice in a single minute, the information obtained from the two accesses can differ because computers can measure weather and change the report constantly.

In addition to resembling a newsstand, Internet also resembles a traditional library because it has tools that aid the search for information. In a typical library, for example, one finds a card catalog and a reference desk. The Internet has similar services that help one find information electronically.

Understanding The Big Picture

Understanding the Internet can be especially difficult for three reasons. First, because few people have experience with computer networking before learning about the Internet, one cannot rely on intuition or background. Second, because models of computers differ, one cannot expect a description of details to apply to all computers. Third, because the Internet is changing and growing rapidly, one cannot easily find a complete description of the services available or the locations of interesting data.

To avoid becoming overwhelmed with details, we will examine the fundamentals of the Internet. Instead of focusing on how to use a particular computer, a particular brand of software, or a particular Internet service, we will consider the basics of how the Internet works and how information services use the basic mechanisms. In essence, we will examine the capabilities of the Internet.

Understanding Internet capabilities makes it much easier to read computer manuals and to use the Internet. In particular, because most computer manuals specify the details of how to accomplish a task without describing why one needs to perform the task, beginners often find them difficult to follow. Knowing how the Internet works and the purpose of each service helps put the details in perspective.

Terminology And Technology

A complex technology, the Internet has spawned a terminology that can be daunting. This book clearly explains the Internet technology using analogies and examples. It shows how the pieces fit together, emphasizing basics instead of details. It discusses the services that the Internet offers, explains the flexibility they provide, and describes how they can be used.

More important, this book introduces technical terminology used for computer networking and the Internet. Instead of providing a list of terms, early chapters present definitions in a historical perspective that shows how communication systems evolved. For example, early chapters explain the difference between digital and analog information. Instead of using computer networks as an example, the chapters relate the terminology to everyday experiences.

Growth And Adaptability

Part of the mystique surrounding the Internet arises from its rapid success. While the Internet has grown, dozens of other attempts to provide the same services have failed to deliver. Meanwhile the Internet continues to expand by adapting to change, both technical and political. We will examine why Internet technology has worked so well and how it has adapted to accommodate change.

Another amazing part of the Internet story is its incredible growth. We will look at how the Internet continues to grow and the consequences of such growth.

The Impact Of The Internet

Perhaps the most significant aspect of the Internet is its impact on society. Once restricted to a few scientists, it is quickly becoming universal. It reaches governments, businesses, schools, and homes worldwide. We will examine how the Internet changes peoples' lives, and what we can expect in the future. In summary, the rest of this book looks at what the Internet is and what it can do for you.

Organization Of The Book

This book is organized into four sections. The first section (Chapters 2 through 6) introduces communication system concepts and terminology. If you already understand digital and analog communication, universal service, and binary data encoding, you may choose to skim this section. The second section (Chapters 7 through 10) reviews the history of the Internet and its incredible growth. The third section (Chapters 11 through 17) describes basic Internet technology and capabilities. It examines how Internet hardware is organized and how software provides communication. Be sure to understand this section; it provides the foundation for later chapters. The final section describes services currently available on the Internet. For each service, it explains both how the service works and how it can be used.

A Personal Note

I still remember an occasion several years ago when a colleague bluntly asked me the question, "What is the Internet?" I had been involved with Internet research for many years, and had written a popular college textbook that described the Internet and the principles underlying its design. I knew many details about the hardware and software systems that comprised the Internet, how the computers were connected, and the details of communication. I also knew most of the researchers who were working on technical improvements. What puzzled me most about the question was the person asking – someone who already knew basic technical details and had a copy of my textbook. What could I say?

As I contemplated the question, my colleague guessed that I misunderstood and said, "I do not want to know about computers and wires. I mean, in a larger sense, what *is* Internet, and what is it becoming? Have you noticed that it is changing? Who will be using it in ten years? What will they do with it?"

The questions were important because they pointed out a significant shift. Early in its history, most users of the Internet were the experts who helped build it. The Internet has outgrown its research beginnings and has become a powerful tool. It is a facility used by almost everyone. It is being used in ways that the experts had not imagined.

Before The Internet

A Gentle Introduction To Communication Systems Concepts And Terminology

2

Telephones Everywhere

Introduction

This chapter introduces the concept of *universal service*. It uses a familiar example to show how the assumption of universal service can affect our view of a communication service, and explains why the Internet will be a necessity when it becomes universal.

A New Communication Service

The Internet is a communication technology. Like the telephone before it, the Internet makes it possible for people to communicate in new ways. However, to the average person living in the 1990s, digital communication seems as distant as telephone communication did to the average person living in the 1890s. We can learn many lessons from the story of telephone service that apply directly to the Internet.

Selling Communication

To understand how a new communication technology infiltrates society, think back approximately a century. Imagine yourself as a salesperson in an average town in the U.S. who has the job of selling telephone service.

All things considered, the economic times you face are full of promise. Excitement and optimism pervade industry. After all, society is experiencing an industrial revolution. Everywhere you find that mechanization has replaced manual labor. The steam engine has replaced water wheels and animals as a source of power; some industries are starting to use engines that run on gasoline. Factories are producing more goods than ever before.

Of course, a telephone salesperson of a century ago would have had little or no firsthand experience using a telephone. Indeed, he or she may have had only a few demonstrations before going out to sell telephone service.

Imagine that you walk into a small company and talk to the owner about telephone service. What can you say? You could tell the owner that the company needs a telephone because it will allow customers to place orders easily. Or you could say that a telephone will allow employees to check with suppliers, order raw materials, or trace shipments that do not arrive on schedule. Maybe you would ask the owner if he or she goes out to lunch with other business owners, and point out that a luncheon could be arranged in a few seconds over a telephone. You could say that a telephone is easy to use. Or, you might take a more serious approach and point out that if fire struck the business, a telephone could be used to reach the firehouse: it might save property or lives.

How do the owners react to your telephone sales pitch? Some are interested; many are skeptical. A few are delighted, but others are angry. Although some will think the idea has merit, many will laugh. Some want to redesign business practices, but most resist. A few want a telephone just because it is new and lends status to their establishment. Despite what they say, most owners believe that they will continue to conduct business without using a telephone.

Limited Access

Selling telephone service without having used it can be difficult. But let's make the task of selling easier. Suppose that you had grown up in a world with telephone service, and that you had used telephones all your life. Then suppose that you were transported back in time almost 100 years and tried to sell telephone service. You might think that it would be easy to convince people to buy telephone service knowing how it can be used, but you would be surprised by what you face.

The first shock you encounter when trying to sell telephone service is learning that the service of a century ago did not work the same way as modern telephone service. Back then, telephone service meant *local* service. Each town or village decided independently when to run wires, hire a switchboard operator, and establish phone service. More important, each town chose a telephone technology that met its needs and budget. As a result, although many telephone systems existed, they were incompatible – running wires from one town to the next did not guarantee that the telephone systems in the two towns could work together. From a business perspective, even if a company installed a telephone, it could not be used to order supplies from other parts of the country. You quickly discover:

Having an independent local telephone service in each town limits the usefulness of a telephone.

High Cost

The second shock you encounter when trying to sell telephone service approximately a century ago is learning that even when it is available, telephone service is expensive. An average family cannot afford a telephone in their home. In addition to buying the telephone itself, many telephone companies charge each subscriber the true cost of installation. The first customer on a given street must pay for running the wires from the telephone office to the street; subsequent customers pay only for running wires to their houses. As a consequence, it is often more difficult to enlist the first subscriber in a given neighborhood than to enlist additional subscribers. More important, for a large part of the population who live in rural areas, telephone service is out of the question.

After many attempts to sell telephone service to individuals fail, you report back to your employer with a conclusion:

Telephone service will not be a viable business until the cost of service becomes low enough for an average family to have a phone installed.

The Difficult Transition

In a world without telephones, convincing a business to install one may seem impossible. If the business cannot use it to call suppliers in remote parts of the country and local customers do not have easy access to a telephone, there is little economic justification for acquiring one. In fact, after thinking about the world of telephone service that we enjoy and the world of telephone service approximately a century ago, you realize:

The single most important idea behind a communication service arises from its coverage – if no one else has the service, it is useless; if everyone else has the service, it is a necessity.

The transition between the two extremes is difficult. It requires businesses and individuals to invest in a new communication technology before the economic benefit is obvious. If they choose a technology that does not catch on, they lose their investment. Even if others adopt the technology, it may have insufficient subscribers to justify economically. Many people remain reticent when a new technology arrives. They wait to see what everyone else will do, hoping to minimize their financial risk.

Ubiquitous Access

Why did everyone in the U.S. eventually choose to subscribe to telephone service? If you are a student of history, you know the answer: because the U.S. government decided that ubiquitous telephone service was important for the country. The governments of most other countries reached the same decision. The U.S. government established a regulated monopoly, American Telephone and Telegraph (AT&T). It mandated that telephone service be available to every home and business, and regulated rates to ensure that telephone service was affordable to the average family. It required the telephone system to reach rural areas as well as cities. More important, the government encouraged AT&T to interconnect all the local telephone services, providing a single, large system.

Because one company owned and operated much of the U.S. telephone network, many tasks were easy. For example, AT&T could specify the technical details of how the phone system in one city interconnected with the phone system in another. Having one company own the system made it easy to deploy new technology. A single company also made it easy to define a global numbering system so that a subscriber in one city could directly dial the telephone number of a subscriber in another city.

In short, the result of the government action was universal telephone service available at a price an average family could afford. Within a few decades, most businesses and a large portion of the population could be reached by telephone. Of course, universal telephone service could have occurred without government intervention; we can only speculate about what might have happened. The important point is not that the government intervened, but that popularity of the telephone surged as universal service became a reality. Businesses understood that universal phone service would mean a change in business procedures. As businesses and individuals started acquiring telephones, it became apparent to everyone that telephones were important. Acquiring one became a necessity. Telephone service changed from a luxury reserved for the rich to something expected by the average family.

> *In the U.S., the telephone system became the communication system of choice in the twentieth century because the government mandate of universal telephone service guaranteed that subscribing would benefit everyone.*

Relevance To The Internet

Like the telephone system, the Internet provides communication. Currently, the Internet falls in the awkward transition period between limited access and universal service. Although connections are growing rapidly, the Internet does not reach everyone. Although the U.S. government has contributed to Internet development, it has not decided to mandate universal service. Thus, unlike the phone system, Internet growth has relied on economics. As a result, growth has proceeded in a haphazard manner. Most Internet subscribers are still universities and businesses, not individuals.

During the transition, convincing someone who has not used the Internet that it offers exciting new possibilities is like trying to sell telephone service before a universal phone system is in place. Often people who see Internet technology smile politely and nod, while thinking to themselves, ''That's all very nice, but how would *I* use it?'' The question is the analogy of someone who has never seen a telephone asking, ''Yes, I see how it works, but whom would *I* call?''

The answer, of course, is that once everyone is connected to the Internet, you will want to use it to contact local schools, businesses, friends, government offices, computational services, data banks, and relatives. A later chapter discusses Internet growth, and shows that the Internet will soon become universal.

3

The World Was Once Analog

Introduction

The Internet can carry many forms of information. This chapter explains analog information, and shows how analog signals can be encoded in digital form. The discussion uses audio as an example.

Sound, Vibrations, And Analog Recording

Highway engineers use a simple mechanism to warn motorists of an approaching toll booth. They install a series of small bumps in the roadway. When a car passes the bumps, the tires vibrate. Humans perceive the tire vibration as sound.

The first mechanical phonographs used the same basic idea to reproduce sound. A pointed stylus, called a *needle*, traveled across the surface of a cylinder or disc that contained small bumps of recorded sound. As the needle ran across the bumps, it vibrated a flat diaphragm, producing vibrations that humans perceive as sound. Figure 3.1 illustrates the idea.

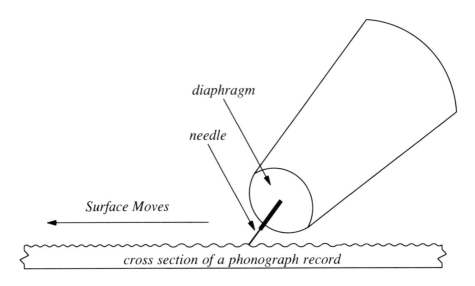

diaphragm

needle

Surface Moves

cross section of a phonograph record

Figure 3.1 An illustration of how bumps on an early phonograph cause a diaphragm to vibrate as the record passes under the needle.

Devices like a phonograph are called *analog devices* because they record and play an exact analog of sound. The bumps on a phonograph recording are exactly analogous to the vibrations that make sounds. For example, the height of the bumps controls the volume. When the sound is soft, the bumps are nearly flat; when the sound is loud, the bumps are higher. If there are no bumps at all, a phonograph produces no sound†.

To summarize:

> *An analog device maintains an exact physical analog of information. For example, bumps on an early phonograph recording correspond to vibrations that we perceive as sound.*

Analog Electronic Devices

Although early phonographs were entirely mechanical, modern equipment that reproduces sound uses electronics. For example, a cassette tape recorder also uses analog technology. The recorder arranges the magnetic material on the surface of a recording tape to be an exact analog of sound. When the sound is loud, more of the magnetic material is aligned than when the sound is soft. In fact, analog can best be understood by thinking about an amount of one substance being proportional to another: the amount of magnetism on a tape is proportional to the volume of sound.

---

†In practice, a phonograph always produces some noise because the recording surface is not perfectly flat; it contains minor scratches that become worse each time the record is played.

When a cassette tape recorder plays an audio tape, an electronic circuit in the tape recorder senses the magnetism on the tape and produces an electric current that is an exact analog of the magnetism. When little magnetism exists on the tape, the current is small. When the tape contains more magnetism, the current is larger. Thus,

> *An electronic device is analog if the amount of electrical current it generates is proportional to its input.*

Many Electronic Devices Are Analog

Many familiar electronic devices use analog technologies. For example, AM or FM radios, stereo systems, and televisions all use analog electronic circuits. In fact,

> *At one time, most electronic devices used analog techniques to store, amplify, or emit pictures or sounds.*

The First Analog Communication

Analog communication was an important part of early telephone systems. The first telephones had two basic parts: a microphone to convert sound into an analog electrical signal and an earpiece to convert an analog electrical signal into sound. Whenever a person spoke into the microphone, the electrical signals carried an analog of the sound along the wire to another telephone where it was converted back into sound. Because the system used analog signals, a loud sound caused more electric current to flow than a soft sound.

> *Early telephones used an analog scheme to send voice from one place to another; the amount of electrical current sent between two telephones was proportional to the volume of sound.*

Analog Is Simple But Inaccurate

Analog devices are the easiest to understand because most of what we do is analog. When a human uses a muscle to open a door, the door moves in an exact analog of the force exerted on it. The volume of a human voice changes in exact analog to the force exerted by the person's diaphragm. Similarly, the pitch of a human voice is an exact analog of the force a person applies to stretch their vocal cords.

Although analog may be natural and easy for a human to understand, analog devices have drawbacks. In general, it is impossible to produce an exact analog of all possible inputs. For example, consider recording the sound of a loud drumbeat on a cassette tape. The magnetism must be aligned at the place the drumbeat occurs. However, because the alignment is limited by the available magnetic material, it is impossible for the magnetism to be high enough to record an arbitrarily loud sound. Furthermore, because playing a cassette wears down the surface, the sound diminishes slightly each time the tape is played.

Inaccuracies also arise because electronic amplifiers are not perfect. An analog electronic device changes its input signal in unintended ways. It may mangle the signal, record it inaccurately, or add background noise. We call the changes *distortion*. For example, one can hear the background noise produced by an audio amplifier when the volume is set at maximum and no input is connected.

In summary:

> *An analog device always distorts the input and adds noise.*

Sending An Analog Signal Across A Wire

Whenever an electric current passes along a wire, some of the signal disappears. Although engineers talk about *signal loss*, energy is not really lost. It is simply converted to heat. The consequence for analog electrical signals is important: as electric current passes along a wire and some of the energy is converted to heat, the signal becomes weaker and weaker. For example, if an electrical signal contains an analog of sound, the volume of the sound will be lower after the signal passes across a long wire than it was at the start.

For an analog telephone system, the signal loss causes a problem. It means that the signal becomes weaker as it travels from one telephone to another. If the telephones are far apart, the signal will be so weak that the sound cannot be heard. In early telephone systems, the signal loss problem was so severe that telephones only worked in a small local area.

As telephone service expanded, telephone companies solved the problem of signal loss by adding amplifiers to the system. Amplifiers were placed periodically along wires, to boost the signal after it became weak. The amplified signal was given enough energy to travel to the next amplifier. Eventually, the signal reached its destination. Figure 3.2 illustrates the idea.

Of course, analog electronic devices are never perfect. Each amplifier along the path between two telephones distorts the signal and adds a little noise that is amplified, along with the signal, by the next amplifier. The analog telephone system included special filters to block distortion and noise, but doing so also meant the system blocked some legitimate sounds. The filters themselves distorted the signal as they eliminated unwanted sounds.

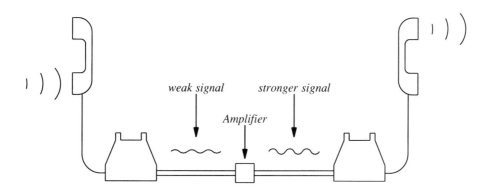

Figure 3.2 Telephone systems that use analog communication need to amplify
the signal if it travels a long distance.

Digital Music

A few years ago, the music industry began selling recordings on a new medium
known as a *compact disc* (CD). Advertisements boast that CDs are better than records
because CDs are *digital*. When CDs arrived, most people had no idea what "digital"
meant, how digital music would sound, or why it was supposed to be better. If a customer asked what digital meant, he or she would receive a simple definition:

> *A technology is* digital *if it uses numbers to record information in-
> stead of a physical analog like bumps on a record or magnetism on a
> tape.*

The Digital Revolution

The digital revolution did not start with the compact disc. The current digital
world became possible when scientists at Bell Laboratories invented a solid state switch
called a *transistor*. The revolution began a short time later when scientists and engineers devised ways to combine transistors in an *integrated circuit*† built out of silicon
crystals.

---

†An integrated circuit is informally called a *chip*.

An integrated circuit consists of many electronic components interconnected by wires, built on a square a few tenths of an inch per side. Through intensive research, manufacturers have found ways to reduce the size of transistors and to make integrated circuits more sophisticated. Currently, a manufacturer can build an integrated circuit that contains several million transistors.

The importance of integrated circuits lies in their economy. Because integrated circuits can be manufactured in mass quantities at low cost, it is now possible to mass produce complex circuits that were too expensive to build using individual components.

Many integrated circuits are designed primarily for use in computers. For example, a microprocessor is an integrated circuit that forms the heart of a modern computer – it contains all the electronic circuitry needed to add, subtract, multiply, divide, or compare numbers. In addition, a microprocessor can fetch numbers from a computer's memory or store results into memory.

Computers Are Digital

Unlike the analog devices discussed earlier, a computer is a *digital device*. It is called "digital" because:

Inside a computer, all information is represented by numbers.

For example, when the user presses a key on a computer keyboard, the keyboard sends a number to the computer. When the computer paints text or graphics on the screen, it does so using numbers.

Because a computer is digital, microprocessors and other integrated circuits built for use in computers work with numbers. Because computer circuits are extremely flexible, they can be used in a variety of ways; because they are inexpensive, engineers have used them in many devices. For example, microprocessors are used in hand-held calculators, automobiles, televisions, refrigerators, microwave ovens, and office equipment. They control heating units, airplanes, cameras, and traffic lights.

Digital Recording

Recording sounds in digital form may seem impossible. After all, we know that sound is a sequence of vibrations of varying pitch and volume. Sound seems to have little to do with numbers. Digital recording only works because computer circuits operate at much higher speeds than the human ear and mechanisms exist that translate between analog and digital signals.

Using Digital To Recreate Analog

To understand digital recording, think of the temperature on a summer day. In the early morning it can be cool, but the temperature rises rapidly following sunrise. Around noon it peaks, and begins to fall in early evening. Suppose you wanted to recreate the exact outdoor temperatures of a summer day inside. Let's assume you have a heat lamp, a dimmer switch that controls the amount of heat the lamp produces, and a thermometer.

To recreate the temperatures that occur on a given day, you must record the temperatures that day. You take a thermometer outside and record the temperature periodically (for example, every half hour). The next day, you take the list of temperatures and the thermometer inside to the heat lamp. By adjusting the dimmer control, you can raise or lower the temperature of the lamp every half hour to exactly match the outdoor temperature of the previous day.

Computer circuits use the same technique when they record sound digitally on a compact disc. A conventional microphone generates an analog electrical signal. The signal travels across a wire to a digital recoder. Inside the recorder, a computer circuit periodically measures the incoming signal and generates a number that tells the level of the signal at that instant. Because a computer circuit operates quickly, it can generate thousands of numbers per second. The set of numbers is saved and transferred to a compact disc. When someone plays the compact disc, a computer inside the player reads the numbers. The computer uses the sequence of numbers to recreate an analog electrical signal that matches the original signal. The output passes through a conventional amplifier to a loudspeaker.

The electronic circuit used to convert an analog signal into a sequence of numbers is known as an *Analog-to-Digital converter*, often abbreviated *A-to-D converter*. An A-to-D Converter measures an electrical signal and produces a numeric value that corresponds to its level. The computer periodically retrieves numbers from the A-to-D converter and saves them. Figure 3.3 illustrates the conversion.

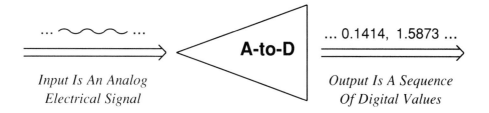

Figure 3.3 An integrated circuit that performs analog-to-digital conversion. The device takes an analog signal as input and produces a sequence of numbers as output.

To play a compact disc, a computer needs an integrated circuit known as a *Digital-to-Analog converter* (D-to-A converter). Figure 3.4 illustrates:

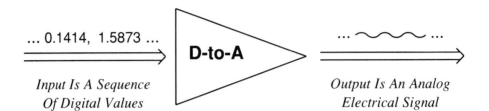

Figure 3.4 An integrated circuit that performs digital-to-analog conversion. The device takes a sequence of numbers as input and produces an analog signal as output.

To reproduce sound from a digital CD, a computer reads the sequence of numbers from the CD and feeds them into the D-to-A converter, which generates an analog electrical signal. The signal can then be amplified and played through a loudspeaker. A computer can send numbers into the converter so quickly that our ears hear the result as continuous sound.

Why Digital?

In essence, a compact disc simply contains a long list of numbers that specify how to reconstruct an analog signal. What makes a CD so fascinating is that it does not ''wear down'' as it is played. Numbers are encoded on a CD so they can be sensed with the light from a laser. Thus, nothing touches the CD itself as it is played. Furthermore, the master recording does not wear down as the manufacturer makes copies – each copy is identical to the original. In addition, a CD does not contain as much background noise as an analog scheme. For example, between songs a CD contains zeroes, meaning that no electrical signal will be produced.

Summary

Sounds are vibrations. The most natural representation of audio information is an analog form in which the amount of a physical quantity varies in exact proportion to the sound. In particular, the height of bumps on a phonograph record or the amount of magnetism on a cassette tape correspond to the loudness of the recorded sound.

Audio information can also be represented using a digital form, which means using a sequence of numbers to represent the sounds. A digital representation is the most convenient form for computers because computers represent everything as numbers.

There are two important ideas to keep in mind throughout the remainder of this book:

- *The chief advantage of using a digital representation arises because the information does not become distorted while being stored, copied, or communicated.*

- *Information, including audio and video, can be encoded in digital form.*

4

The Once And Future Digital Network

Introduction

This chapter discusses the concept of digital communication, and shows how digital information can be encoded for transmission using only two basic symbols.

The World Was Once Digital

The previous chapter asserts that, at one time, most of the electronic devices in the world were analog. Indeed, they were. Before the compact disc appeared, AM and FM radios, stereos, telephones, and televisions all used analog electronic circuits. Surprisingly, the earliest electronic communication devices were not analog. Decades before the first telephones made analog communication popular, the world used digital communication!

Nearly 150 years ago, it was possible to send a message from one town to another in a matter of minutes. The technology was known as a *telegraph*, and became so popular that telegraph lines spread quickly across the country.

A telegraph operates on the same principle as a wall switch that controls an overhead electric light. The switch is located at a convenient height on the wall, remote from both the source of power and the light itself. A pair of wires that reach the switch carry power to the switch and current back to the light. When the switch is in the "off" position, the circuit is open and no current flows to the light. When the switch is in the "on" position, the circuit is complete and current flows to the light.

The basic telegraph also operates using a switch with wires running to it. In the telegraph, however, distances are much longer: the switch is located in one town and the device it operates is located in another. In addition, a telegraph does not use light. Instead, a telegraph uses a small electrically operated device that makes an audible click when it receives electric power. To send a message across the telegraph, a person in one town must move the switch back and forth while a person in another town listens to the clicking device.

To an untrained person, a telegraph sounds like an unending series of clicks with no perceptible pattern. Some of the clicks have a short duration (i.e., the switch was held down a very short time), while other clicks are longer. Sometimes, short pauses occur before the clicks begin again. A trained telegraph operator can distinguish individual letters among the clicks, and can transcribe a message on paper as fast as it arrives.

A Telegraph Is Digital

A telegraph is a digital device because it uses clicks to send the individual characters of a message instead of sending a signal that is an exact analog of the input. To summarize:

> *The telegraph is a digital technology because it transfers discrete clicks instead of a continuously varying signal.*

Morse Code

Samuel Morse invented a code that became popular among telegraph operators. Morse code is simply a way to represent letters and words using a series of clicks and pauses. For example, Morse code uses one short click followed by one long click to represent the letter *A*.

When assigning code values, Morse tried to use short sequences for letters that occurred frequently. The result is that one can send a message faster using Morse's code than codes that are not planned as carefully. For example, in common English text, the letter **E** occurs more frequently than any other letter. Morse code uses a single, short click to encode *E*.

Short clicks are called *dots* and long clicks are called *dashes*. During transmission a short pause occurs after the dots and dashes that comprise a single letter, and a longer pause occurs after each word. A trained operator uses the pauses to detect when each letter and word ends.

Letters And Digits In Morse Code

In addition to codes for all the letters, Morse specified codes for the digits zero through nine and a few punctuation symbols as Figure 5.1 shows.

A	• —	X	— • • —
B	— • • •	Y	— • — —
C	— • — •	Z	— — • •
D	— • •	0	— — — — —
E	•	1	• — — — —
F	• • — •	2	• • — — —
G	— — •	3	• • • — —
H	• • • •	4	• • • • —
I	• •	5	• • • • •
J	• — — —	6	— • • • •
K	— • —	7	— — • • •
L	• — • •	8	— — — • •
M	— —	9	— — — — •
N	— •	,	— — • • — —
O	— — —	.	• — • — • —
P	• — — •	?	• • — — • •
Q	— — • —	;	— • — • — •
R	• — •	:	— — — • • •
S	• • •	,	• — — — — •
T	—	—	— • • • • —
U	• • —	/	— • • — •
V	• • • —	) or (	• — — — • —
W	• — —		

Figure 4.1 Examples of Morse code, which uses a unique sequence of dots and dashes to represent each letter, digit, or punctuation symbol.

Morse did not assign a code to all possible symbols. For example, there is no code for a dollar sign or for a percent sign, even though such characters do occur in written text.

Users Did Not Encounter Morse Code

Although all messages passed across a telegraph in Morse code, only telegraph operators needed to know it. A person who wanted to send a telegram wrote the message on a piece of paper and handed it to an operator. The message itself could be written in any language. In fact, people often abbreviated words because the amount of money a telegraph provider charged to deliver a telegram depended on the length of the message sent.

Transmission across a telegraph system involved two operators. A skilled operator could translate text directly to Morse code or Morse code directly to text. At the sending end, the operator read a message from paper and tapped out Morse code. At the receiving end, the operator listened to the Morse code and wrote the text. After the message was received, it was delivered to the intended recipient.

Three ideas from the telegraph are relevant to the Internet:

- It is possible to encode all letters and digits using only two basic code values: dot and dash.

- A code used for message transmission defines a basic alphabet of characters that can be sent; the code can be useful even if it does not include all possible characters.

- A customer of a telegraph service never encountered or understood the underlying encoding scheme.

Virtually Instant Communication

When the telegraph was invented, it seemed like magic. Until then, sending a message to a remote location meant using a human courier, usually on horseback. Suddenly, the world changed, and it became possible to learn about events as they occurred. With a telegraph, for example, people located far away from a financial market could learn about current stock prices and could send orders to buy or sell stock. People far from the location where ballots were counted could learn the results of an election immediately. Travelers could stay in touch with friends or family at home.

Speed Is Relative

Although the telegraph changed the world because it was so fast compared to a courier, we would think of communication by telegraph as relatively slow. Imagine communicating with a friend via telegraph instead of telephone. After you write a message, you must hand it to a telegraph operator and wait while the operator translates it into Morse code. Only the best operators can send more than a dozen words per minute. Furthermore, both the sending and receiving operators must be equally adept for a transfer to succeed. If the receiver misses a character or word, he or she must ask the sender to transmit it again. As a result, holding a dialogue via telegraph is inconvenient and slow.

It should be obvious why the telephone caused so much excitement. Instead of writing a message and passing it to an operator, a person on one end of a telephone call can speak directly to the other party. The telephone system immediately carries the speaker's voice to the other end, and conveys something that cannot easily be expressed in written form: emotions. Hearing a voice, it is possible to distinguish anger from humor or reticence from excitement.

Telephone communication became popular quickly. Many scientists and engineers working on communication systems abandoned the slow, digital telegraph and spent their time working on analog technology for telephones.

The Telephone Became Digital

Although voice communication may seem inherently analog, many modern telephone systems use digital encoding for voice transfer. At one end, the system converts an analog voice signal into a series of numbers similar to the numbers on a compact disc. Computers transfer the numbers across the phone network, where they are converted back into an analog signal.

Using digital technology to carry voice has a significant advantage for the telephone company. To understand why, consider a phone call. Initially, a long-distance telephone call required a human operator in one town to contact an operator in another, and for them to agree to hook wires together to complete the call. AT&T replaced the manual scheme with a mechanism that used dialing to connect wires automatically. To place a call, a subscriber only needed to dial the destination number. As the subscriber dialed, the telephone sent digital pulses that the dialing system used to connect the call to the specified destination.

When the dialing mechanism was first built, the telephone company used two sets of wires, one set carried the digital signals used for dialing and the other set carried analog signals used for voice communication. Over time, engineers merged the voice and dialing systems. As a result, modern telephone systems are almost entirely digital.

Relevance To The Internet

Like the early telegraph, the Internet provides digital communication. Because computers store information in digital form, digital communication works well in a computer network. When the information moves from one computer to another, a digital mechanism saves time and effort.

Binary Encoding Of Data On The Internet

The Internet is like a telegraph in another way: it uses exactly two values to encode all data items. While the values used in Morse code are commonly called dot and dash, we usually think of the values used in the Internet as zero and one, the two ''digits'' of the binary number system. In the Internet, as in most computer systems, the values are known as *bits*†. The next chapter explains the modern equivalent of Morse code used on the Internet. It describes the sequences of bits used to represent individual letters.

Encoding in bits is not surprising because almost all computers use bits to encode data. Even though the Internet encodes data in bits, the details are completely hidden from the user. Like a person who sent a message using a telegraph, a person who uses the Internet never sees the underlying binary encoding.

> *Although the Internet uses a binary encoding for all data transferred, users usually remain completely unaware of the encoding.*

Summary

The Internet is similar to its early predecessor, the telegraph, in three ways. First, the Internet provides digital communication service. It allows one to transfer a set of numbers from one computer to another. Numbers stored in a computer can be used to encode almost any information including the letters in a document, sounds, or pictures. Second, like the telegraph, at the lowest level the Internet encodes all data using two values. The Internet uses zero and one, the two binary digits. Third, the Internet hides the details of data encoding from the user.

---

†The term *bit* is an abbreviation for *binary digit*.

5

Basic Communication

Introduction

Computer networks interconnect computers so they can exchange data. Although modern computer networks are complex combinations of hardware and software, early computer networks were much less sophisticated.

This chapter outlines the development of basic communication technologies, and shows how networks evolved. It introduces terminology and explains how modems work. The concepts defined here are important throughout remaining chapters.

Communication Using Electricity

Since the discovery of electricity, inventors, scientists, and engineers have worked on ways to use electrical signals for communication. The principles discovered have resulted in fast, reliable communication systems. Our knowledge of digital communication can be divided into roughly three historical stages. The first stage focused on the properties of signals on wires. The second stage focused on how to use signals to send bits and how to organize the bits into characters. The third stage focused on how to detect and correct errors that occur during transmission.

Signals On Wires

Researchers first studied how electrical signals pass across wires. They learned, for example, that an electrical signal reflects from the end of a metal wire the same way that light reflects from a mirror (the reason that many modern networks require a terminator at the end of every wire). They also learned that electrical signals lose energy as they pass across a wire (the reason that modern networks either limit the length of interconnecting wires or use electronic devices to amplify signals). They learned that an electrical signal in a wire emits electromagnetic radiation that can interfere with signals in nearby wires (the reason that high speed networks and cable TV connections use a special cable that encloses the wire in a metal shield).

Information Coding

Once researchers understood sending electrical signals on wires, they studied ways to encode information in electrical signals. Much of the work focused on finding ways to encode the human voice for transmission across telephone lines with minimum distortion, but many of the techniques apply to communication in general.

Researchers discovered a technique known as *modulation* that transmits voice well. To use modulation, the sender must have a device called a *modulator*. The modulator begins with a basic electrical signal that oscillates back and forth regularly. The basic oscillating signal is called a *carrier*. The modulator uses a second signal (e.g., one generated by a human voice speaking into a telephone), to change the carrier slightly. At the receiving end of the wire, a *demodulator* device performs the reverse function, which is known as *demodulation*. The demodulator is tuned to expect the carrier. By measuring how much the incoming signal deviates from a perfect carrier, the receiver can recover the second signal (the human voice). After they determined the range of pitch for the human voice, scientists found a carrier signal sufficient to carry audible information.

MODEM: A Modulator And A Demodulator

The principle of modulation is still in use in modern communication systems – before two computers in the Internet can communicate across a long cable, they need a modulator at one end and a demodulator at the other. A customer can install wires within a building, or lease wires from a telephone company between two buildings, across a town, or across a country. Electrically, the leased wires do not connect to the phone system; whoever leases the wires can only use them for private communication. When a customer uses a set of wires for communication, the customer must install a device at each end of the connection. The device is called a *modem* (an abbreviation for *mod*ulator/*dem*odulator). In fact, a leased communication circuit always contains two independent sets of wires, one set for data traveling in each direction. A modem contains both a modulator that it uses to send information, and a demodulator that it uses for arriving information. Figure 5.1 illustrates the concept.

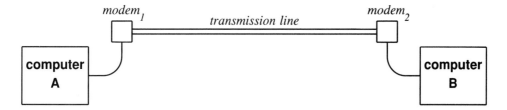

Figure 5.1 Illustration of modems that use modulation to send data across a transmission line. When a computer interacts with a modem, it sends and receives digital data; the modem encodes the data for transmission.

Modems are also available that allow communication over an ordinary dial-up telephone connection. A dial-up modem contains additional circuitry that can dial a phone number or answer an incoming call. The user must instruct a modem on one end to dial a phone number and a modem on the other end to answer the call. Once a call has been accepted, both modems can begin transferring data.

A dial-up modem uses an audible tone as the carrier when it encodes data (the carrier is the high-pitched sound one hears in a telephone handset when a modem is in use on the phone line). Whenever a computer sends data, the sending modem modulates the carrier tone by changing the pitch. The receiving modem monitors the carrier, and decodes the data when the carrier changes.

Modems Allow Two-Way Traffic

Most modems permit data to be sent between them in both directions. Recall that each modem contains both a modulator and a demodulator. Furthermore, the modems are designed so they either use two different carrier signals or agree to take turns sending data. In either case, data appears to flow in both directions simultaneously.

To summarize:

> *A modem is a device needed for communication across a dial-up telephone connection or for long distance communication across a wire. A modem supports two-way communication because it contains a modulator for the signal being sent and a demodulator for the signal being received.*

A Character Code For Digital Information

As they studied voice transmission, researchers also considered transmission of digital information. They found ways to encode the basic values of a bit in an electrical signal (e.g., using a positive voltage to encode *1* and negative voltage to encode *0*). In addition, they devised a sequence of bits to represent each letter and digit.

Although the character codes used on modern computer networks use two basic values, they differ from Morse code because each character is assigned a code with the same number of bits. For example, Morse code uses a single dot for the letter *E* and three dots for the letter *S*. By contrast, most modern character codes assign a sequence of seven 0's and 1's to each letter. Having a uniform number of bits for all characters makes character processing faster and the hardware less expensive. It also simplifies character storage because each character occupies a constant number of bits regardless of the specific character.

The *American Standard Code for Information Interchange* (*ASCII*) is among the most popular and widespread character codes used throughout the computer and network industry. ASCII defines a bit sequence for most characters used in English: upper and lower case letters, digits, punctuation, and a few miscellaneous symbols such as the mathematical symbols for less than, greater than, equal, plus, and minus.

The details of the ASCII encoding are unimportant because most people who use computers or networks never see the encodings. However, the examples shown in Figure 5.2 will help clarify the idea.

A 1000001	S 1010011	a 1100001	s 1110011
B 1000010	T 1010100	b 1100010	t 1110100
C 1000011	U 1010101	c 1100011	u 1110101
D 1000100	V 1010110	d 1100100	v 1110110
E 1000101	W 1010111	e 1100101	w 1110111
F 1000110	X 1011000	f 1100110	x 1111000
G 1000111	Y 1011001	g 1100111	y 1111001
H 1001000	Z 1011010	h 1101000	z 1111010
I 1001001	0 0110000	i 1101001	. 0101110
J 1001010	1 0110001	j 1101010	, 0101100
K 1001011	2 0110010	k 1101011	? 0111111
L 1001100	3 0110011	l 1101100	) 0101001
M 1001101	4 0110100	m 1101101	{ 1111011
N 1001110	5 0110101	n 1101110	/ 0101111
O 1001111	6 0110110	o 1101111	& 0100110
P 1010000	7 0110111	p 1110000	+ 0101011
Q 1010001	8 0111000	q 1110001	- 0101101
R 1010010	9 0111001	r 1110010	= 0111101

Figure 5.2 Examples of the ASCII encoding. The upper and lower case
letters each have a code. Users never see the encoding.

ASCII uses the 7-bit sequence 1000101 to represent the letter ''E'', the sequence
1010011 to represent the letter ''S'', and the sequence 0101100 to represent a comma.
To summarize:

> *Many networks use the ASCII code when sending textual information*
> *in digital form. ASCII assigns a 7-bit code to each letter and digit.*
> *Most users never see ASCII because it is an internal detail that*
> *remains hidden.*

Detecting Errors

Much of the early work on digital communication focused on error detection and correction. Researchers studied the errors that occur when sending electrical signals across a wire, and found ways to detect the errors. For example, they knew that natural phenomena like lightning can cause random electrical signals to appear on wires and become confused with signals that carry information. They also found that electrical signals on wires can become distorted when the wire carrying them passes through a strong magnetic field (e.g., near an electric motor in a household appliance).

When electric or magnetic interference disrupts signals on a wire, data can be damaged or lost. For example, if voltage is used to represent a bit, a bolt of lightning that strikes near a wire can cause the voltage to change even if lightning does not hit the wire directly. The point to remember is:

> *When using electrical signals to communicate digital information, electrical or magnetic interference can cause the value of one or more bits to be changed.*

To guard against corruption of information caused by random electrical noise, researchers devised mechanisms to detect and correct the problem. For example, they found that they could detect small errors if they added an extra bit to a character's code and set the extra bit to *1* if the character had an odd number of *1*s, or to *0* if it had an even number of *1*s. In essence, the sender sets the extra bit so that each character has an even number of bits set to *1*.

The extra bit is called a *parity bit*. Character *E* will be assigned parity bit *1* because its 7-bit code, `1000101`, contains an odd number of *1* bits. However, character *S* will be assigned parity bit *0* because its 7-bit code, `1010011`, contains an even number of *1* bits.

To make parity checking work, a receiver must test the parity of each incoming character. The receiver examines all the bits that arrived, including the parity bit. The receiver declares that an error occurred if it finds an odd number of bits turned on, and declares that the character arrived undamaged otherwise. If electrical interference changes one of the bits during transmission, the receiver rejects the character as damaged because it will find an odd number of bits turned on.

Although parity checking helps find minor problems, it does not guarantee that all errors will be detected. To understand why, think of the bits for a character traveling across a wire. Random electrical interference can cause some bits that start out as *1* to change to *0*, or it can cause some bits that start out as *0* to change to *1*. If it happens that in a given character, the electrical interference changes an even number of *1* bits to *0*s, the parity bit will still appear to be correct. Similarly, if the noise changes an even number of *0* bits to *1*s the parity will also appear to be correct. As an extreme case, think of what happens if a strong magnetic field changes all bits of a character to zero. The result appears to have correct parity. The point is:

> *Adding a parity bit to each character code before transmission can help the hardware detect errors that occur when transmitting the character across a network. However, parity alone is not sufficient to detect all possible errors; more powerful techniques are needed.*

Indeed, the Internet error checking techniques detect errors that parity alone cannot. In the rare case that bits become damaged in transit, the receiver declares that an error occurred, and the communication software handles the problem.

Summary

Researchers have studied the properties of electrical signals on wires, and have learned how to use electrical signals to encode information like voice. In addition, researchers have found ways to use electrical signals to encode digital information by sending bits. They devised codes that assign each character a unique string of bits. In particular, they devised the ASCII code that many computers and computer networks use.

Researchers devised a transmission scheme of particular importance that uses modulation to encode information for transmission. Modulation starts with a carrier, an oscillating signal such as an audible tone, and uses information to change the carrier slightly before transmission. The receiver extracts the information by measuring how the incoming signal deviates from a perfect carrier.

A device that provides modulation and demodulation is called a modem; modems are used for sending information a long distance across wires or when sending information across a dial-up telephone connection. Modems are currently used on almost all transmission lines throughout the Internet.

Researchers also studied transmission errors and found mechanisms like the parity scheme that hardware can use to detect when electrical interference has damaged bits during transfer. Although parity can help detect errors, it does not solve the problem completely. The Internet uses more powerful error detection techniques.

6

The Local Area Network Arrives

Introduction

Motivated by the need for better telephone communication, much of the early work on communication focused on ways to span large geographic distances. Indeed, researchers still study the problem of long-distance communication and look for ways to improve transmission. In the late 1960s and early 1970s, new networking technologies emerged that had a more immediate impact on the average person. This chapter examines the new technologies, and describes how they changed the economics of computing.

Motivation

Known as *Local Area Network* (LAN) technologies, the new networks were motivated by two trends. First, computers had grown smaller and less expensive. In place of large bulky mainframe computers that cost several million dollars, groups began acquiring smaller, less expensive computers called *minicomputers*. Second, people began to understand that computers could help with many of the tasks in an ordinary office.

Low-cost minicomputers changed computing. When computers cost more than a million dollars, an organization could aspire to have only one computer. As computers became inexpensive, however, it became obvious that each organization could benefit from having several computers. It became equally obvious that organizations with many computers needed to move data among them to facilitate information sharing.

Interchangeable Media

The first data transfers from one computer to another involved removable media storage devices, usually magnetic tapes or disks. Although the early disks were physically large and bulky, they worked like modern floppy disks. An operator placed a blank disk into a disk drive attached to a computer, and arranged for the computer to write data on it. The operator then moved the disk to a disk drive attached to another computer, and instructed a second computer to read the data.

A Computer Consists Of Circuit Boards

To understand how computer networks were formed, one must understand the basics of how computers are built. Inside a computer, electronic components reside on thin, flat rectangular boards called *circuit boards*. Each circuit board contains both electronic components and the wires that connect them.

Not all computers have the same circuit boards. When someone buys a computer, he or she must choose among various options; the options selected determine which circuit boards the computer will contain. For example, one person can choose to purchase a printer and a video camera for their computer, while another person chooses a CD player and two disks. A vendor installs the appropriate circuit boards to create the computer that the customer ordered.

Circuit Boards Plug Into A Computer

To make installing circuit boards easy, computer manufacturers build a computer so it contains a set of sockets. Figure 6.1 illustrates the sockets one might see in a computer.

Wires connect the sockets to each other and to other parts of the computer. For example, some of the wires in each socket carry electric power to the circuit board. The computer uses other wires to carry data.

Each circuit board contains a plug that exactly matches a socket inside a computer. In addition, each circuit board that controls an external device (e.g., a printer) has an additional cable that connects to the device. Assembling a computer means plugging a set of circuit boards into the computer's sockets. Plugging in a circuit board is not difficult – many people who own personal computers add or replace circuit boards to upgrade their computer.

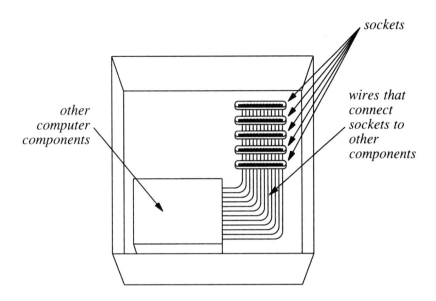

Figure 6.1 Illustration of the components visible in a computer when the cover has been removed. A circuit board can plug into each socket; wires connect the sockets to other components.

Connecting One Computer To Another

The first hardware that engineers built to transfer data between two computers electronically consisted of two circuit boards connected by a cable as Figure 6.2 illustrates.

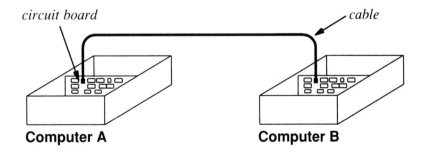

Figure 6.2 Illustration of an early computer communication system formed using two circuit boards plugged into sockets in two computers.

Once communication circuits have been plugged into the computers and connected by a cable, the computers use them to transfer data electronically. The circuit boards operate like an Input/Output (I/O) device (e.g., like a disk). To communicate, one computer writes data to its circuit board as if it were writing the data to a disk. The electronic circuits on the two boards cooperate to move the data between them, and then the other computer reads data from its circuit board as if it were reading the data from a disk.

The chief advantage of a direct connection from one computer to another is speed. Because the sockets in a computer provide the fastest path to the computer's memory, circuits can be built that move data from one computer to another quickly.

The chief disadvantages of a direct connection are inconvenience and cost. The method is expensive because one must install costly new circuit boards in each pair of computers that are interconnected. It is inconvenient because it requires considerable effort to add a new computer to the set. Furthermore, if two computers are not the same, it may be impossible to find a pair of circuit boards to interconnect them. Connecting computers directly is also inconvenient because the computers must be running to make communication possible. For example, Figure 6.3 shows three computers connected by two communication links. In the figure, computer *B* must be running before computer *A* can send a message to computer *C*.

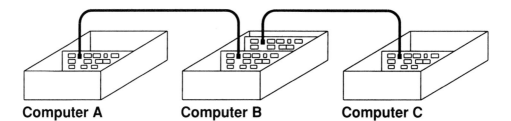

Computer A   **Computer B**   **Computer C**

Figure 6.3 Two pairs of interface boards connecting three computers. Each
new computer added to the set requires a new pair of interface
boards and an additional cable.

LAN Technologies

LAN technologies solve the problem of computer communication in a way that is convenient, inexpensive, and reliable. Instead of connecting one computer directly to another, LAN technologies use hardware to interconnect multiple computers. The "network" exists independent of the computers themselves. If one computer connected to a LAN is down, other computers can still communicate.

LAN technologies are designed for use across short distances. In general, one can think of *LAN* as meaning "within a building." Because LANs only need to span short distances, it is possible to transmit an electrical signal that remains strong enough to reach the end of the LAN before it experiences any significant loss. Therefore, LANs do not need amplifiers to boost signal strength.

In many LAN systems, the network consists of a single, long cable to which each computer attaches. Figure 6.4 illustrates how multiple computers attach to a LAN.

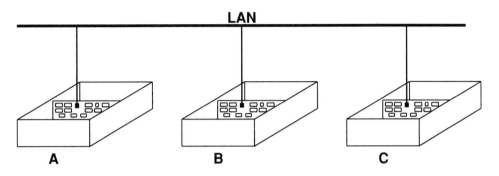

Figure 6.4 Computers attached to a LAN communicate directly without sending data through intermediate computers. The LAN interface
hardware differs from the interface hardware used for a direct
connection.

In an office building, the cable forming a LAN can run along a hallway ceiling. At each office along the hall, a separate cable connects a computer in the office to the main cable in the hall. All the electronic circuits needed to communicate across the LAN are contained in the computers; the LAN itself is merely a long wire.

Because most LANs do not contain electronic components, they are highly reliable. The hardware in an individual computer can fail or the connection between that comput-er and the LAN can be broken, but the LAN usually continues to operate.

To summarize:

> *A computer communication technology is classified as a* Local Area
> Network (LAN) *if it provides a way to interconnect multiple comput-*
> *ers across short distances. LANs are inexpensive, highly reliable, and*
> *convenient to install and manage.*

Connecting A Computer To A LAN

To connect to a LAN, a computer needs network interface hardware. From the computer's point of view, a LAN interface operates like the interface for an I/O device. Physically, the network interface hardware consists of three parts: a circuit board that plugs into the computer, a cable that connects the circuit board to the LAN, and hardware that attaches the cable to the LAN.

The processor in a computer uses the network interface to access the LAN. It can request that the interface send a message to another computer over the LAN or read the next incoming message.

> *A computer needs additional hardware to connect it to a local area network. The hardware consists of a circuit board that plugs into the computer and a cable with associated hardware that attaches the circuit board to the LAN. Once connected, a computer uses the network interface to send and receive data.*

A LAN remains independent from the computers it connects. For example, the format of data and the speed at which data traverses the LAN does not depend on the computers that attach. In each computer, the network interface circuit board places data in the form required by the LAN, and compensates for differences in speed between the computer and the network. To do so, the network interface usually contains a microprocessor and a small amount of high-speed random access memory. The interface uses the high-speed memory to hold each incoming or outgoing message so it can be transferred to the LAN at the speed the network uses, and can be transferred to the computer at the speed the computer uses.

For example, when computer A sends a message to computer B, it does not send the message directly from its memory across the LAN. Instead, computer A moves the message to its network interface. The network interface in A transmits the message across the LAN to the network interface in computer B at the speed the LAN uses. After the network interface on B has received the message, it moves a copy into B's memory. The two computers do not need to operate at the same speed as each other or as fast as the LAN because only the network interface circuits are used during transmission or reception of data. The important idea is:

> *Because each computer attached to a LAN contains interface hardware that isolates the computer from the LAN, the speed of the LAN does not depend on the speed of computers that attach to it. As a result, heterogeneous computers can communicate across a LAN.*

The Importance Of LAN Technology

LAN technologies changed the way people used computer networks. Before LAN technologies were available, people thought of computer communication as a way to cross large geographic boundaries. Once LAN technologies emerged, people began to use networks to connect machines within a room or within a building.

The most significant change that LAN technologies produced was resource sharing. Before LAN technologies, a computer existed in a self-contained island. Each computer had a specific set of I/O devices like printers and disks, and each computer had one copy of the software that users could access. Once LAN technologies became available, a set of computers could share resources like printers.

The ability to share resources changed the economics of computing dramatically. Because a network connection was much less expensive than a set of I/O devices, it became sensible to hook many computers to a network and to use the network to provide shared access to the I/O devices. To summarize:

> *Local area networks changed the economics of computing because they made it possible to use inexpensive computers that shared access to resources like printers and disks.*

Relationship To The Internet

When the Internet project began, Local Area Network technologies were just emerging. Xerox Corporation had given several universities a prototype version of a new LAN technology that had been developed in one of its research labs. Called *Ethernet*, the technology was destined to become the leading LAN technology.

Internet researchers imagined a future in which LAN technology would become inexpensive and widely available. They assumed, for example, that each organization would use one or more LANs to interconnect all its computers. They designed the Internet with the assumed future in mind. As it turned out, the assumption was correct.

A Brief History
Of Internet Time

**...how the Internet
grew from its humble
beginnings to become
the largest network
in the world**

7

Internet: The Early Years

Many Independent Networks

By the late 1970s, computer networking began to blossom. Several computer manufacturers introduced small minicomputers with sufficient computational power to handle many users. Because such computers are inexpensive, each department in a large organization can afford one.

To interconnect minicomputers and to permit the rapid transfer of information among them, many organizations began installing Local Area Networks. Because LAN technology is both inexpensive and easy to install, an individual department can purchase, install, and operate a LAN for their machines without consulting a central administration.

The Proliferation Of LANs

Allowing each group within an organization to build and operate a computer network has both advantages and disadvantages. When granted independence, a group can choose a network technology appropriate for their needs. They can budget funds to pay for the LAN installation and operation. They can decide who has access, and can devise policies regarding network use.

Allowing autonomy can also have severe disadvantages. Most important, because not all computer vendors supply interface hardware for all types of networks, allowing groups to act independently can encourage a proliferation of many LAN technologies.

Facts About LANs

To understand how and why local area networks have proliferated, one must understand three facts:

1. Engineers have devised many LAN technologies.

    LAN hardware can be designed to achieve a combination of speed, reliability, ease of installation, capacity, and cost. Engineers have designed network hardware for several combinations.

2. LAN performance determines cost; high performance LANs are expensive.

    As one might expect, hardware that transfers data faster costs more money. The consequence is that a given group may choose to save money by acquiring a LAN that has lower performance. Indeed, it is possible to install some LANs with only trivial cost.

3. A particular LAN technology may only work with specific computers.

    Recall that bus interface hardware is needed to connect a given computer to a LAN. A computer vendor may not offer interface hardware for all types of LANs. In particular, when a computer vendor develops a LAN technology, the vendor usually only sells interfaces for its computers. Even when the LAN technology is developed by a company that does not sell computers, the company usually only sells bus interface hardware for the most popular computers.

Fact *3* suggests that when a group decides to acquire and install a LAN, choices may be limited by the availability of products. If the group owns a set of computers, they must verify that interface hardware is available for each computer. Fact *2* suggests that the choice of a LAN technology may depend on economics. Two groups within an organization can choose different LAN technologies if they have different amounts of money to spend. Finally, Fact *1* suggests that there are many possible technologies from which to choose.

The consequence of the above facts is simple: because each group in an organization can choose a technology that best meets its needs, most large organizations have many LAN technologies in use. Some are chosen for speed, others for ease of installation or maintenance, and still others for minimum cost. To summarize:

> *A LAN technology is chosen for its speed, ease of use, and the availability of interfaces for specific computers. Most large organizations use many LAN technologies.*

LANs Are Incompatible

The disappointing news about LAN technologies can be summed up succinctly:

Various LAN technologies are completely incompatible.

That is, multiple LANs cannot just be plugged together. For example, suppose a given organization has two LANs, one in the shipping department and one in the accounting department. Further suppose that someone needs to transfer information from a computer in the shipping department to a computer in the accounting department. Connecting the two LAN cables does not solve the problem.

There are several technical reasons why one cannot plug together multiple LANs. First, a given LAN technology is engineered to operate over a limited distance. Each technology specifies a maximum cable length (e.g., one popular technology specifies that the cable must be 500 meters or less). Adding more distance to a LAN can result in a malfunction. Second, each LAN technology has its own specification for electrical signals like voltage and frequency; different LAN technologies may be electrically incompatible. Third, each technology has a way of encoding information (e.g., a form of modulation); the encoding used by one LAN system does not make sense to another.

Wide Area Technologies Exist

In addition to LAN technologies, another form of computer networking emerged in the 1960s and 1970s. Scientists and engineers devised ways to build networks that connected multiple computers across large geographic distances. Called *Wide Area Networks (WANs)* or *long-haul networks*, the long-distance technologies use the same basic mechanisms as earlier long-distance systems. For example, WANs use modems to send signals across long-distance transmission lines. However, WANs do more than connect two computers across a single transmission channel – a WAN uses computers to unify a set of transmission lines into a coordinated system. To do so, a WAN includes a small, dedicated computer at each site that attaches to the transmission line and keeps the network operating independently from the computers that use it. The dedicated computer receives an incoming message that arrives from another site and delivers it to one of the local computers. It accepts a message from any of the local computers and sends the message across a transmission line toward the destination. To summarize

A Wide Area Network technology (WAN) differs from a set of disjoint transmission lines because the WAN includes an additional special-purpose computer at each site that connects to the transmission lines and keeps communication independent of the computers that use the WAN.

To understand how a WAN can be useful, imagine a company with offices in four cities: New York, Chicago, Los Angeles, and Austin. The company can install a WAN that links computers in each office. Physically, the WAN might consist of three leased transmission lines: one from Chicago to New York, another from Chicago to Los Angeles, and a third from Chicago to Austin, plus a small, dedicated computer at each site. Conceptually, the WAN functions much like a LAN except that it operates more slowly. It allows all the attached computers to communicate.

A WAN understands how transmission lines interconnect computers, and handles the details of passing messages automatically. In the example above, when a computer in Los Angeles sends a message to a computer in Austin, the message must pass through Chicago. However, the message does not pass through the company's computers in Chicago – it only passes through the special purpose computer that is part of the WAN hardware. From the company's point of view, a computer in Los Angeles can communicate with a computer in Austin even when the company's computers in Chicago are temporarily shut down.

Few WANs, Many LANs

Although WAN technologies became available in the 1970s, early WANs cost much more than LANs. To compare, think of the cost of a LAN. By installing a single cable in a building, a company can create a LAN that interconnects many computers. Furthermore, once the cable is in place, the company can add a connection to a new computer, incrementally growing the LAN as needed.

Unlike the low cost LAN, a WAN requires more planning and significantly more hardware. To install a WAN, a company must lease long-distance transmission lines as well as acquire modems, special-purpose computers, and the software used by a WAN. The company also needs interface hardware that connects each of the company's computers to the WAN. Because transmission lines and dedicated computers that form a WAN were expensive in the 1970s, only a few companies used WANs. Although more companies use WANs today, LANs still remain much less expensive and more popular than WANs.

WANs and LANs Are Incompatible

Scientists and engineers have invented a variety of WAN technologies. Each technology has an independent design, chosen for reliability, speed, distance spanned, and cost. Each technology chooses the details of voltage and signal modulation techniques. Thus, most WAN technologies are electrically incompatible with one another; one cannot create a larger network merely by plugging wires from one type of WAN into another.

Many companies choose a single WAN technology and use it to link all their sites, so incompatibility among WANs is not usually a severe problem. However, a serious problem can arise because WANs are also electrically incompatible with LANs. Most companies have more than one computer at each site and use a LAN to connect the computers at a given site. If the company installs a general-purpose WAN to connect the sites, the WAN can only attach to one computer at each site. Other computers at the site cannot communicate directly across the WAN because incompatibility keeps the WAN isolated from the LAN.

To summarize:

> *Many Local Area Network and Wide Area Network technologies exist, and most are incompatible with each other. One cannot produce a usable large network merely by interconnecting the wires from two different networks.*

The Desirability Of A Single Network

Anyone who uses multiple computers that connect to two or more separate network systems understands how inconvenient the scheme can be. For example, if one computer attaches to a LAN and another attaches to a WAN, neither has access to all resources in the organization. A computer attached to a WAN can access resources and information on remote machines, but cannot easily access information on local machines. A computer attached to a LAN can access resources and information on local machines, but cannot access information on remote machines. Simple tasks that require local access (e.g., printing output on a local printer) are tedious or impossible for machines that only connect to a WAN. At the same time, tasks that require access to remote parts of the company (e.g., access to a remote database), are impossible for machines that only connect to a LAN. In some organizations, a user who needs access to both local and remote services must have two keyboards and two display screens on their desk. Transferring data between the two computer systems can be awkward and time consuming.

In the best of all worlds, each computer in an organization has access to all resources. Of course, policies on use may restrict the set of resources a given computer or user can access, and systems try to keep resources secure from unauthorized use. However, it should be unnecessary to manually transfer data from one network to another. It should also be unnecessary to force users to move from one computer to another merely to access different resources.

The Department Of Defense Had Multiple Networks

By the late 1960s, the U.S. Department Of Defense became interested in using computer networks. Because the idea of computer networking was new, little was known about how to build networks or how they could be used. Through the *Advanced Research Projects Agency (ARPA)*†, the military funded research on networking using a variety of technologies. By the late 1970s, ARPA had several operational computer networks and had begun to pass technology on to the military. ARPA projects included a wide area network called the *ARPANET* as well as networks that used satellites and radio transmission for communication.

ARPA realized the military would face a problem that many organizations with multiple network systems faced: each network connected a set of computers, but no path existed between computers on separate networks. In essence, each network formed an isolated island that connected a set of computers, with no path between the islands.

Connecting Disconnected Machines

ARPA research examined how to interconnect all the machines from a large organization. ARPA started with a few basic ideas, awarded grants to researchers in both industry and academia, and arranged for the researchers to cooperate in solving the problem. Researchers discussed their findings, and generated new ideas at regular meetings.

Instead of allowing researchers to engage in theoretical discussions, ARPA encouraged them to apply their ideas to real computers. ARPA chose researchers interested in experimental work, and insisted that they build prototype software to test their ideas.

The Internet Emerges

A key idea in the ARPA research was a new approach to interconnecting LANs and WANs that became known as an *internetwork*. The term is usually abbreviated *internet*‡, and is applied to both the project and to the prototype network that was built. To distinguish their internet from other internets, researchers working on the ARPA project adopted the convention of writing *internet* in lowercase when referring to internetworks in general, and writing *Internet* with an uppercase I when referring to their experimental prototype. The convention persists. The key point is:

> *ARPA funded research to investigate ways to solve the problem of incompatible networks. Both the project and the prototype system that researchers built became known by the name* Internet.

---

†ARPA was called the *Defense Advanced Research Projects Agency (DARPA)* during the latter 1980s and early 1990s.

‡Chapter *12* discusses the structure of an internet in detail and shows how the Internet connects multiple networks.

The ARPANET Backbone

The ARPANET was especially important to the Internet project, and was often called the *backbone* network because it was the central WAN that tied researchers together. Each researcher working on the Internet project had a computer connected to the ARPANET.

Although having a Wide Area Network in place helped researchers communicate, the ARPANET became a key part of the Internet project because it allowed researchers to attach more than one computer at each site. Researchers took advantage of the feature and used ARPANET for two purposes. First, they used the ARPANET like a conventional WAN to connect a computer at each site. Second, they added an additional connection at each site, and arranged to use the additional connection to experiment with new ideas. Thus, the ARPANET served as both a standard network that permitted researchers to move data among sites involved in the project, and as an experimental network that allowed researchers to evaluate new network software and applications.

Internet Software

Computer software forms an important part of the technology that makes it possible to interconnect networks†. ARPA's Internet project produced many innovations to make networking more general and efficient. Researchers worked individually and in groups to invent, test, and refine new ways of making computers communicate. The research produced software that made communication possible and useful.

Although the software consists of many programs that interact in complex ways, researchers wanted the software to form an integrated system. They studied the interactions among various programs to ensure that the actions taken by one program did not conflict with actions taken by others. The end result is a smooth, apparently seamless software design. The parts work together so well that most users do not sense the underlying complexity.

The Name Is TCP/IP

Two pieces of the Internet software stand out as particularly important and innovative. The *Internet Protocol* (*IP*) software provides basic communication. The *Transmission Control Protocol* (*TCP*) software provides additional facilities that applications need. In informal discussions, researchers identify the entire set of Internet communication software by the initials of these two important parts; usually the term is written with a slash between the names: *TCP/IP*‡.

When a more formal name is needed for the set of software specifications, researchers use *The TCP/IP Internet Protocol Suite*. The formal name is more accurate because it points out that the entire set contains more than just the two protocols. In the

---

†Chapters *13* through *16* discuss the software that makes internetworking possible and efficient.

‡One pronounces the name by spelling out the letters ''T-C-P-I-P''.

end, however, the simpler name has persisted – both vendors who sell the technology as well as users who acquire and install it use the term *TCP/IP*.

The Shock Of An Open System

To encourage vendors to adopt Internet technology, ARPA decided to make the research results public. Whenever a researcher discovered a new technique, measured network performance, or extended the TCP/IP software, ARPA asked that the researcher document the results in a report. All the specifications needed to build TCP/IP software, and all the experience installing and using it were documented. ARPA made the reports available to everyone.

ARPA's practice of publishing network specifications was surprising because most commercial companies that had devised network technologies kept their discoveries private. In fact, many companies had filed patent applications to guarantee that no other company could use the same techniques. The idea derived from standard business practice:

> *Prevailing opinion suggested that a company selling computer networks could achieve maximum profits by protecting their technology with patents.*

The idea seems to make sense. After all, if a vendor only allows its own brand of computers to attach to its brand of network, sales should increase. The vendor merely needs to convince an organization to use its network technology, and the organization will be forced to buy the vendor's computers.

In the mid-1970s major computer companies that sold network systems only offered interface hardware that could connect to their own computers. The technologies included various combinations of LANs and WANs. Computer professionals apply the term *closed* to proprietary systems to suggest that they are closed to outsiders (i.e., they exclude computers designed by other vendors).

From its inception, the Internet project aspired to produce an *open* system that permitted computers from all vendors to communicate. The open philosophy meant that researchers published all discoveries about the Internet and all specifications needed to build TCP/IP software.

> *A network system is closed if a company owns the technology and uses patents and trade secrets to prevent other companies from building products that use it. By contrast, the Internet is an open system because all specifications are publically available and any company can build a compatible technology.*

Open Systems Are Necessary

Computer companies found that, despite their efforts to sell closed systems, customers began to acquire several brands of computers. Advances in processor and memory hardware made new computer designs possible. Plummeting costs made personal computers affordable. Organizations like the U.S. military realized that as computer technology evolved, vendors would continually offer new models. Furthermore, not all software worked on all computers. A large organization usually has many brands and models of computers because it needs software systems and computers for many purposes. Only an open network system can be used to interconnect computers from multiple vendors. In summary:

> *A large organization needs an open network system because it acquires computers from multiple vendors; using a closed network system restricts the computers that can connect to the network.*

TCP/IP Documentation Is Online

Most of the researchers that ARPA chose for the Internet project already had experience using computer networks. They had helped design and build the ARPANET, and had devised applications that used it. They knew they could use the ARPANET to exchange technical information. Soon after the Internet project began, they decided to keep all technical documents in computer files accessible over the ARPANET.

Initially, the researchers planned to issue reports in two steps. After a report was written, it would be made available to other researchers for comments. After a short time, the author would incorporate all comments and issue a final report. To implement the two steps, researchers established two series of reports. When a report was first issued, it was labeled *Request For Comments* (*RFC*). After other researchers sent the author comments and the report was polished, it was labeled *Internet Engineering Note* (*IEN*).

Unfortunately, the best laid plans often go astray. Researchers found that some of the initial reports were sufficient and did not need revision or improvement. Other reports were rewritten completely, but reissued as an RFC for another round of comments. Most researchers found it more productive to continue investigating new ideas than to edit old reports. In the end, RFC reports became the official record of the project and the IEN series was dropped. The irony is that each of the documents that specifies the technology of the largest, most successful computer network in history has a label that implies the work is unfinished and the author is still waiting tenuously for comments. To summarize:

For historical reasons, the documents that define TCP/IP and related Internet technology are called Requests For Comments.

Researchers working on the Internet project had access to all Requests For Comments documents because they were stored on a computer attached to the ARPANET. Each RFC was assigned an integer number, and an index was kept that listed the title of each number. At any time, a researcher who wanted to know the details of a particular piece of Internet software could use the ARPANET to retrieve the RFC that contained the information. If the researcher did not remember which RFC was needed, they could retrieve the index.

Keeping the project documentation accessible across the network enabled everyone working on the project to coordinate their activities and keep software up-to-date with the specifications. More important, rapid communication among the researchers increased the speed at which the project progressed.

Because RFCs that documented the technical details of TCP/IP and the Internet project were accessible over the ARPANET, work on the project proceeded more quickly.

As the Internet project progressed, the technology reached a stage where prototype software could be deployed and tested. A fledgling Internet was born. One of the first applications that researchers devised for the new Internet was a mechanism that could be used to access RFCs. In fact, almost all the initial applications for the Internet provided some form of communication among the researchers building it.

The Military Adopts TCP/IP

By 1982, a prototype Internet was in place and the TCP/IP technology had been tested. A few dozen academic and industrial research sites had been using TCP/IP regularly. The U.S. military started to use TCP/IP on its networks.

In the beginning of 1983, ARPA expanded the Internet to include all the military sites that connected to the ARPANET. The date marked a transition for the Internet as it began to change from an experiment to a useful network.

Summary

The Internet began as a research project funded by ARPA. Researchers studied ways to interconnect computers that used various kinds of networks. The name *Internet* refers to both the project and the prototype network system that researchers built.

Known by the name *TCP/IP*, the software used to make the Internet operate contains many complex computer programs that work together to provide communication. The software works so well that it hides the details of the underlying hardware and provides the illusion of a seamless system.

The Internet is an *open* system because the specifications needed to build TCP/IP software or use the Internet are available to everyone. Researchers who devised the Internet published technical information in a series of reports that describe the Internet and the TCP/IP software it uses. For historical reasons, each document in the series is labeled *Request For Comments*.

A Personal Note

Recently, while I was attending a technical conference, two attendees stepped into a crowded elevator carrying on a loud, animated conversation. One of them explained to the other that the Internet had been started as a secret government project to upgrade the ''hot line'' (the telephone system that ran between Washington and the Soviet Union during the years of the cold war). I wanted to interrupt the conversation, but I hesitated. The attendee doing most of the talking explained for the benefit of everyone in the elevator that the military had to cover up the project when Congress heard about it and decided to investigate the cost. He suggested that the military worked out an agreement with a large corporation. He said that the corporation paid money that was put into the treasury and, in exchange, the corporation received the technology. I wanted to interrupt and explain, but the attendee concluded emphatically that the whole episode clearly explained why the corporation's stock prices dropped rapidly during the preceding year. The pair left chattering and nodding in agreement.

When I stepped off the elevator, I was amused and puzzled. Later, I realized that something significant had happened. The Internet had become a powerful force quickly. To newcomers, it seemed vast, strange, and intimidating. Novices were shocked and ready to believe almost anything, including preposterous tales. Others were ready to invent a mythology that could explain it.

8

A Decade Of Incredible Growth

Introduction

During the decade from 1983 to 1993, the Internet changed from a small, experimental research project into the world's largest computer network. When the decade began, the Internet connected a few hundred computers; ten years later, the Internet connected over a million computers. This chapter chronicles the growth of the Internet and the changes that accompanied it. It concludes by explaining some of the consequences that arise from the Internet's incredible rate of growth.

Disseminating The Software

By 1980, the Internet was becoming a viable network system. Experimental TCP/IP software was available for several brands of computers. A handful of universities and research labs had copies of the TCP/IP software, and were using it every day. The Internet reached researchers at a dozen academic and industrial research labs.

Before the U.S. military could use the Internet for production work, however, the technology needed to become more robust. The software needed to be polished and tested, and the whole system needed more tuning. ARPA considered the next step in its research program carefully.

Meanwhile, Back In Computer Science

While ARPA worked on the Internet research project, another technology came from a research lab and swept the computer science community: the *UNIX Operating System*. Although vendors now use the term *operating system* when referring to the simple support software that comes with a personal computer, computer scientists use the term to describe the complex software that manages the computer, controls I/O devices, and provides file storage on multi-user computers. Operating systems for sophisticated computers are so complex that scientists and engineers spent years in the 1960s trying to understand them. Computer vendors sold proprietary operating systems for each of their computers.

A team of computer scientists at Bell Telephone Laboratories built a new operating system in the early 1970s. They called it *The UNIX Timesharing System*. Because Bell Laboratories used a variety of computers, the researchers built the system to be general – they designed the software carefully so it could be moved to new computers easily.

Bell Labs allowed universities to obtain copies of the UNIX system for use in teaching and research. Because they were interested in measuring its portability, Bell Labs provided source code and encouraged universities to try running it on new machines. As a result, the UNIX system became one of the first operating systems that students could study.

A group of faculty and graduate students from the University of California at Berkeley became interested in the UNIX system. They wrote application programs and modified the system itself. They added new features and experimented with programs that used a Local Area Network. To make the work available to other universities, researchers at Berkeley established a software distribution facility to mail out computer tapes that contained a copy of their software. The Berkeley version of the UNIX system, often called *BSD UNIX*†, became popular at other universities.

The Internet Meets UNIX

ARPA realized that the Berkeley software distributions reached many universities, and decided to use it to disseminate Internet software. They negotiated a research contract with Berkeley. Under the terms of the contract, ARPA gave researchers at Berkeley a copy of the TCP/IP software that had been developed as part of the Internet project. Berkeley incorporated the software into their version of the UNIX system, and modified application programs to use TCP/IP.

When Berkeley issued its next major software distribution, most computer science departments received TCP/IP software at virtually no cost. Although only a few computer science departments had computers connected to the Internet, most of them had a Local Area Network or were about to install one. They knew that their students needed to study networking. They also knew that using a network would make computing easier because it would allow users to share resources like printers.

---

†The acronym BSD stands for *Berkeley Software Distribution*.

For many departments, TCP/IP was the first viable networking software they had encountered. It offered a low-cost, efficient way to provide a departmental network and a technology that could be studied in classes. Thus, in a short time, most computer science departments had TCP/IP software running on their Local Area Networks. The point is:

> *Computer science departments in universities received TCP/IP software along with a release of UNIX system software from U. C. Berkeley. Although only a few departments had computers connected to the Internet, most of them used TCP/IP on their Local Area Networks for teaching, research, and production computing.*

The U.S. Military Makes A Commitment

In the early 1980s, the Internet operated reliably. It interconnected academic and research sites. More important, the Internet demonstrated that the basic principles of internetworking were sound. Convinced of the Internet's viability, the U.S. military started to connect computers to the Internet and to use TCP/IP software.

In 1982, the U.S. military chose the Internet as its primary computer communication system. Consequently, a cutoff date was planned. At the beginning of 1983, the ARPANET and associated military networks stopped running old communication software. All connections were switched to use TCP/IP, and any computer that did not understand TCP/IP could not communicate. The point is:

> *Although the U.S. military funded Internet research and eventually chose to use the Internet, internetworking was developed and tested at civilian sites.*

The Internet Doubles In Size In One Year

Before the U.S. military started switching its computers to TCP/IP, the Internet interconnected approximately two hundred computers. One year later, it had doubled in size. In retrospect, the increase seems trivial. It involved hundreds, not thousands of computers. At the time, however, the increase was significant.

As one might expect, the increase in Internet size uncovered limits in the computer software. For example, some parts of TCP/IP contain lists of other computers and the addresses used to access them. As new computers joined the Internet, the lists became too large; the software had to be changed to accommodate longer lists. Unlike modern computers, the computers in use in the early 1980s had a small amount of memory; researchers could not increase sizes arbitrarily. Any computer memory devoted to a list was unavailable for I/O or other programs. As a result, using more memory for lists meant the computer system ran slower.

At first, researchers made small increments to the software. They increased the capacity by ten or twenty percent, but soon found that it was insufficient. As the Internet continued to grow, the process of changing the software kept pace.

In addition to uncovering limitations in the software, the Internet growth revealed limits in manual and clerical procedures. For example, each time a new computer was added to the Internet, several people had to take action. Someone had to review the reasons for the connection and its relationship to the project before approving the connection. Someone else had to assign a name to the computer and then enter it in a database. Finally, someone had to make a physical connection between the computer and the network.

During the period of rapid growth, researchers were busy updating the software and had little spare time to help with manual procedures like registration; the duties began to pass to a professional staff. We can summarize what happened:

> *As new computers were added to the Internet, it doubled in size in a single year. The rapid growth forced researchers to tune administrative procedures as well as the software.*

Every Computer Science Department

In the late 1970s, many computer scientists recognized the importance of networking. A small group of researchers proposed a networking project to the *National Science Foundation (NSF)*†. Their goal was to devise a network that could connect all computer science researchers.

After reviewing the proposal and asking the group to revise it, the National Science Foundation funded a project to build the Computer Science Network. The project, which also had support from ARPA, became known as *CSNET*.

To reach all computer scientists in the country, CSNET had to contend with the problem of providing network service to a variety of institutions. Because large institutions could afford to pay more, CSNET encouraged them to run TCP/IP software and connect to the Internet. For smaller institutions that could not afford direct connections, CSNET devised ways to provide limited network services at much lower cost.

By the time the U.S. military selected the Internet as a primary computer communication system, many of the top computer science groups in industry and academia were already using it. Over the next few years, CSNET worked to provide Internet connections to computer science departments. As a result, by the mid-1980s, many computer scientists had Internet access.

---

†NSF, a U.S. federal agency, is responsible for funding research and education in science and engineering.

Graduate Students Volunteer Their Time

Connecting major computer science research groups to the Internet had an interesting effect. Many computer scientists are professors who work in universities, where they also teach classes and advise students. The professors talked to students about the Internet project, the technology and software that it used, its success, and the remaining research problems. The professors' enthusiasm was contagious.

Students became interested in learning more about TCP/IP and the Internet. Graduate students who were searching for research topics began to investigate the technical details of TCP/IP software. They studied ways to extend the Internet technology, and devised experiments to measure its capabilities. They considered new applications, and found ways to extend the functionality. The result was synergistic: students gained valuable knowledge and experience with computer networks, while their creative energies helped advance Internet technologies.

The IAB evolves

Research scientists working on the Internet held regular meetings to discuss new ideas, review the technology, share discoveries, and exchange technical information. ARPA decided that with the Internet growing rapidly, the group of scientists should have a more formal structure and more responsibility for coordinating TCP/IP research and Internet development. It renamed the group the *Internet Activities Board*. Following military tradition, the board became known by its acronym, IAB. Among networking professionals, it is still called the *IAB*.

ARPA appointed a chairman of the IAB, who was given the title *Internet Architect* (although the Internet was already growing too rapidly for a single person to seriously consider devising an architectural plan). Another member of the IAB was designated as the *RFC Editor* and given responsibility for reviewing and editing all RFCs before they were published. Others scientists on the IAB were each assigned a specific problem to investigate.

To study an assigned problem, each member of the IAB gathered volunteers from the research community to serve on a *task force*. The IAB member served as the task force chairperson, interacted with the task force members, and represented the task force at meetings of the IAB. Each task force held meetings to discuss ideas, resolve issues, generate new approaches, and report on experiments. If a task force reached a consensus on a new approach, members would build prototype software to demonstrate how their ideas worked in practice, and then would generate and submit a specification as an RFC.

The IAB guided the development of the Internet for many years. In 1989, it was reorganized to add representatives from commercial organizations. The IAB's duties and interactions with other groups were reorganized again in 1992, when it became part of the *Internet Society*. The IAB divested some of its technical responsibilities, passing more control to subordinate groups, and leaving the board as the ultimate arbiter of policies and standards. At the time of its second reorganization, the IAB kept the acronym, but changed its name to the *Internet Architecture Board.*

The IETF

Among all the task forces established by the IAB, one stands out: the *Internet Engineering Task Force (IETF)*. The IETF has survived reorganizations, and remains active. In fact, the IETF has grown so large that its subgroups have been partitioned into a dozen areas of interest, with a manager assigned to coordinate groups within each area. The IETF holds open meetings approximately three times per year, rotating the location among Europe, the U.S., and the Pacific rim. When it holds a meeting, hundreds of people attend, most from commercial companies. They are all volunteers who attend to hear about the latest developments and participate in efforts to refine and improve the software.

The IETF had as its original charter the problem of short-term Internet development. It now has responsibility for much of the technical direction, including adoption of specifications for new communication software or revisions of old software. Most RFCs now originate within the IETF from committees called *working groups*. To summarize:

> *The group responsible for guiding the research and development of the Internet is known as the* Internet Architecture Board *(IAB). The primary subgroup responsible for technical matters is known as the* Internet Engineering Task Force *(IETF).*

Doubling Again In A Year

During the years following the military's decision to use the Internet, growth continued. In 1984, the Internet almost doubled in size again. However, size alone does not tell the story: government agencies other than ARPA began to use the Internet and to support research. For example, the *Department of Defense (DOD)* and the *National Aeronautics And Space Administration (NASA)* used TCP/IP on some of their networks, and would soon connect more networks to the Internet.

The Internet Improves Science

By the mid-1980s, the National Science Foundation (NSF) recognized that eminence in science would soon demand computer communication. Before computer networks, scientists exchanged ideas by publishing them in scientific journals. It took many months, sometimes years, between the time a scientist submitted a manuscript and the time a final version appeared in print.

Computer communication changed the way scientists do research. Scientists connected to the Internet can exchange documents or experimental data instantly. In fact, scientists can use the Internet to disseminate data as an experiment proceeds, making it possible for many other scientists to analyze the results without traveling to the site of the experiment. More important, scientists can use the Internet for informal discussions that are not published.

NSF Takes A Leadership Role

Recognizing how important the Internet was becoming to science, NSF decided to use some of its money to fund Internet growth and the TCP/IP technology. In 1985, NSF announced that it intended to connect researchers at *100* universities to the Internet. They advised the U.S. Congress of their plan, and received additional money to support networking. NSF consulted experts in the field, devised a plan, and began a program that resulted in major changes to the Internet.

Scientists often use sophisticated, high-speed computers called *supercomputers* to analyze data from their experiments. Because supercomputers are expensive, NSF had previously established five supercomputer centers around the country. A scientist working on an NSF project could use the nearest supercomputer center to analyze data.

NSF took the first step by building a Wide Area Network that interconnected computers at its five supercomputer centers. The network used TCP/IP, and provided a connection to the Internet. Named *NSFNET*, the network was much smaller, and not any faster, than the ARPANET. Scientists found the network useful, but not exciting.

Target: All Of Science And Engineering

NSF knew that the small network they built would not replace the ARPANET; it was only the beginning. While scientists began using the initial network to access the supercomputers, NSF made plans for a major new program. The program had an ambitious goal:

> *NSF decided that to keep the U.S. competitive, it needed to extend network access to every science and engineering researcher.*

Although NSF was impressed with the functionality that the Internet provided, it knew that the ARPANET did not have sufficient capacity to achieve the goal. Clearly, the Internet needed a new Wide Area Network.

NSF's Approach

NSF decided to use its funds to create a major new Internet that had significantly more capacity than the existing Internet. After examining available technologies and reviewing its budget, NSF decided that it could not afford to pay for the entire project. Instead, it decided to offer partial support, in the form of federal grants. Companies and other organizations submitted written proposals to NSF to request funding to work on the project.

NSF divided the grants into two types. First, NSF funded a group that wanted to build and operate a new high-speed Wide Area Network to connect parts of the Internet. The new WAN had to replace parts of the ARPANET as well as the original NSFNET. Second, NSF funded groups that wanted to interconnect computers in a small region and attach them to the new WAN. For example, NSF thought that each state might choose to apply as a group. Originally, the groups were referred to as *NSF Regional Networks*. Later, when it became clear that some of the groups spanned large geographic areas, NSF began referring to them as *NSF Mid-Level Networks*.

Because most universities or companies already had LANs connecting their computers, NSF decided to use its funds to help pay for long-distance connections; individual companies and schools paid for their own internal networks.

The NSFNET Backbone

NSF used a competitive bidding process when it awarded a grant for the new Internet WAN, which became known as the *NSFNET backbone*. In 1987, it asked for proposals and used a panel of scientists to help assess them. After considering the alternatives, NSF selected a joint proposal from three organizations: IBM, a computer manufacturer; MCI, a long-distance telephone company; and MERIT, an organization that built and operated a network connecting schools in Michigan.

The three groups cooperated to establish a new Wide Area Network that became the backbone of the Internet in the summer of 1988. MCI provided long-distance transmission lines, IBM provided the dedicated computers and software used in the WAN, and MERIT operated the network. Most people referred to the new backbone using the same name applied to its predecessor, *NSFNET*.

A Major Reorganization

Eventually, as traffic on the new WAN reached capacity, NSF approved reorganizing the network slightly and tripled the capacity of each transmission line. Figure 8.1 shows the results: a wide area network backbone that spans the country.

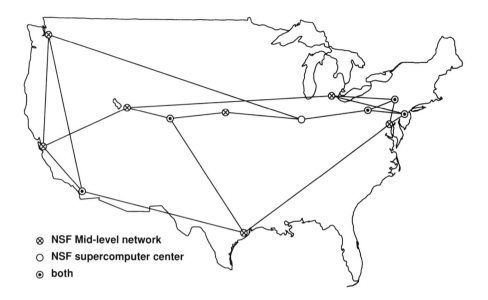

Figure 8.1 The Wide Area Network that formed the backbone of the Internet
before 1992. Funding came from NSF, IBM, MCI, and MERIT.

The ANS Backbone

By the end of 1991, it became clear that the Internet was growing so fast that the
NSFNET backbone would soon reach its capacity. NSF realized that the federal
government could not afford to pay for the Internet indefinitely. They wanted private
industry to assume some responsibility. To solve the problem, IBM, MERIT, and MCI
formed a nonprofit company called *Advanced Networks and Services* (*ANS*).

During 1992, ANS built a new Wide Area Network that forms the current Internet
backbone. Known as *ANSNET*, the new WAN uses transmission lines with 30 times
the capacity of the NSFNET backbone it replaced.

ANSNET differs from the former NSFNET backbone in a significant way. ANS,
not the federal government, owns the transmission lines and computers that comprise
the network. Transferring ownership to a private company is one of the first steps toward commercialization and privatization of the Internet.

Exponential Growth

As NSF connected scientists and engineers, the Internet grew incredibly fast. In
1983, the Internet connected 562 computers. Ten years later, it connected over
1,200,000 computers and was growing quickly. Such staggering growth can best be understood by considering individual computers:

*By early 1994, the Internet was growing so fast that on the average, a
new computer was added to the Internet every 30 seconds. Furthermore, the rate continues to increase.*

Although the Internet did not grow at exactly the same rate in all years and most of
the computers were added late in the decade, a trend of doubling can be identified. In
round numbers the Internet has experienced sustained growth of approximately *10* percent per month, doubling in size approximately every *10* months. Mathematicians call
such growth *exponential.* The table in Figure 8.2 illustrates growth from 1983 to 1994.

Year	Approximate Number Of Computers On The Internet
1983	562
1984	1024
1985	1961
1986	2308
1987	5089
1988	28174
1989	80000
1990	290000
1991	500000
1992	727000
1993	1200000
1994	2217000

Figure 8.2 Estimates of computers connected to the Internet each year from
1983 to 1994. In 1988, the higher speed NSF backbone made
possible more rapid growth.

Exponential growth has some interesting properties. For example, although the Internet has been around for many years, exponential growth means that approximately
half the people connected to the Internet have gained access in the past year. Interestingly, that same statement could have been made in 1983 or in 1989. In fact, the following summarizes the decade of incredible growth:

*At any time during the decade from 1983 through 1994, approximate-
ly half the Internet growth occurred in the previous 12 to 14 months.*

Another way to look at exponential growth puts it in terms of an individual. In the
beginning, a person who acquires access to the Internet feels like a novice. It seems as
if many people have had access for a long time. After a year, the individual can feel
content knowing that over half the Internet users have gained access more recently.

Extending the time scale for exponential growth makes one appreciate it more. Three years after an individual gains access, over *87%* of all Internet users have gained access more recently. In six years, the figure reaches *98%* percent. Six years ago we thought the Internet was huge; it represents less than *3* percent of the current Internet.

A Commercial Assessment

Phenomenal growth has been both a curse and an opportunity. On one hand, it haunts groups who are responsible for operating the Internet and pushes engineers who must plan new technologies that accommodate expansion. On the other hand, it provides an incredible opportunity for vendors who sell TCP/IP and Internet technologies.

A decade ago, most implementations of TCP/IP software were found in universities or computer science research laboratories. Now, businesses use TCP/IP. Entire new industries have arisen; they sell products and services that connect homes and businesses to the Internet. More important, companies have begun selling services that deliver information across the Internet.

The End Of Growth

The Internet cannot continue to grow indefinitely. Although the technologies have managed to accommodate an incredible expansion, exponential growth must end soon. At its current growth rate, for example, the Internet will outpace worldwide production of computers. Furthermore, current Internet technology can connect a maximum of 4,294,967,296 computers†, which is approximately twenty times as large as the number of computers in existence, but only about two-thirds of the world's population. When will growth slow to less than exponential? When will it stop?

At various times in the past, people have predicted the imminent collapse of the Internet by observing that some small piece of the technology was reaching its limit. A few years ago, for example, someone predicted that the Internet could not survive past March of 1993. The predictions of doom have been incorrect. Each time the traffic has approached the capacity of a backbone network, a new backbone technology has been found with significantly more capacity. When the traffic approached the capacity of the dedicated switching computers that comprise the Internet, faster computers were found with significantly more processing power. While researchers agree that growth cannot continue unchecked, few are willing to venture a guess about the future.

---

†The limit arises because the numeric addresses TCP/IP uses to identify computers must be less than 4,294,967,296.

9

The Global Internet

Introduction

Because it spans many countries, people often refer to the Internet as *The Global Internet*. This chapter describes the scope of the Internet, and gives examples of how it reaches much of the world.

Early ARPA Networks

Although ARPA is an agency of the U. S. Government and most of the network research ARPA funded focused on U. S. participants, a few of the research networks included connections to other countries. For example, ARPA used satellites to experiment with communication to sites in Norway and England.

As ARPA concentrated research funding on the Internet project, it used existing connections outside the U.S. to test Internet technology on a larger scale. Thus, those sites became the first foreign sites to have Internet access.

Electronic Mail Among Computers

While ARPA researchers worked on the Internet, other U. S. researchers also experimented with networking. Many of them had used electronic mail for communication with other users on a single timesharing computer. They realized that if a computer had access to basic communication, its electronic mail system could be extended to send messages to users on other machines. The researchers built software that used the dial-up telephone system to connect computers, and soon had electronic mail systems on multiple machines interconnected.

Extending electronic mail connections to machines outside the U. S. was trivial. Because the voice telephone network adheres to a set of standards, systems in multiple countries all interoperate. Thus, researchers did not need to add additional hardware to make communication possible. Like its U.S. counterpart, a foreign computer required only a modem and a copy of the software to enable communication.

One early computer network technology that offered electronic mail over the dial-up telephone system came with the UNIX system from Bell Laboratories. Called the *Unix to Unix Copy Program* or *UUCP*, the program handled the details of interacting with a modem, dialing the destination computer's telephone number or accepting incoming calls, and transferring electronic mail messages across the connection. UUCP ''networks'' arose as owners of machines agreed to cooperate in the exchange of electronic mail.

BITNET

Not everyone had a UNIX system. Researchers who used IBM mainframe computers invented a network that permitted those systems to exchange electronic mail as well. Called *BITNET*, the network grew from a grass roots effort. Technologies like UUCP and BITNET have been adopted in many countries, and some examples of such networks still survive†. For example, although the following countries do not have an Internet connection, they can communicate over a BITNET connection:

Bahrain, Colombia, Guadeloupe, Iran, Panama, Saudi Arabia.

In addition, many countries have access to electronic mail through UUCP or similar technologies. Figure 9.1 lists the set of countries that have only electronic mail connections.

Networks In Europe

As computer technology emerged, Europeans began to establish computer networks. Most countries of Europe have an organization known as the *Post, Telegraph, and Telephone* (*PTT*). The PTTs are agencies of the government, and have control over many forms of communication including computer networking.

PTTs and other telephone companies have experience working together. To ensure that all telephone systems throughout the world are compatible, they formed an organization to create standards. Officially, named the Telecommunication Section of the International Telecommunication Union, the organization usually is known by its acronym, *ITUT*‡. The ITUT publishes documents that contain technical specifications for telephone systems. For example, the documents specify such details as voltages used on telephone lines as well as international agreements for the assignment of telephone numbers.

---

†The *European Academic And Research Network*, *EARN*, uses BITNET technology.

‡The ITUT was formerly named the *Consultative Committee for International Telephone and Telegraph*, *(CCITT)*.

Armenia	Jamaica	Peru
Aruba	Kazakhstan	Philippines
Azerbaijan	Kenya	Re'union
Barbados	Kiribati	Saint Lucia
Belarus	Kyrgyz Republic	Samoa
Belize	Lesotho	Senegal
Bermuda	Lithuania	Seychelles
Bolivia	Macau	Solomon Islands
Botswana	Macedonia	Sri Lanka
Burkina Faso	Madagascar	Suriname
Cameroon	Malawi	Swaziland
China	Mali	Tajikistan
Congo	Malta	Tanzania
Cook Islands	Mauritius	Togo
Cote d'Ivoire	Moldova	Tonga
Cuba	Mozambique	Trinidad and Tobago
Dominican Republic	Namibia	Turkmenistan
Ethiopia	Netherlands Antilles	Uganda
Faroe Islands	New Caledonia	Uruguay
French Guiana	Nicaragua	Uzbekistan
French Polynesia	Niger	Vanuatu
Georgia	Nigeria	Vietnam
Ghana	Niue	Virgin Islands
Grenada	Pakistan	Yugoslavia
Guatemala	Papua New Guinea	Zambia
Indonesia	Paraguay	Zimbabwe

Figure 9.1 Countries in 1994 that could send or receive electronic mail over computer networks, but did not have direct connections to the Internet or BITNET.

When the PTTs became interested in computer networks, they asked the ITUT to create a network standard that would guarantee compatibility. The ITUT convened a committee that produced a standard for computer networking. The result is a network technology known as *X.25*, that is used throughout Europe.

Because the PTTs in Europe followed the ITUT recommendation, it was difficult for European groups to experiment with alternatives like TCP/IP, which is used in the Internet. The point is:

Many countries in Europe adopted the X.25 technology for computer networks because PTTs controlled networking and followed ITUT's recommendation for computer networks in the same way that they followed ITUT's recommendations for voice networks.

Despite the restrictions imposed on networking, a few researchers in universities and research labs have managed to develop experimental networks. In the United Kingdom, for example, a network known as the *Joint Academic NETwork* (*JANET*) has been operational since the 1970s. With funding from IBM, universities in several European countries established a network called the *European Academic And Research Network* (*EARN*).

EBONE: A European Backbone

In 1991 several European countries had experimental networks using TCP/IP; a few had connections to the Internet. Most of the experimental networks connected computers at universities or research labs. Groups throughout Europe organized themselves into a cooperative. Their goal was to form a high-speed European backbone network that connected the members and extended the Internet to each. Figure 9.2 shows a diagram of the resulting European backbone network, called the *EBONE*.

In 1994, the European backbone organization consists of *21* members, each of whom pays an annual fee. In exchange for its fee, the member receives reliable network connectivity to other sites and to the US portion of the Internet. The central organization uses the fees to pay the costs associated with maintaining the backbone network. For example, the organization must pay for leased transmission lines (including transmission lines that connect to the U. S.), hardware, and a staff to operate the backbone. To summarize:

> *The EBONE is a WAN that spans Europe and connects sites to the global Internet.*

EBONE Is The Top Level

As in the U. S., the European portion of the Internet is organized in a three-level hierarchy. The EBONE provides the top level that interconnects the countries. In addition, a region has one or more regional networks that form the second level of the hierarchy. Each regional network interconnects multiple sites, often inside a single country, and also connects them to the backbone. At the third level, an individual site can have a local network that interconnects multiple computers at the site.

When two computers at a single site communicate, they use the local network. Communication between computers at two sites within a single region relies on regional network connections. When a computer in one region communicates with a computer in another, the data passes up to an EBONE site, across the EBONE, and into the other region.

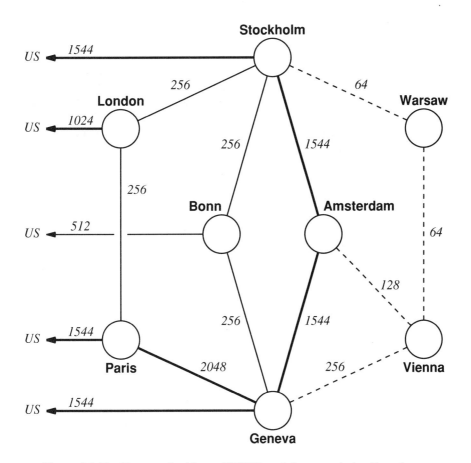

Figure 9.2 The European backbone, EBONE, and the transmission lines that connect it to the U.S. portion of the Internet in 1994. Each transmission line is labeled with its capacity in thousands of bits per second. High-capacity lines are darkened; proposed connections are dashed. Each site on the backbone connects to a large set of computers in its country or region.

Internet On Other Continents

The Internet connects countries on all continents. For example, it covers all of North America and Western Europe, much of South America, Australia, and parts of Asia, Africa, and Antarctica. In addition it reaches several countries in Eastern Europe and the former Soviet Union. Figure 9.3 lists countries currently connected by the global internet.

Antarctica	Estonia	Korea	Slovakia
Argentina	Fiji	Kuwait	Slovenia
Australia	Finland	Latvia	South Africa
Austria	France	Liechtenstein	Spain
Belgium	Germany	Luxembourg	Sweden
Brazil	Greece	Malaysia	Switzerland
Bulgaria	Greenland	Mexico	Taiwan
Canada	Guam	Netherlands	Thailand
Chile	Hong Kong	New Zealand	Tunisia
Costa Rica	Hungary	Norway	Turkey
Croatia	Iceland	Poland	Ukraine
Cyprus	India	Portugal	United Kingdom
Czech Republic	Ireland	Puerto Rico	United States
Denmark	Israel	Romania	Venezuela
Ecuador	Italy	Russian Federation	
Egypt	Japan	Singapore	

Figure 9.3 Countries or regions with computers connected to the global Internet in 1994.

The World Of Internet

The map in Figure 9.4 provides a graphic illustration of how the Internet covers much of the world. A copy of this map also appears on the inside front cover of this book.

A Personal Note

As the Internet grows, I receive messages from many places around the world. A dozen years ago, I was pleased to receive messages from England and Canada because it was thrilling to imagine network connections that reached to foreign countries. I was surprised the first time someone in the Soviet Union sent me electronic mail because, at the time, I assumed that such communication was forbidden. I was also pleased the first time I heard from someone in faraway places like Australia, Japan, India, and China.

Although the thrill of foreign communication has faded over the years, I am still pleased to hear from remote places. For example, I was intrigued by a message from South Africa that asked a technical question about TCP/IP because people studying the details of computer network technologies seemed incongruous with the events reported on the evening news. Now, of course, communication arrives from around the world. After all, the Internet is global.

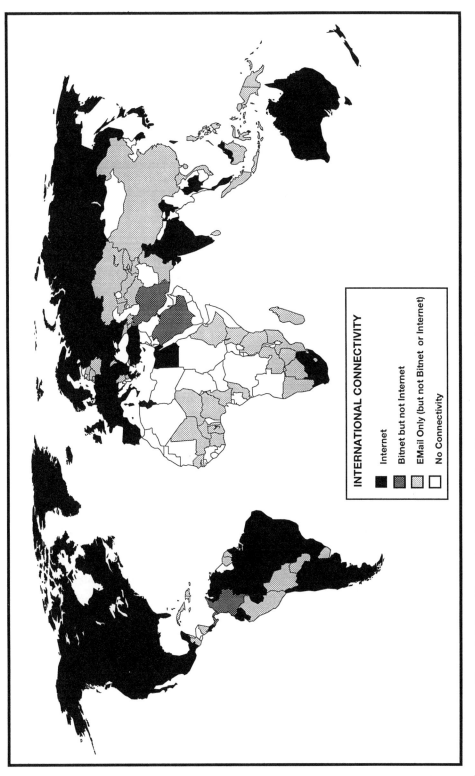

Figure 9.4 A world map that shows countries with one or more networks connected to the Internet in 1994.

INTERNATIONAL CONNECTIVITY

■ Internet

▨ Bitnet but not Internet

░ EMail Only (but not Bitnet or Internet)

□ No Connectivity

10

A Global Information Infrastructure

Introduction

The previous chapter describes some of the long-distance connections that comprise the Internet, and shows how it reaches around the world. Its significance does not arise from size alone, however, it arises because the Internet offers a new global infrastructure that is changing the way people interact. This chapter reviews how previous advances in infrastructure have changed society, and shows what we can expect from the Internet.

Existing Infrastructure

Originally, the term *infrastructure* referred to permanent installations established by the military, usually fortifications used for defense. Currently, it refers to any basic foundation on which society depends. For example, a power distribution system that supplies electricity to homes and businesses is an important part of the infrastructure in industrialized nations.

Each new infrastructure changes society. Before currency was invented, all business transactions involved barter. A person with goods or services for sale had to trade for other goods or services. The two parties negotiated the terms of an exchange; each negotiation began independently from previous negotiations, and the value of an item depended on how much a single individual needed the item. Currency introduced the concept of price, and allowed everyone to translate the value of goods or services into a common form.

Transportation infrastructures changed the way businesses operate. Before society had an overland transportation infrastructure, companies could only choose locations close to raw materials, workers, and customers. Railroads changed society because they made it economical to ship raw materials or manufactured goods long distances. The railroad infrastructure meant companies could locate factories far from the raw materials they use and far from the customers they serve.

A second major change to the U. S. transportation infrastructure occurred when the U. S. government installed an interstate highway system across the country. Originally designed to provide mobility for military equipment, the Interstate system provides high-speed highways that span multiple states, and make it possible to travel to any part of the country quickly. Although railroads existed previously, the interstate system added fundamental new infrastructure because it dramatically increased the speed of transportation to outlying areas as well as the number of locations that could be reached. As a result of the interstate system, long-distance travel by car or truck became an economical alterative to travel via railroad; the trucking industry expanded. The point is:

> *New infrastructure makes new industries possible; the interstate highway system provides an example.*

Communication Infrastructure

Communication infrastructure has been dominated by a series of advances. In ancient civilizations, messengers carried all communication by foot. More recently, messengers rode on animals. Then, people discovered that they could send signals across long distances faster using smoke or the light of a fire. In many cases, governments established communication systems primarily for emergencies (e.g., to communicate information about an invading army). Consequently, only government officials were authorized to use the communication system.

Postal Mail Service

Modern civilizations have a postal mail service that delivers letters. Two advances in infrastructure accompanied the adoption of a postal mail system. First, because postal mail permits a message to be addressed to an individual, it means that any individual served by the mail system can receive a letter. The idea has become known as *universal delivery*. Second, in most modern societies the postal system permits any individual to send a letter; communication is no longer reserved for heads of state or other dignitaries. To summarize:

The modern postal mail service adopted the notion of universal delivery and made it available to all. Any individual can send a letter to any other individual.

Of course, ''universal'' only includes the individuals covered by the postal system. For example, a given country can decide to limit postal mail to those individuals within the country. Doing so encourages individuals within the country to communicate, while discouraging foreign correspondence. The result of such limitation is a closed community: individuals in the country share the benefits of easy communication, while individuals outside the country do not have easy access to it. In general:

The scope of an infrastructure defines a closed community that shares the benefits it offers.

Telegraph

The telegraph introduced a major change in communication technology because it used electric current to carry information. More important, it changed the basic communication infrastructure because it provided high-speed message delivery. Although it had been possible to send a letter almost anywhere using the postal system, delivery required many days or weeks. In contrast, an intercity transfer via telegraph required only minutes. High-speed delivery made it possible to conduct business in ways that were impossible by mail.

The telegraph changed the basic communication infrastructure because it introduced high-speed message delivery.

Telephone

The modern telephone system introduced additional changes in the communication infrastructure. Telephones extended the electronic communication to individuals, and made communication instantaneous.

To understand the significance of individuals having direct access to the infrastructure, remember how a telegraph worked. To send a message, an individual wrote the message and carried it to the telegraph office (or hired a messenger to carry it). An operator then translated the message to code and transmitted it. At the receiving site, the operator wrote down each incoming message and then passed it to a messenger who delivered it to the recipient. As a result, the transfer process involved three or four individuals other than the sender and receiver.

Unlike a telegraph system that uses a single telegraph machine to serve an entire town, a modern telephone system has one telephone in each home or office and permits one individual to communicate directly with another. Because a telephone call reaches an individual without intervening messengers, people have invented new ways to use the telephone that were not possible with the telegraph. Because individuals have direct access to the technology, they use it more frequently.

The telephone also provides instantaneous access. To understand the significance of instantaneous access, think about our example of a telegraph again. Imagine trying to hold a conversation using a telegraph. A sender cannot know whether the intended recipient is currently available (e.g., whether the recipient is out of town), whether the recipient needs time to think about an answer, or whether the recipient did not receive the message. With a telephone, a person communicates with another party directly. Instantaneous communication makes conversation possible, just as if the two parties were physically adjacent.

> *Telephones changed the communication infrastructure by extending communication services to individual homes and offices, and by providing the instantaneous communication needed for interactive conversations.*

The Current Approach

It should be obvious to anyone who reads newspapers that the Internet is not the only available communication service that links computers. In fact, so many groups have organized computer networks that permit computers to exchange information, that the choice is confusing. For example, people talk about such offerings as CompuServe, Prodigy, USENET, America Online, and others. Some are new; others have been in operation for years.

Why are so many companies eager to offer computer network services? The answer, of course, is that they expect to turn a profit. Most entertainment and communication companies understand that it is possible to blend computers, television, and telephones. They realize:

- The set of potential subscribers is large.
- Many potential subscribers own personal computers.
- Potential subscribers are eager to try computer networks.
- Potential subscribers are willing to spend money for network services.

To capture a large market, most companies have designed their network services so they appeal to a mass audience. For example, one service offers school children tutoring in the form of self-paced learning. Another allows an individual to inquire about current stock prices.

While each of the services that network companies offer seems interesting, the idea has a fundamental limitation: because the hardware and software have been optimized for a particular service, the cost of adding new services remains high. For example, some communication services offer subscribers access using modems and a dial-up telephone connection. Because the software has been optimized for use through a dial-up connection, changing it to support high-speed network connections can be complicated.

To summarize:

> *Although many commercial computer networks exist, most have been optimized for a limited set of services, making it difficult to add new types of service.*

The Internet Was Designed To Be General

Unlike most commercially available computer networks, the Internet was not designed for a specific set of services. Instead, software that provides services over the Internet is built in two functional parts. The first part contains basic software needed to allow computers to communicate. It can be used by any service. The second part consists of applications that provide high-level services. As a result:

> *Because the basic Internet communication facilities are both general-purpose and efficient, almost any network application can use the Internet.*

The Internet Offers Diverse Information Services

When an individual first encounters the Internet, they usually use a specific service. Sometimes, people expect the Internet to be completely different from anything they have used before, and are surprised to learn that the Internet offers many of the same services available in other networks. One can send electronic mail or read notices on bulletin boards. In addition, one can obtain information ranging from weather maps to a list of recent jokes.

Although an individual user examines the information and services available on the Internet at a given time, people who designed the Internet understood that the technology could not be designed for a specific set of services. It had to support a wide variety of services, many of which had not been invented when the basic technology was designed. In short,

> *The Internet offers a wide variety of services. Most of the services currently available had not been invented when the Internet was designed.*

TCP/IP Provides Communication Facilities

TCP/IP software provides the basic communication facilities used on the Internet; TCP/IP forms the base on which all services depend. Its flexibility is the key to Internet success. Because TCP/IP is general purpose and efficient, it can support many services. Because TCP/IP is flexible and robust, it can be used with many underlying communication technologies. Most important, its flexibility has allowed scientists and engineers to use TCP/IP with computers, networking technologies, and services that did not exist when TCP/IP was designed.

In essence, TCP/IP provides a general-purpose communication mechanism on which many services have been built. It has been flexible enough to withstand exponential growth for nearly a decade, to tolerate computers and network technologies that were unimaginable when it was defined, and to support constantly changing services. In summary:

> *The Internet is a global information infrastructure. Although it offers many services, the Internet's chief advantage lies in the design of TCP/IP software that has accommodated changes in computers, networks, and services.*

A Personal Note

We live in a university town, so it did not surprise me when my teenage daughter found a summer job in one of the physics labs at the university. At dinner one evening shortly after she started work, she announced that as part of her summer job she was learning to use a computer program called ''gopher'' that worked over the Internet.

I was surprised at the casual way that she talked about the Internet. She did not view the Internet as a grand computer science research project; she viewed it as a service, exactly the same way one views a telephone system. She used the Internet without understanding or caring about the underlying technology. The Internet had become part of the infrastructure.

Inside The Internet

An Explanation Of The Underlying Technology And Basic Capabilities Of The Infrastructure

11

Packet Switching

Introduction

This chapter begins an exploration of the basic communication technology that the Internet uses. It describes the fundamental mechanism all computer networks use to transfer data, and explains why the scheme works well. Succeeding chapters show how the Internet uses the mechanism. Understanding how networks function is important because it explains which high-level services are possible.

Sharing Saves Money

Computer networks do not usually dedicate a single wire to each pair of communicating computers. Instead, the network system arranges for multiple computers to share the underlying hardware facilities. Economics motivates sharing:

> *Arranging for multiple devices to share a single transmission path lowers cost because it uses fewer wires and fewer switching machines.*

Sharing Introduces Delays

Sharing a transmission path is not a new idea, and is not limited to computer networks. For example, some stores require customers to share a transport mechanism. The store is divided into two sections, a main showroom for customers and a warehouse for the inventory. A slow-moving conveyor belt connects the two areas.

When a customer places an order, the order is sent to the warehouse where a clerk assembles the ordered items onto the conveyor belt, which carries them to the showroom. Such stores often require a clerk to finish sending items from one order before moving to the next one.

Normally, the shared conveyor system works well because each order is small. If one customer orders a chess set and then another orders a toaster, the chess set will arrive on the conveyor before the toaster. When a large order appears, however, the shared conveyor can delay many orders. Imagine, for example, that after ordering a toaster, a customer finds the conveyor belt busy transporting *48* folding chairs. Because the store does not permit mixing orders on the conveyor, the customer must wait for all the chairs to arrive before receiving the toaster.

The point is:

> *Granting one party exclusive access of a shared transport path can be impractical because it can delay all other parties.*

Sharing Wires

In a computer network, the transmission path between two computers consists of wires†. Many years ago, engineers designing computer hardware and telephone systems came to the same realization: because only one data transfer can occur on a given wire at a given time, multiple devices that share a wire must wait to use it. For example, in some early telephone systems, subscribers on a street all shared one telephone line. If two neighbors were talking to each other, their conversation prevented a third person from making a call. Similarly, when two computers attached to a given network transfer data, all other computers are forced to wait until the transfer completes.

Selectable Channels

Engineers have devised several solutions to the problem of shared resources. Cable television systems use one of them. A cable company transmits multiple signals on a single wire by using multiple *channels*. Technically, the encoding uses a scheme similar to the one described for modems in Chapter *5*: each channel is assigned a unique frequency, and a carrier at that frequency is modulated to encode information for the channel. The cable company then mixes the encoded signals for all channels and transmits them across the cable.

A television receiver contains the electronic circuitry needed to separate incoming signals by frequency. At any time, a person watching the television tunes it to a specific channel. The television receiver extracts the signal for the selected channel from those that arrive over the cable, and ignores signals on other channels.

---

†Although optical glass cable can also be used, we will use the term ''wire'' to keep the text readable.

Sharing By Taking Turns

While it is possible to build a computer network technology that uses multiple channels to mix signals on a shared wire, most network technologies do not. Instead, they use a variation of the conventional idea of taking turns. Access to the shared resource proceeds by allowing one computer to use the network at a time. As we can see from the conveyor belt example above, the rules of sharing must be defined carefully or a single computer can delay others by using the shared cable for an arbitrarily long time.

To avoid long delays, network technologies limit the amount of data that a computer can transfer on each turn. The idea, which was invented in the 1960s, is called *packet switching*, and the unit of data that can be transferred at one time is called a *packet*. Figure 11.1 illustrates how computers use packet switching.

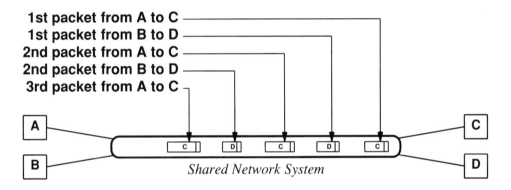

Figure 11.1 An example sequence of packets transferred across a packet switching network as computer *A* communicates with computer *C*, while computer *B* communicates with computer *D*.

In the figure, four computers attach to a network. Assume that computer *B* is sending data to computer *D* while computer *A* is sending data to computer *C*. Both *A* and *B* divide outgoing messages into packets, and then take turns sending the packets. First *A* sends one packet to *C*, then *B* sends one packet to *D*. After *B* sends its packet, *A* sends a second packet, and so on. If *A* has less data to send than *B*, its transfer will complete and *B* can send remaining packets without interruption.

Packet Switching Avoids Delays

Both LANs and WANs use packet switching. To understand how packet switching avoids delays, think of the conveyor belt analogy. Suppose that clerks in the warehouse fill orders by sending an item from one order, then an item from another order, and so on. If a customer orders one small item, it will be placed on the conveyor quickly. If a customer orders 48 folding chairs, only one chair from that order will be entered on the conveyor before an item from each of the other orders is entered.

The same idea holds for computers. A computer can divide data into pieces easily. If A needs to send a long message to C, the computer divides the message into many packets. If B has a short message for D, the message will fit into a single packet or a few packets. After A sends one packet of its message, B can send its packet. Thus, B need not wait for A to finish before it has an opportunity to send packets. Consequently, short messages need not wait for long transfers to complete.

Each Packet Must Be Labeled

Each packet sent across a network originates at one computer and is destined for another. The hardware watches as packets pass across the network. Whenever the hardware detects a packet destined for its local machine, it captures the packet. The hardware places a copy of the packet in the computer's memory, and informs the computer that a packet arrived.

To enable network hardware to distinguish among packets, each packet follows the same format. The packet includes a *header* at the beginning, and data at the end. Think of the header as a label that specifies which computer sent the packet and which computer should receive the packet.

Computers Have Addresses

Each computer on a network has a unique number known as the computer's *address*. To identify the pair of communicating computers, the header at the beginning of a packet contains two important addresses: the address of the computer that sent the packet and the address of the computer to which the packet has been sent. The sender's address is called the *source address*, while the receiver's address is called the *destination address*. Network hardware always uses the numeric addresses to send or receive packets.

The numbers used for addresses depend on the specific network technology. Some technologies use numbers containing a few digits, while others use numbers of *16* digits. The important idea is:

Each computer attached to a network is assigned a unique number called its address. *A packet contains the address of the computer that sent it and the computer to which it is sent.*

Packets Are Not All The Same Size

Although packet switching technologies limit the amount of data in a packet, they allow the sender to transmit any size packet up to the maximum. For example, some network applications allow a user to interact with a remote system by sending keystrokes. Such applications often send a single keystroke in a packet as soon as the user types it on the keyboard. Other applications that have larger amounts of data to transfer choose larger packets.

Packet Transmission Seems Instantaneous

In most packet switching networks, packet transfer occurs quickly. For example, a typical LAN can transfer one thousand large packets between two computers in a second; it takes slightly less time to send small packets. To a human, events that require thousandths of a second seem instantaneous. For example, several people can use computers that attach to a single, shared network without perceiving delay. While one user runs a word processing application on a remote computer, another can access a remote database. Each user types input, uses a mouse, and experiences exactly the same response as if the program were run locally.

To summarize:

A packet switching system permits multiple pairs of computers to communicate across a shared network with minimal delay because it divides each conversation into small packets and arranges for the computers that share a network to take turns sending packets.

Sharing Is Automatic

Packet switching technologies allow computers to send data at any time. One computer can begin to send packets before others are ready to use the network. As long as only one computer needs to use the network, it can send packets continuously. As soon as a second computer becomes ready to send data, sharing begins. Both computers take turns so each receives a fair share of the network. If a third computer becomes ready, all three share the network equally. The network also adjusts sharing when a computer stops sending data. For example, if three computers share a network equally and one of them finishes sending data, the remaining two computers take turns.

More important, a computer does not need to know how many other computers are using the network simultaneously. The key point is:

> *Because packet switching systems adapt instantly as computers be-*
> *come ready to send data or others finish sending data, each computer*
> *receives a fair share of network resources at any given time.*

Network Hardware Handles Sharing

Interface hardware handles sharing automatically. That is, network sharing does not require any ''computation,'' nor do computers need to coordinate before they begin using a network. Instead, a computer can generate a packet at any time. When a packet is ready, the computer's interface hardware waits its turn and then transfers the packet. Thus,

> *From a computer's point of view obtaining fair access to a shared*
> *network is automatic – the network hardware handles all the details.*

Many Devices Can Use Packet Switching

Devices such as cash registers, video cameras, bar code scanners, and magnetic strip readers can all connect to a packet switching network. Many vendors also sell printers that connect to a network. Because a single network printer can be accessed by all computers on a network, using network printers can reduce costs: each computer does not need a separate printer.

A device like a printer requires special hardware to attach it to a network. In particular, each device attached to a network must contain a small computer, usually a microprocessor. The computer receives packets from the network that contain instructions to control the device. Conceptually,

> *Although many types of devices can connect directly to a computer*
> *network, each such device must contain a small computer that handles*
> *communication.*

Relevance To The Internet

Like most computer networks, the Internet is a packet switching system. Internet hardware includes physical wires shared among multiple users. Packet switching allows many communications to proceed simultaneously, without requiring an application to wait for all other communication to complete. As a consequence, whenever a user transfers data across the Internet, network software on the sending machine divides the data into packets, and network software on the receiving machine must reassemble the packets to produce the data. For example, a document from a word processor must be divided into packets for transfer across the Internet, and then reassembled into a complete document at the receiving side. To summarize:

> *All data is transferred across the Internet in packets. A sender divides a message or document into packets and transfers the packets across the Internet. A receiver reassembles the original message from the packets that arrive. Packets from many machines traverse the Internet at the same time.*

Summary

The fundamental technique that computer networks use to ensure fair access to shared network resources is known as packet switching. Before data can be transferred across a network it must be divided into packets. Each packet contains a header that specifies the computer to which the packet should be delivered; the destination is specified using a number known as the computer's address. Computers that share access to a network take turns sending packets. On each turn, a given computer sends one packet. Although devices like printers can connect to a network, such devices must contain a microprocessor to handle network communication.

12

Internet: A Network Of Networks

Introduction

The previous chapter describes packet switching and shows why dividing long messages into short packets lowers delays for computers that share a transmission path. This chapter describes how multiple packet switching networks can be interconnected to form an Internet that functions like a single, large network.

Network Technologies Are Incompatible

Many packet switching technologies exist because each has been designed to meet constraints of speed, distance, and cost. Inexpensive networks usually operate at lower speeds than expensive networks. Designers do not attempt to make all designs compatible – details such as the electrical voltages and the numbers assigned as computer addresses often differ. Consequently, one cannot form a large network merely by connecting the wires of two or more smaller networks.

To understand the consequences of incompatible technologies, consider a large enterprise that has two, incompatible local area networks in use. For example, suppose the accounting department uses one type of network and the production department uses another. When the accounting department needs information that resides on a computer in the production department, the information must be written to an external storage device (e.g., a floppy disk), and transferred manually. If both networks could be interconnected, the information could be transferred from one computer to another at electronic speed without requiring a person to transport a disk; interconnecting networks saves time and money.

Coping With Incompatibility

There are two possible solutions to the problem of network incompatibility:

- Choose a network technology that suffices for the entire enterprise, and mandate that the enterprise use the chosen technology.

- Allow groups to choose the network technology that best fits their needs and budget, and then find a way to interconnect all types of networks.

The first solution has several drawbacks. It can be impossible to find a single network technology that handles all the needs of an enterprise. Even if such a technology exists, cost may be prohibitive. More important, requirements can change when a new group within an enterprise needs a network. If every group in the enterprise must use the same type of network, changing the technology to accommodate one group means replacing all existing installations. We can conclude:

> *It is impractical, and may be economically infeasible, to require all computers in an enterprise to use the same network technology.*

The Internet uses an approach that allows each group to select the network technology that best meets the group's needs. To accommodate multiple network types, the Internet provides a mechanism to interconnect arbitrary networks and the software to transfer data across the connections.

Two Fundamental Concepts

Two simple ideas will help explain some of the technology used to interconnect networks within the Internet. The first reveals how it is possible to solve the problem of distant connections; the second reveals how it is possible to connect networks that are incompatible.

A Connection To A Network Can Be Extended

Each computer that attaches to a Local Area Network needs a cable that connects from the computer to the LAN. Although the cable between a computer and a LAN is usually short (e.g., a few inches or the distance of one hallway in an office building), it can be extended. Figure 12.1 illustrates three ways that a computer can connect to a remote network.

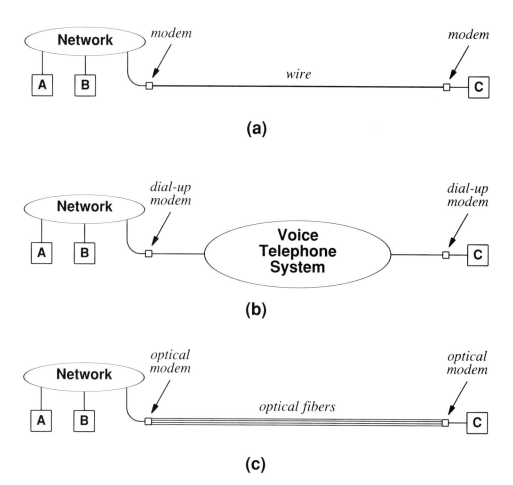

Figure 12.1 Three ways to extend the connection between a computer and a
network: (a) two modems with wires connecting them, (b) two
modems that communicate across the voice telephone system,
and (c) two optical modems with glass fibers connecting them.

Chapter 5 discusses how modems can be used to send data across a wire or across
the telephone system. Instead of wires or telephone connections, many modern communication systems use flexible glass fiber to provide connections across long distances. Called a *fiber optic* connection, the technology requires optical modems that
use light instead of electricity to carry data. At the sending end, an optical modem contains a laser that converts data from a computer into pulses of light and sends the pulses
down the fiber. At the receiving end, an optical modem senses the pulses of light and
turns them back into data for a computer.

The fiber optic approach has the advantage of permitting long distances (e.g., across a campus or between towns). An optical fiber has three interesting properties that explain why it is so useful. First, because the fiber is flexible, it can be installed similar to any cable. Second, because the fiber is made from glass, light can travel through it. Third, because the fiber is constructed to reflect light back inside, the light intensity does not diminish much as it travels along (i.e., almost no light escapes from the sides of the fiber).

A Computer Can Have Multiple Connections

The second idea that will help explain internet technology is straightforward: a given computer can connect to two or more networks. Chapter 6 explains that a computer contains a circuit board that connects the computer to a network. In fact, a computer can have multiple circuit boards that each connect it to a network; the networks do not all need to use the same technology. After a computer has been connected to multiple networks, it can send or receive packets from any of them.

Using A Computer To Interconnect Networks

The Internet uses special-purpose computers to interconnect networks. Figure 12.2 illustrates the concept. Computers used to interconnect networks have standard hardware. Like a conventional computer, they include a central processor, memory, and network interfaces. Also like conventional computers, they come in a variety of sizes and speeds. The smallest, least powerful models cost only a few hundred dollars; powerful models that can interconnect multiple networks cost tens of thousands of dollars.

Although they use conventional hardware, computers that interconnect networks do not use conventional software. Because they are busy handling network interconnections, such computers do not include application programs. For example, an interconnecting computer does not run word processing spreadsheet applications. Instead, such a computer has only special purpose software that performs tasks related to the job of interconnecting networks. In fact, interconnecting computers are configured so they start the needed software automatically whenever they are powered on. As a result, they automatically restart after a power failure, and normally do not require any human intervention.

To summarize:

> *Computers that interconnect networks are dedicated to the interconnection task. Although they use conventional hardware, they run special-purpose software that starts automatically when the system is powered on and remains operating at all times.*

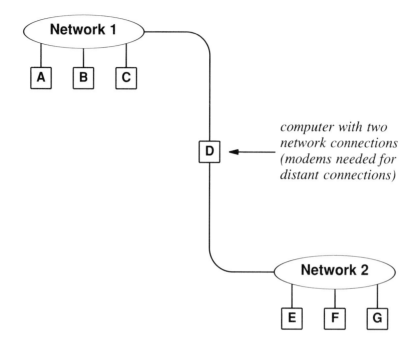

Figure 12.2 A computer, *D*, used to interconnect two networks. The networks can be the same type or different types.

Interconnecting Computers Pass Packets

A computer that interconnects networks has one major task to perform: it forwards packets from one network to the other. The next chapter describes how packet forwarding works, but the idea is simple: the computer receives a packet sent to it across one network, and sends the packet on to its destination across the other network. For example, in Figure 12.2, computers *A* and *G* do not attach to the same network. If computer *A* generates a packet for computer *G*, it sends the packet to *D*, the computer that interconnects the networks. *D* receives the packet from Network *1* and then uses Network *2* to send the packet to *G*.

Interconnecting Computers Are Called Routers

Software on a computer that interconnects networks needs to know to which network each computer connects so it can determine where to send packets. In the case of two networks, the decision is straightforward – when a packet arrives over one network, it should be sent over the other. In the case of a computer that interconnects three networks, however, the decision is complex. When a packet arrives over one network, software on the computer must choose one of the other two networks.

The process of selecting a network over which to send a packet is called *routing*, and the dedicated computers that interconnect networks and perform the task are called *routers*. The next chapter discusses the details of routing in the Internet.

Routers Are The Building Blocks Of The Internet

Although many people think of the Internet as a single, giant network to which many computers attach, it is not. Instead, the Internet consists of thousands of computer networks, interconnected by routers. Each computer attaches to one of the individual networks. When a computer on one network communicates with a computer on another network, it sends packets through a router. To summarize:

> *The Internet is not a conventional computer network. It consists of thousands of computer networks interconnected by dedicated, special-purpose computers called* routers.

Routers are used in many ways throughout the Internet. For example, a router can interconnect two Local Area Networks in a single building or even in a room. Using a pair of modems to reach a distant network, a router can interconnect the Local Area Networks in two buildings or across a campus. Because a router can interconnect diverse technologies, it can interconnect a Local Area Network and a Wide Area Network.

Routers Accommodate Multiple Types Of Networks

Because a given router can interconnect networks that use different hardware technologies, the router architecture permits the Internet to contain multiple types of networks. Each small group can use whichever LAN technology is best suited to its performance needs and budget. It then uses a router to connect its network to the Internet. A large organization can purchase routers to interconnect its networks into a private internet. By adding one additional router, the organization can connect its private internet to the global Internet.

Connecting multiple types of networks is important for two reasons. First, because the Internet connects many organizations of diverse size, networking needs, and budgets, the organizations use diverse network technologies. Second, and more important, because computer networking is an active area of research, technologies keep changing. Many of the hardware technologies currently used in the Internet did not exist when the Internet began, and many technologies in use now will be replaced in the future. The Internet could not survive if it did not permit multiple types of networks.

Routers Can Interconnect WANs And LANs

Routers explain how the Internet can use both Wide Area Networks and Local Area Networks. A national Wide Area Network, for example, provides an efficient long-distance technology that connects many sites. Often, the term *backbone network* is used to describe a major WAN to which other networks attach. The backbone reaches some, but not all sites; such locations are called *backbone sites*. Figure 12.3 illustrates the architecture.

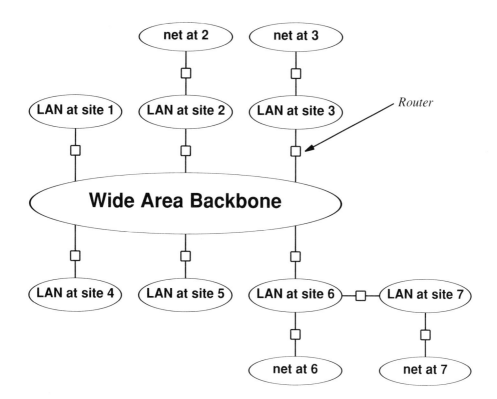

Figure 12.3 An example of a wide area backbone. At each backbone site, a router connects a local area network to the backbone. At some sites, additional routers connect additional networks. Networks at site *7* do not connect directly to the backbone.

As Figure 12.3 illustrates, a router at each backbone site connects the backbone WAN to a Local Area Network. The router at a site provides a path between computers attached to the site's LAN and computers attached to LANs at other sites. A given site can also use additional routers to connect additional networks either at the site or at other sites. In Figure 12.3, for example, site *2* has two routers and two networks. Three routers attach to the LAN at site *6*: one connects to the backbone, another connects to a second network at the site, and a third connects to a LAN at site *7*.

Usually, the least expensive way to connect a new network to the Internet involves finding the closest Internet site and connecting a router between one of its networks and the new network. However, not all sites are authorized to provide connections. In addition, it may be impossible to cross political boundaries (e.g., to form a connection between networks in two different countries).

Dial-up Access For Personal Computers

Previous sections describe the Internet as an interconnection of networks. However, many people who cannot afford a direct network connection use the telephone system to access Internet services. To do so, their computer must have a dial-up modem, which plugs into the phone system like an ordinary telephone. In addition, their computer must have software to use the modem. When the software runs, it uses the modem to place a telephone call to a modem that connects to a computer attached to the Internet. The remote computer answers the call and provides access to Internet services. Figure 12.4 illustrates the idea.

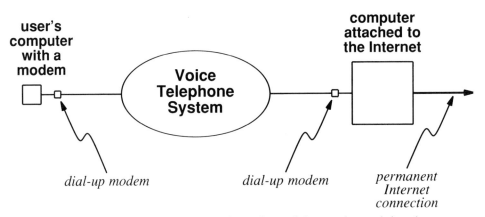

Figure 12.4 Access to Internet services using a dial-up modem and the telephone network. Private individuals often choose dial-up access because it costs less than a permanent Internet connection.

Interconnecting Networks Was Revolutionary

Using a dedicated computer to interconnect two networks may not seem like a fundamental idea, but it is. Before Internet technology appeared, a company needed to choose one network technology for all computers or have several, independent networks. Routers enable a company to allow each group to choose an appropriate network technology, while providing a way to interconnect the networks.

Summary

Although to a user it appears to be a single, large network, the Internet consists of thousands of computer networks interconnected by dedicated computers called routers. Because a router can interconnect two networks that use different technologies, a router can connect a LAN to another LAN, a LAN to a WAN, or a WAN to another WAN. Because it is made up of networks interconnected by routers, many people refer to the Internet as a *network of networks*.

Using routers to interconnect networks produced a revolution. It permits connections among multiple types of networks, and allows each group in an organization to choose a network technology that best suits the group's needs and budget.

13

IP: Software To Create A Virtual Network

Introduction

The previous chapter describes the Internet as a network of networks, formed by using special-purpose computers called routers to interconnect networks. Of course, merely connecting hardware together does not make an Internet. Interconnected computers need software before they can communicate. This chapter describes the basic software that makes the hardware behave like a single, large network.

Protocol: An Agreement For Communication

It is impossible for two humans to communicate unless they agree to speak a common language. The same holds true for computers – two computers cannot communicate unless they share a common language. A *communication protocol* is an agreement that specifies a common language two computers use to exchange messages. The term derives from diplomatic vocabulary, in which a protocol specifies the rules under which a diplomatic exchange occurs.

A computer communication protocol defines communication precisely. For example, a protocol specifies the exact format and meaning of each message that a computer can send. It also specifies the conditions under which a computer should send a given message, and how a computer should respond when a message arrives.

Basic Functionality: The Internet Protocol

A key communication protocol used in the Internet is called, appropriately, the *Internet Protocol*. Usually abbreviated *IP*, the protocol specifies, in great detail, the rules that define the details of how computers communicate. It specifies exactly how a packet must be formed, and how a router must forward each packet on toward its destination.

Each computer that connects to the Internet must follow the rules of the Internet Protocol. When it creates a packet, a computer must use the format IP specifies. When a computer receives a packet, the packet will be an exact copy of the packet that was originally sent, still in IP format. Furthermore, each router in the Internet expects packets to adhere to the IP format as they pass from one network to another.

IP Software On Every Machine

Computer hardware does not understand IP. Therefore, attaching a computer to the Internet does not mean it can use Internet services. To communicate on the Internet, a computer needs IP software. Indeed, every computer that uses the Internet must run IP software.

IP is fundamental: all Internet services use IP to send or receive packets. Because IP is fundamental, each computer usually has a single copy of IP software that all applications share. On sophisticated computers, the operating system keeps a copy of the IP software in memory at all times, ready to send or receive packets. In summary,

> *Because all Internet services use the Internet Protocol, a computer must have IP software before it can use the Internet.*

Internet Packets Are Called Datagrams

To distinguish between Internet packets and packets for other networks, we call a packet that follows the IP specification an *IP datagram*. The name was chosen to provide intuition about how the Internet packet delivery service handles packets. As it suggests, the Internet handles datagrams in much the same way that a telegraph office handles telegrams. Once the sending computer creates a datagram and starts it on a trip through the Internet, the sender is free to resume processing in the same way that a person is free to perform tasks after sending a telegram. A datagram travels across the Internet independent of the sender, just as a telegram travels to its destination independent of the person who sent the message. To summarize:

Each packet sent across the Internet must follow the format specified by the Internet Protocol. Such packets are called IP datagrams.

The Illusion Of A Giant Network

Although the Internet Protocol defines many communication details, it has an important purpose. Once every computer on the Internet has IP software installed, any computer can create an IP datagram and send it to any other computer. In essence, IP transforms a collection of networks and routers into a seamless communication system by making the Internet function like a single, large network. Figure 13.1 illustrates the idea.

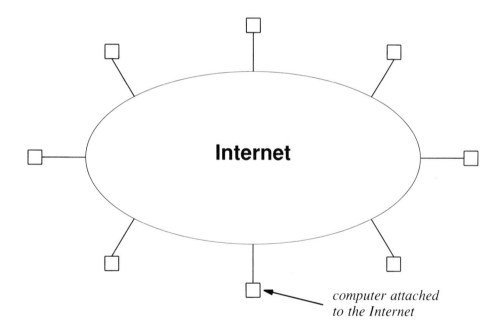

computer attached
to the Internet

Figure 13.1 The view of the Internet that IP software provides. Users and application programs treat the Internet like a single large network that allows arbitrary numbers of computers to communicate.

Computer scientists use the term *virtual* to describe technologies that present the illusion of larger, more powerful computational facilities than the hardware provides. The Internet is a *virtual network* because it presents the illusion of a single, large network. Although the Internet is a network of networks, IP software takes care of the details and allows users to think of "the Internet" as a single network. Users remain unaware of the Internet's networks and routers, just as telephone subscribers remain unaware of the wires and switches that comprise the telephone system.

The point is:

> *The Internet operates like a single network that connects several million computers. IP software allows any computer to send an IP datagram to any other computer.*

The Reality Of Internal Structure

Although users believe the Internet to be a single large network, the Internet contains a complex internal physical structure that users never see. Figure 13.2 illustrates the concept.

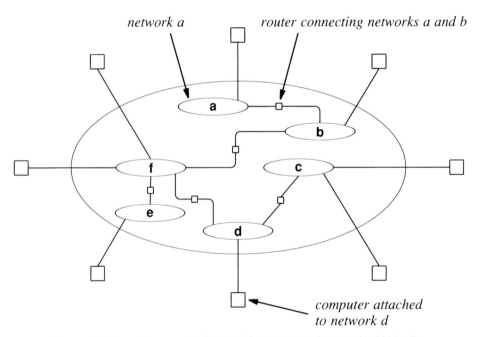

Figure 13.2 A small example of the physical structure that remains hidden inside the Internet. Each computer attaches to a single network; routers interconnect the networks.

When a datagram travels across the Internet from one computer to another, it must follow a physical path. At each step along the path, the datagram either travels across a physical network or through a router to another network. Eventually the datagram reaches its final destination.

Datagrams Travel In Packets

The IP datagram defines a standard format for all Internet packets. Choosing a standard packet format may seem like a wonderful idea because it means an Internet packet is not limited to the packet format used by the underlying network hardware. More important, it means that the Internet packet format does not depend on one particular network technology.

Unfortunately, defining a standard Internet packet format also has a disadvantage. Each network technology defines its own packet format, and a given computer network only accepts and delivers packets that adhere to the format for its technology – network hardware simply does not understand the IP datagram format.

How can the Internet send IP datagrams across networks that do not recognize the IP datagram format? The easiest way to imagine a datagram transfer is to consider how overnight shipping services handle letters. Assume someone has written a letter, placed it in an envelope, and written the name of the intended recipient on the outside. The letter is much like an IP datagram. Suppose the sender asks an overnight shipping service to deliver the letter. The overnight service requires that the letter be placed inside one of their envelopes, and that the name and address of the recipient be written on the outside in the format they specify. The outer envelope is analogous to a *network packet*.

Both the inner and outer envelopes contain a recipient name. Although the names usually agree, they need not be identical. Consider what happens if the sender knows the exact office address of a secretary at the recipient's place of business but not the exact office address of the individual to whom the letter is addressed. The sender can mail the overnight parcel to the secretary for delivery. In such cases, the inner address and outer address differ. When the parcel arrives at the address on the outer envelope, the secretary named on the outer envelope opens it and forwards the letter.

Datagram transmission follows the same pattern. The Internet sends an IP datagram across a single network by placing it inside a network packet. As far as the network is concerned, the entire IP datagram is data. When the network packet arrives at the next computer, the computer "opens" the packet and extracts the datagram. The receiver examines the destination address on the datagram to determine how to process it. In particular, when a router determines that the datagram must be sent across another network, the router creates a new network packet, "encloses" the datagram inside the packet, and sends the packet across another network toward its destination. When a packet carrying a datagram arrives at its final destination, local software on the machine opens the packet and processes the datagram.

Every Computer Is Assigned A Unique Address

To make datagram routing and delivery possible, each computer attached to the Internet must be assigned a unique address. Like addresses used by conventional networks, the addresses used on the Internet are numeric. One computer must know the address of another computer before it can communicate, just as a person must know someone's telephone number before calling them on the phone.

Internet Addresses

The unique number assigned to a computer is called its *Internet address*, often abbreviated *IP address*. Each computer, including routers, needs to be assigned an IP address before the computer can communicate on the Internet. When an organization connects to the Internet, it obtains a set of IP addresses for the organization's computers from the Internet authority. If the organization acquires a new computer, an address from the set is assigned to the new machine.

An Odd IP Address Syntax

Internally, a computer stores an IP address in four binary units called *bytes*. Although the exact internal form is unimportant, it helps explain why IP addresses are expressed in an odd syntax. When an application program needs to display an IP address for a human, or when humans need to type an IP address to a program, the binary address is expressed in a form that is easy for humans to understand: it is written as four decimal numbers separated by periods. For example, the IP address of one particular computer is:

$$128.10.2.1$$

The IP address of another computer is:

$$192.5.48.3$$

Fortunately, users seldom need to type or see IP addresses; most application programs allow humans to enter a name when specifying a computer†.

---

†Chapter *16* explains the computer names one must enter.

IP Addresses Are Not Random

IP addresses are like telephone numbers in another way: the assignment of numbers is not random. Instead, IP addresses are assigned so that all computers on the same network have the same prefix. The address assignment has been chosen to make it efficient to route IP datagrams through the Internet.

An Example Trip Through The Internet

An example may help clarify how IP software works. Consider the example internet that Figure 13.3 shows.

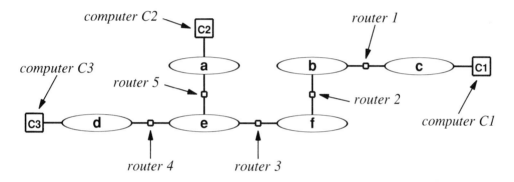

Figure 13.3 An example internet with six networks and three computers attached.

Imagine that computer *C1* needs to communicate with computer *C3*. To begin, IP software on *C1* must create an IP datagram. Each datagram has a field that specifies the sender's IP address and a field that specifies the destination's IP address. The datagram that *C1* creates contains *C3*'s IP address as the destination and *C1*'s IP address as the sender's (source) address.

Because the two computers do not attach to the same network, any datagram traveling between them must pass through a router. *C1* sends the datagram across network *c* to router *1*. Router *1* examines the datagram's destination address, *C3*, to determine where to send it. Because the destination lies beyond network *b*, router *1* sends the datagram across network *b* to router *2*. Router *2* examines the destination address and sends the datagram across network *f* to router *3*. Router *3* must make a choice between routers *4* and *5*. It chooses to send the datagram across network *e* to router *4* because router *4* leads to the destination†. Router *4* finds that it can deliver the datagram to its final destination, *C3*, by sending across network *d*. If *C3* sends a datagram back to *C1*, the new datagram follows the same path in the reverse direction.

---

†When a router must choose between two paths that both lead to the destination, the router chooses the shortest path.

Of course, computer networks and routers transfer datagrams at incredibly high speed. If the networks in our example are local area technologies, the entire time required for a datagram to traverse the Internet and a reply to come back takes only a few thousandths of a second. A human perceives the time required for a complete round trip to be instantaneous. Even if some of the networks are distant, the delays can be so short that a human does not notice. As a result, the Internet is so effective when transferring datagrams that it appears to operate like a single, large computer network.

Summary

The Internet Protocol, IP, specifies the basic rules that a computer must follow to communicate across the Internet. IP defines the format of Internet packets, which are called IP datagrams. IP also defines an address scheme that assigns each computer a unique number used in all communication. More important, IP software makes an interconnected set of networks and routers operate like a single, large network.

Each computer on the Internet must have IP software that allows it to create and send IP datagrams. Each router also has IP software that knows how to forward datagrams to their destination. When a datagram arrives at a router, the IP software chooses the path that will lead to the datagram's destination.

14

TCP: Software For Reliable Communication

Introduction

The previous chapter discusses the Internet Protocol and describes how IP software on computers and routers makes it possible to send an IP datagram from any machine on the Internet to any other. This chapter continues the discussion of basic Internet communication software. It examines the second major communication protocol, TCP.

A Packet Switching System Can Be Overrun

Chapter *12* describes packet switching, the basic technique used by most modern computer networks. Recall that packet switching allows multiple computers to communicate without delay because it requires that the computers divide data into small packets. Packet switching systems, like those used in the Internet, need additional communication software to ensure that data is delivered. To understand why, consider the miniature internet that Figure 14.1 illustrates.

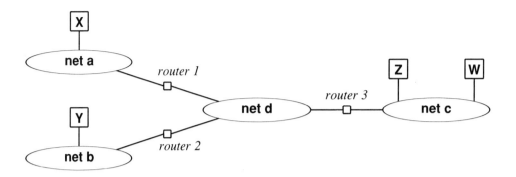

Figure 14.1 An example internet with four networks connected by routers. If
each network has the same capacity, packets from networks *a*
and *b* cannot flow to network *d* at full speed.

Suppose computer *X* sends packets to computer *W* at the same time computer *Y*
sends packets to computer *Z*. Network *d* lies on the path from *X* to *W* as well as on the
path from *Y* to *Z*. Furthermore, all four networks have the same capacity. Suppose that
each network can handle 5000 packets per second. Also suppose that computers *X* and
Y both generate 5000 datagrams per second. Router *1* and router *2* each receive 5000
datagrams per second. Both routers need to send all the datagrams they receive across
network *d* to router *3*. Unfortunately, network *d* can also handle only 5000 packets per
second.

To understand the problem, imagine that each network is a road, that each router is
an interchange that connects two roads, and that all roads have the same speed limit.
Figure 14.2 illustrates how cars traveling on roads correspond to packets traveling on an
internet. Imagine that both roads *a* and *b* are packed with cars traveling at the speed
limit. If all the cars from roads *a* and *b* attempt to merge onto road *d*, a traffic jam
results.

On a roadway, cars stop when a traffic jam occurs. In the example internet, however, datagrams cannot stop. Each second, 5000 datagrams arrive from one network,
5000 from another, and only 5000 datagrams can be sent to their destinations. Where
do the extra 5000 datagrams per second go when they cannot squeeze onto network *d*?
The routers discard them! Of course, each router has memory, and can store some of
the datagrams in memory in case of temporary congestion. However, a router only has
enough memory to hold a few thousand datagrams. If datagrams continue to arrive faster than they can leave, the router must discard datagrams as they arrive until the
congestion clears.

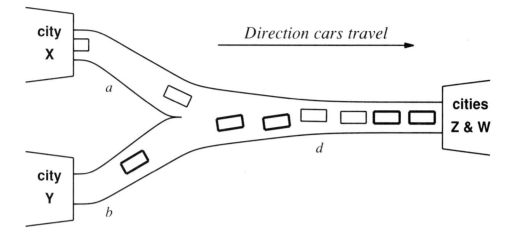

Figure 14.2 Cars from two roads merging onto another road are analogous to packets from two networks merging onto a third network. The diagram only shows cars traveling left-to-right, from cities *X* and *Y* to cities *Z* and *W*.

TCP Helps IP Guarantee Delivery

Because the Internet uses packet switching hardware that can become overrun with datagrams, the designers knew that additional communication software was needed. To handle the problem, they invented the *Transmission Control Protocol* (*TCP*). TCP makes the Internet reliable. All computers that attach to the Internet run IP software; most of them also run TCP software. In fact, TCP and IP are so important and work together so well that the entire set of communication protocols the Internet uses is known as the *TCP/IP* protocol suite.

TCP solves several problems that can occur in a packet switching system. If a router becomes overrun with datagrams, it must discard them. As a result, a datagram can be lost on its trip through the Internet. TCP automatically checks for lost datagrams and handles the problem. The Internet has a complex structure with multiple paths that datagrams can travel. When the hardware in a router or network system fails, other routers start sending datagrams along a new path analogous to the way cars detour around a problem on a highway. As a result of the change in routes, some datagrams can arrive at the destination in a different order than they were sent. TCP automatically checks incoming datagrams and puts the data back in order. Finally, network hardware failures sometimes result in duplication of datagrams. As a result, multiple copies of a datagram can arrive at the destination. TCP automatically checks for duplicate datagrams and accepts only the first copy of data that arrives.

To summarize:

> *Although IP software allows a computer to send and receive datagrams, IP does not handle all the problems that can arise. A computer using the Internet also needs TCP software to provide reliable, error-free communication.*

TCP Provides A Connection Between Computer Programs

Conceptually, TCP allows computer programs to interact analogous to the way people interact when they use a telephone. A program on one computer specifies a remote program and initiates contact (the equivalent of using a telephone number to place a call). The called program must accept the incoming call (the equivalent of answering the phone). Once contact has been established, the two programs can send data in either direction (the equivalent of holding a telephone conversion). Finally, when the programs finish, they terminate the session (the equivalent of hanging up the telephones). Of course, because computers operate at much higher speeds than humans, two programs can establish a connection, exchange a small amount of data, and then terminate the connection within a few thousandths of a second. To summarize:

> *TCP software makes it possible for two computer programs to communicate across the Internet in a manner similar to the way humans use a telephone. Once the programs establish a connection, they can exchange arbitrary amounts of data and then terminate communication.*

The Magic Of Recovering Lost Datagrams

Detecting and removing a duplicate copy of a datagram is a relatively easy task. Because TCP includes an identification of the data in each datagram, the receiver can compare the identification in an incoming datagram with the identification of data already received. If a duplicate copy of data arrives, the receiver ignores it.

Recovering from datagram loss is more difficult. To understand why, consider the example internet shown in Figure 14.1; datagrams can be lost in a router in the middle of the internet while neither the original source computer nor the final destination computer experiences trouble. TCP handles the problem by using timers and acknowledgements. Whenever data arrives at its final destination, TCP software on the receiving machine sends an *acknowledgement* back to the source. An acknowledgement is a short message that specifies which data arrived.

A sender uses acknowledgements to guarantee that all data arrives. Whenever TCP software sends data, it starts a timer using the computer's internal clock. The timer works like an alarm clock – when the timer expires, it notifies TCP. If an acknowledgement arrives before the timer expires, TCP cancels the timer. If the timer expires before an acknowledgement arrives, TCP assumes the datagram was lost and sends another copy.

TCP Retransmission Is Automatic

Many computer communication protocols use the scheme of starting a timer and resending data if an acknowledgement fails to arrive before the timer expires. TCP's scheme differs from the one used by other protocols because it works across the Internet. If the destination computer resides close to the source (e.g., in the same building), TCP only waits a short time before retransmitting the datagram. If the destination computer resides far from the source (e.g., in another country), TCP waits a longer time before retransmitting. Furthermore, the timeout mechanism is completely automatic – TCP measures current delays on the Internet and adjusts the timeout automatically. If many computers begin to send datagrams and the Internet slows down, TCP increases the time it waits before retransmitting. If conditions change and datagrams begin to flow across the Internet quickly, TCP automatically decreases the timeout. Experience has shown that in a large Internet, a communication protocol must change the timeout automatically to achieve efficient data transfer.

TCP's ability to automatically adjust timeout values has contributed much to the success of the Internet. In fact, most Internet applications could not operate without TCP software that adapts to changing conditions. Furthermore, careful measurements and experience have shown that TCP software can adapt to changes in the Internet extremely well – although many scientists have tried to devise improvements, no one has produced a better protocol.

TCP And IP Work Together

It is not a coincidence that TCP and IP work well together. Although the protocols can be used separately, they were designed at the same time to work as part of a unified system, and were engineered to cooperate and to complement each other. Therefore, TCP handles the problems that IP does not handle without duplicating the work that IP does. The point is:

> *A computer connected to the Internet needs both TCP and IP software. IP provides a way to transfer a packet from its source to its destination, but does not handle problems like datagram loss or delivery out of order. TCP handles the problems that IP does not. Together, they provide a reliable way to send data across the Internet.*

Often, vendors sell a single package that includes software for TCP, IP, and a few related communication protocols. Collectively, the set is known as *TCP/IP software*.

Summary

Although IP software provides basic Internet communication, it does not solve all problems that arise. Like any packet switching system, the Internet can become overrun if many computers send data at the same time. When computers send more datagrams than the Internet can handle, routers must discard some of the incoming datagrams.

IP software does not detect missing datagrams. To handle such communication errors, a computer must also have TCP software. TCP eliminates duplicate data, ensures that data is reassembled in exactly the order it was sent, and resends data when a datagram is lost.

The problem of data loss is especially difficult because loss can occur in the middle of the Internet, even when the networks and routers adjacent to both the source and destination computers do not experience problems. TCP uses acknowledgements and timeouts to handle the problem of loss. The sender retransmits data unless an acknowledgement arrives before the timer expires. TCP's scheme for timeout works across the Internet because TCP changes the timeout automatically depending on whether the destination is close or far away from the source.

15

Clients + Servers = Distributed Computing

Introduction

Previous chapters describe the TCP/IP communication protocols that work together to provide reliable data delivery across the Internet. This chapter describes how application programs use TCP/IP software to provide services across the Internet. It shows that, despite their diversity, all applications on the Internet follow a single organizational model. Later chapters discuss specific examples of services and show how the model applies in practice.

Large Computers Use Networks For Input And Output

Early computers were large and expensive. As a result, most companies could only afford a single computer. When networks first appeared, companies used the technology to connect remote I/O devices to their computer. For example, some remote sites included a printer plus one or more terminals, each with a keyboard and display. Although a remote device connected to the single central computer across a network, the central computer controlled the device completely. The arrangement in which a large, central computer controlled small I/O devices at remote sites led to the term *master-slave* networking.

Small Computers Use Networks To Interact

As newer technologies emerged, computers became inexpensive. Powered by microprocessors, personal computers and scientific workstations appeared. Although small, a personal computer contains much more than a keyboard and a display. It also has the ability to process information.

Personal computers use networks in new ways. First, because a personal computer contains the processing power necessary to send and receive packets, it can communicate with any other computer on its network. Second, because a personal computer does not depend on a large, central computer for control, it can act independently. To emphasize the symmetric relationship among computers that communicate with one another, scientists use the terms *peer-to-peer networking* or *distributed computing*.

Peer-to-peer networking refers to network technologies that permit arbitrary communication among computers. The Internet is a peer-to-peer technology because it does not distinguish among connected computers. A personal computer can contact another personal computer as easily as it can contact a large mainframe. A large mainframe computer can contact another large mainframe, a medium-size computer, or a small personal computer.

Distributed computing refers to any computation that involves two or more computers communicating over a network. The computation need not involve arithmetic or numbers. For example, when two computers exchange electronic mail, they engage in a form of distributed computing because multiple computers cooperate to send and deliver the message.

To summarize:

> *Because modern computer networks allow large or small computers to initiate interaction and to interact arbitrarily with other computers, we use the term* peer-to-peer networking. *Distributed computing refers to any interaction among computers that share access to a peer-to-peer network.*

Distributed Computing On The Internet

The Internet offers an amazing diversity of services that each involve a form of distributed computation. For example, one can send a message to a friend, retrieve a file, browse through directories, search a database, print a document, transmit a FAX, or listen to music.

The diverse variety of available services means the Internet offers equally diverse styles of interaction. In some cases, a user interacts with another human. In other cases, a user interacts with a remote computer program that offers a service. In still others, two computer systems communicate without human intervention. Interactive services allow a user to remain connected for hours or days. Other services need only milliseconds to supply requested information, and terminate communication almost immediately. Some services allow users to fetch information, while others allow users to store or update information. Some services involve only two computer systems, one that sends a request and another that supplies a response; other services involve several computers.

A Single Paradigm Explains All Distributed Computing

Despite the wide diversity among Internet services and the apparent differences in their use, the software that implements a service always uses a single scheme. The scheme is called *client-server computing*. Client-server computing is not limited to the Internet – it forms the basis for distributed computing.

The idea behind client-server computing is quite simple: some computers on the Internet offer services that others access. For example, some servers manage files that contain information. A client program can contact such a server to request a copy of one of the files. Other servers manage multiuser games. An individual who wants to play one of the games must use a client program to contact the server and participate in the game.

To understand how a single paradigm can encompass the diversity of services, one needs to know three basic facts.

- Programs communicate.

  People who use the Internet often say that their computer has communicated with another computer. Although such statements occur frequently in informal conversations, they hide a technical detail. Computers do not communicate with other computers – only programs can communicate. A program running on one computer uses protocol software to contact a program on another computer and exchange messages. On the Internet, the two programs must use TCP/IP protocol software. While the distinction between computers and the programs running on them may seem trivial, it is important because it explains how a single computer can engage in multiple conversations with other computers.

- TCP/IP does not create or run application programs.

  Although the Internet can transfer data from one point to another, it does not automatically start a program on the receiving machine. In a sense, the Internet works like a telephone system – it allows one program to call another, but the called program must answer the call before communication is possible. Thus, two programs can only communicate if one of them starts running and agrees to answer calls *before* the other program contacts it.

- Computers can run multiple programs.

  Even the slowest, smallest computers can run more than one program at a time. It may seem strange to think about a computer running more than one program because most computers contain a single processor. However, an operating system keeps multiple programs running by switching the processor among them rapidly. It allows the processor to work on one program for a short time, then it moves the processor to another program for a short time, and so on. Because a computer's processor can execute several million operations per second, switching it among multiple programs gives a human the impression that the programs all run at the same time. For example, a user can have three activities in three separate regions on the display that each appear to proceed simultaneously.

Knowing that programs communicate and that a computer can run multiple programs at one time explains an apparent mystery: how a single computer can provide service to multiple users at the same time. Many Internet services use multiple copies of a program to permit multiple users to access the service simultaneously. For example, a single computer can receive and store incoming electronic mail from many other computers at the same time. To do so, it creates multiple copies of the program that accepts incoming e-mail. Each computer that sends mail communicates with a single copy of the program. Because the processor can switch among the copies rapidly, all transmissions appear to proceed simultaneously.

To summarize:

> *Communication across the Internet always occurs between a pair of programs; one initiates a conversation, and the other must be waiting to receive it. Because a given computer can run more than one program at the same time, a single computer can appear to engage in multiple conversations simultaneously.*

Programs Are Clients Or Servers

Each computer program that communicates can be classified in one of two categories. Any program that offers a service belongs in the *server* category; any program that contacts a service belongs in the *client* category.

Usually, people who use Internet services run client software. For example, a typical application program that uses the Internet to access a service becomes a client. The client uses the Internet to communicate with a server. For some services, the client interacts with the server using one request. The client forms a request, sends it to the server, and awaits a reply. For other services, the client engages in a long-term interaction. The client establishes communication with the server, and then continuously displays the data received from the server, while it transmits keystrokes or mouse input to the server.

A Server Must Always Run

Unlike client software, a server program must always be ready to receive requests. A client can contact a server at any time; the server has no warning. Usually, server programs only run on large computers that allow multiple servers to execute simultaneously. When the system first begins execution, it starts one or more copies of each server program running. A server continues to execute as long as the computer continues to run.

If a computer loses power or the operating system crashes, all servers running on the computer are lost. When the computer that offers a service crashes, clients actively using a server on that computer will receive an error message. Any client that attempts to establish communication with a server while the computer is down will also receive an error message.

Summary

Unlike older networks that connected terminals to large, central computers, the Internet provides peer-to-peer networking. It allows an arbitrary computer to communicate with any other computer.

The Internet offers a wide variety of services that use many styles of interaction. Despite apparent differences among the available services, all software on the Internet uses the same general structure. The structure is known as client-server computing.

In a client-server environment, each program must be classified as a client or as a server. A server program offers a service. Usually, computers that offer services start the server software running automatically when the computer is powered on. The server remains running, ready to accept an incoming request at any time. Users usually run client software when they access a service. A client program contacts a server, sends a request, and displays the server's response.

16

Names For Computers

Introduction

The previous chapter describes client-server interaction used by Internet services. This chapter describes an important Internet service that allows humans to use alphabetic names for machines in place of numeric addresses. It explains the naming scheme and describes how software uses client-server interaction to convert a computer's name into the computer's numeric address.

People Prefer Names To Numbers

Recall that the Internet assigns each computer a numeric value called an IP address, and that every packet sent across the Internet contains the IP address of the computer to which it has been sent. Like a telephone number, an IP address is a multi-digit number. Also like a telephone number, an IP address can be difficult to remember and enter correctly. When written in decimal, for example, an IP address contains ten digits.

Instead of IP addresses, people prefer to use alphabetic names for computers. The Internet accommodates such names. First, it allows each user to name their machine. Second, it allows a user to enter a computer's alphabetic name in place of the computer's IP address. Third, it provides a service that automatically translates a computer's alphabetic name to the computer's numeric address. We will explore name translation after considering how computer names are assigned.

Naming A Computer Can Be Difficult Or Fun

The name assigned to a computer can affect the way people react toward it; a name creates a sense of personality. For example, some people choose a name for their computer that conveys a sense of pride in their work. Others choose a name that conveys their sense of frustration. When someone hears a computer's name, they often infer something about the machine or its owner.

Names for computers attached to the Internet vary widely. For example, people have chosen the names of geographic locations, characters in movies, actors, colors, oceans, corporations, characters from mythology, and famous people. The names of planets like *Mercury* or *Saturn* remain popular. In fact, in 1994 the most popular name for a computer on the Internet was *venus*.

Of course, using a common word as the name of a computer can seem frivolous. Some people choose names that identify the type of computer, and simply add a suffix to distinguish multiple machines. For example, both the series *pc1*, *pc2*, ... and the series *mac1*, *mac2*, ... rank among the top names used in the Internet.

A group of co-workers can adopt a naming scheme for their computers. For example, one group uses the names of trees. Their computers are named *birch*, *elm*, *oak*, and so on. Often, a naming scheme relates to a group's profession. Computers owned by a group of chemists could be named after the elements (e.g., *hydrogen*, *helium*, and *oxygen*), while a group of computers owned by physicists could be named after particles (e.g., *proton*, *quark*, *neutrino*, and *positron*).

Some people have fun choosing a name for their computer. At one university, computers were named *up* and *down*, making it possible for the statement "down is up today" to be true. You may be surprised to learn that *hobbes* is the 38th most popular name for a computer on the Internet until you learn that *calvin* ranks 45th. Sometimes a computer and its owner share the same name, making it possible to joke about the machine or the person. For example, if both a computer and its owner are named *John*, one can say "John is down" or "I find it difficult to work with John."

Computer Names Must Be Unique

Although most people prefer to use a short name for their computer, longer names must be used on the Internet to avoid assigning the same name to multiple computers. Two computers with the same name would create a significant problem because communication software could not distinguish between them. The point is:

> *Each computer on the Internet must have a unique name or the name would not distinguish the computer from all others.*

Suffixes On Computer Names

To make names unique, the Internet naming mechanism uses a familiar idea: it extends each name by adding additional strings. We think of the additional strings as a suffix appended to the name. The full name of a computer consists of its local name followed by a period and the organization's suffix.

While among humans, additional parts of a name identify a person's family or place of birth, additional names on the Internet identify the organization that owns the computer. Unfortunately, multiple organizations sometimes have similar or related names. To allow multiple organizations to use similar names without conflict, the Internet scheme further qualifies each name by giving the type of the organization. For example, because the Internet authority classifies Purdue University as an *edu*cational institution, it approved the suffix:

purdue.edu

for the names of all computers at Purdue. If a company named *Purdue Gumball Corporation* asks to use *Purdue* in the names of its computers, the Internet naming authority will assign it a suffix that designates it as a *com*mercial enterprise. For example, it might be assigned:

purdue.com

The suffix *purdue.com* clearly distinguishes the company from the university.

If both Purdue University and Purdue Gumball Corporation each name one of their computers *groucho*, the suffixes guarantee that the two computers will have unique full names†:

groucho.purdue.edu

and

groucho.purdue.com

The point is:

> *Because a suffix appended to the name of a computer identifies the organization that owns the computer and the type of the organization, the full names of any two computers owned by separate organizations are guaranteed to differ from one another.*

---

†In Internet terminology, a computer is called a *host*, and a computer's full name is called a *hostname*.

Names With Many Parts

Although the examples above imply that computer names always have three parts (local, organization, and organization type), they seldom do. The Internet naming scheme allows names to contain multiple parts. Once the Internet assigns a suffix to an organization, the organization can choose to add additional parts to the names of computers. Often, each organization decides that names for all its computers will contain a computer name and a department name followed by the organization suffix. Adding an additional level to names solves an important problem:

> *Because the Internet permits organizations to add additional parts to computer names, each group in the organization is free to choose the primary names for its computers. The full names of any two computers in separate groups are guaranteed to differ.*

Like the computer science departments at many other universities, the Computer Science Department at Purdue University uses the 2-letter abbreviation *cs* to denote the department. Thus, the suffix *cs.purdue.edu* appears on the names of all computers in the CS Department. For example, a computer named *groucho* in Purdue's Computer Science Department has the full name:

groucho.cs.purdue.edu

The computing center at Purdue University uses the abbreviation *cc*, so a computer named *groucho* at the computing center has the full name:

groucho.cc.purdue.edu

Domain Names Outside The US

Although most domain names in the United States end with *.edu* or *.com*, other countries have chosen to follow alternative schemes. Most append the 2-letter country code to each domain name. For example one computer at the Interop company in Japan is named:

interop.co.jp

because *jp* is the internationally recognized 2-letter county code identifier for Japan. Similarly, domain names for computers in Germany end in *de*, those in Canada end in *ca*, and those in the United Kingdom end in *uk*. Each country chooses how to further divide domain names. For example, because the United Kingdom has chosen *ac* to denote academic institutions, a computer at the University of York in England has the name:

minster.york.ac.uk

Translating A Name To An Equivalent IP Address

Recall that the Internet communication software must use IP addresses when it sends and receives datagrams. Although people can refer to a computer by name, the name must be translated into an IP address before an application program can communicate with a program on the named computer. The Internet offers a service that translates names to IP addresses automatically. The names described above are called *domain names*, and the software that translates a domain name to an IP address is called the *Domain Name System* (*DNS*). Whenever an application program encounters a computer name (e.g., when a user enters the name of a computer on the keyboard), the application uses the domain name system to translate the name into an IP address. It then uses the IP address in all communication.

The domain name system uses the client-server approach described in the previous chapter. Each organization operates a domain name server that contains the list of all computers in that organization along with their IP addresses. When an application program needs to translate a computer's name into the computer's IP address, the application becomes a client of the DNS. It contacts a domain name server, and sends the server an alphabetic computer name. Sending a domain name server a computer's name is equivalent to asking,

What is the IP address for this name?

The server looks up the answer, and returns the correct IP address.

Domain Name System Works Like Directory Assistance

The easiest way to understand the operation of the domain name system is to think about directory assistance in the telephone system. To place a telephone call, the caller must use a telephone number. If the caller knows a person's full name, address, and city, the caller can obtain the person's telephone number from the directory assistance service. To do so, one calls directory assistance for the correct city, and specifies the person's name. The directory assistance operator replies by giving the person's telephone number.

Of course, a directory assistance operator does not know all the telephone numbers in the world. If one needs the telephone number of a person in another country, for example, directory assistance does not have an answer. However, the directory assistance in one country can supply the telephone number of directory assistance in a foreign country.

The domain name system works similar to the way directory assistance does. A given server does not store the names and addresses of all possible computers in the Internet. Instead, each server stores the names of computers at only one company or enterprise. When an application on a computer in France needs to know the IP address of a computer in California, the application sends its request to a domain name server in

France. The server in France does not know the answer, but knows how to contact the appropriate domain name server in California.

Computer Name Lookup Is Automatic

Consider an example. Suppose that a user sitting at a computer in France needs to communicate with computer *hobbes* located at company *XYZ* in California. The user must specify the computer's name. For example, the full name might be:

hobbes.xyz.com

Before an application program running in France can communicate with computer *hobbes*, it needs to obtain *hobbes*'s IP address. To find the address, the application uses the Internet's domain name system.

Does an application program in France need to know the address of the domain server for company *XYZ*? No, the domain name system is completely automated. A computer on the Internet only needs to know the location of one domain name server, usually a local one. The domain name server handles the lookup automatically. Figure 16.1 illustrates the communication.

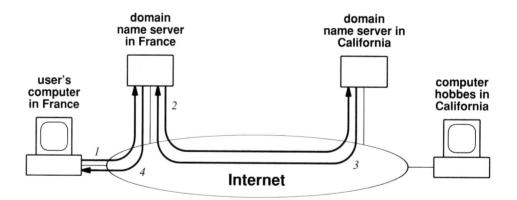

Figure 16.1 To communicate with a remote computer, an application program asks a local domain name server for the remote computer's IP address. If the local domain name server does not know the answer, it contacts a remote domain server automatically. Numbers on the arrows tell the order of the four steps taken.

As the figure shows, finding the IP address for a remote name takes four steps. First, an application program on a computer in France places the name *hobbes.xyz.com* in a message and sends it to the local domain name server in France. The application is asking the server,

> *What is the IP address of the computer named hobbes at company XYZ?*

Second, the domain name server in France contacts the domain name server at company *XYZ*. Third, the server at company *XYZ* responds by sending an answer. Fourth, the local domain name server in France sends the answer back to the original computer. Note that the domain name service performs all four steps without contacting computer *hobbes* similar to the way directory assistance can provide someone's telephone number without calling that person.

Although the domain name system may send several messages across the Internet, obtaining a response does not take long. In many cases, a response takes less than a second. Speed is important because name lookup often occurs when a user enters the name of a computer to be contacted. The user must wait while the domain name system finds the computer's IP address. As soon as the domain name system responds, the application program can begin sending packets directly to the computer.

To summarize:

> *A computer on the Internet only needs to know the location of one domain name server. A program becomes a client of the domain name service when it sends a computer's name to the local domain name server. The local server answers the request by translating the name into an IP address. Although the server may contact remote servers to obtain the information, the client receives an answer from the local server.*

IP Addresses And Domain Names Are Unrelated

Syntactically, domain names resemble IP addresses. An IP address is written as four numbers separated by three periods, while a domain name consists of alphabetic strings separated by periods.

Appearances can be deceiving. Although they may look similar, the individual parts of names and addresses are completely unrelated. An IP address contains four parts because a 32-bit binary number can be divided into four *8*-bit sections. A domain name contains multiple parts because an organization can choose to add zero or more items to its suffix to allow individual groups within the organization to choose the same primary names for computers.

Confusion arises because some domain names contain exactly four parts. For example, the Internet's Domain Name Service translates the name:

arthur.cs.purdue.edu

to the IP address:

128.10.2.1

However, the string *arthur* is not related to *128*, nor are any of the other parts of the name related to parts of the IP address. To keep the distinction clear, think of a person's name and their telephone number. Letters or groups of letters in a person's name have no relationship to groups of digits in their telephone number (e.g., a person's first name is unrelated to the initial group of digits in the person's telephone number).

Summary

Because humans prefer using names instead of numbers, the Internet allows people to assign a name to each computer, and provides an automated system that can translate a name into an equivalent IP address.

Many application programs that use the Internet permit users to enter names for remote computers. The application becomes a client of the domain name service by sending a name to the local domain name server in a request message. The server translates the name to an IP address, automatically contacting other servers if needed.

A computer's name consists of multiple alphabetic strings separated by periods. The computer's primary name comes first, and a suffix that designates the organization that owns a computer comes last. Additional strings can occur in the name if the organization has added supplementary names to identify groups within the organization.

Although both the names used for computers and their IP addresses are written as strings of characters with periods separating them, items in a computer's name are unrelated to items in the computer's IP address just as characters in a person's name are unrelated to digits in their telephone number.

17

Why The Internet Works Well

Introduction

Previous chapters describe the basic Internet technology, including TCP/IP software. This chapter considers reasons for the Internet's success and the lessons that can be learned.

The Internet Works Well

The Internet is a marvel of technical accomplishment. The basic TCP/IP technology has accommodated growth and changes that the original designers did not imagine. While the number of computers on the Internet has grown exponentially, TCP/IP technology has accommodated the increase in size. When traffic on the network also grew exponentially over the previous decade; TCP/IP technology tolerated the additional packets. Although computers now operate 200 times faster than the computers that existed when TCP/IP was first built, new computers can communicate across the Internet with each other and with older computers. Despite an 800% increase in the speed of the central internet WAN, TCP/IP protocols have not changed; the same design continues to operate correctly at the higher speed.

Why is TCP/IP technology so successful? How could a technology from a research project become the foundation of the world's largest computer network system? What lessons have we learned from the Internet project? Obviously, no single technical decision results in the overwhelming success of a complex system like the Internet. However, a poor design choice can ruin an otherwise excellent plan. Remaining sections of this chapter examine some of the best design choices in TCP/IP and draw lessons from the Internet project.

IP Provides Flexibility

The Internet Protocol provides the flexibility needed to accommodate a wide range of underlying network hardware. For example, IP can use:

- Wide Area Network technologies or Local Area Network technologies.
- Networks that operate at the highest speeds or networks that operate at the slowest speeds.
- Networks that guarantee no packet loss or networks that provide only best-effort delivery.
- Wireless networks that use radio for communication, networks that send signals across wires, or networks that send signals across glass fibers.
- Combinations of the above.

In summary, IP allows the Internet to include almost any type of computer communication technology.

The secret of IP's success stems from a tolerant approach. Because it does not demand much from the network hardware, IP tolerates almost any mechanism that can send bits from one location to another. In terms of the design:

> *The Internet Protocol accommodates many types of hardware because it makes almost no assumptions about the underlying network hardware.*

Although IP makes minimal assumptions about networks, all implementations of IP must use exactly the same rules for communication. To ensure compatibility among implementations of TCP/IP, complete specifications for the protocols have been written in documents informally called *standards*. TCP/IP standards include an exact specification of how to send IP datagrams on each type of network. Whenever a new network technology appears, a new Internet standard document is written that describes how to use the technology with TCP/IP. The specifications form an important part of Internet literature because they guarantee that all computers and all routers use exactly the same format when sending a datagram across a network. Thus,

> *Because TCP/IP standards documents specify the exact way to send IP datagrams on a given type of network, computers and routers from multiple vendors always agree on the details.*

TCP Provides Reliability

TCP and IP form a complementary pair that work together well. TCP handles communication problems that IP does not handle, and provides applications with reliable communication.

Interestingly, TCP needs to compensate for differences among the various types of network hardware that IP can use. For example, although sending a datagram across a satellite channel takes tenths of seconds, sending a datagram across a LAN takes only one or two thousandths of a second. A single copy of the TCP software must handle both. Similarly, although a LAN seldom or never drops packets, a Wide Area Network can lose a significant portion. TCP software must be able to use either technology efficiently.

TCP also handles the most difficult problem found in packet switching systems: rapid changes in the performance. Computers tend to send information in bursts – the computer remains quiet for a while, then emits data for a short time, and then resumes its quiet state. For example, when a user first starts an application, the application may need to interact with a server (e.g., to fetch a file or to obtain the first screen of information). If the user stops to think, move the mouse, or enter data on the keyboard, the application stops communicating with the server. Although the Internet has sufficient capacity to handle datagrams sent among many computers, it can become temporarily overloaded and slow down if too many computers send a burst of datagrams at exactly the same time.

Like other packet switching systems, the Internet can experience bursts of traffic or idle periods. If many computers happen to emit datagrams at the same time, a temporary traffic jam slows down delivery. TCP must watch for delays and know to wait until the congestion clears.

The secret of TCP's success arises from the way it automatically adapts to change.

> *Because it constantly monitors conditions on the Internet and automatically adapts, TCP makes reliable communication possible even though Internet experiences temporary congestion.*

TCP/IP Software Was Engineered For Efficiency

In any complex computer system, engineers must choose among a variety of possible designs, TCP/IP protocols have been carefully designed to run efficiently. For example, TCP/IP is designed so it does not require extensive computation when sending or receiving a packet. In addition, TCP/IP is designed so it does not send more than the minimum network packets required to communicate.

The efficient design permits TCP/IP software to run on small, slow computers as well as fast, large computers. Thus, TCP/IP works well on personal computers that do not have as much processing power or memory as large computers.

TCP/IP Research Emphasized Practical Results

Scientists and engineers working on the Internet project took a practical approach to research. Instead of discussing vague possibilities, they decided to build, test, and measure a working communication system. They used experimental evidence to judge all new proposals and ideas. For example, before any new addition to the TCP/IP specifications was approved, two programmers had to build and test software on at least two types of computers. Furthermore, the programmers had to demonstrate that the two implementations could communicate.

In a keynote address at the *INTEROP 92* conference, David Clark‡ characterized the style of development used for TCP/IP and the Internet as *rough consensus and working code*. The phrase captures a simple idea: although much of TCP/IP arose from a consensus among researchers, no idea was accepted until it had been implemented and demonstrated.

To emphasize pragmatics and to make implementations interoperate, researchers working on the Internet project urged one another to design software that tolerated errors or unexpected packets. They challenged one another to build software that would anticipate possible mistakes or flaws in the software on other computers, and tried carefully not to violate the Internet specifications.

Implementation and testing always preceded TCP/IP standardization. Writing and testing programs often uncovered ambiguities and omissions in the design or documentation, and forced designers to correct problems early. As a result, considering the complexity of the protocols, TCP/IP standards documents have had few problems.

The Formula For Success

Many people who encounter the Internet project and success of the TCP/IP technology ask, "What lessons were learned?" Some ask more pointedly, "How can I repeat the success with research projects at my organization?"

Even from an insider's perspective the questions are difficult to answer because the project involved many people working together over several years. Here are a few highlights:

- TCP/IP protocol software and the Internet were designed by talented, dedicated people.

- The Internet was a dream that inspired and challenged the research team.

- Researchers were allowed to experiment, even when there was no short-term economic payoff. Indeed, Internet research often used new, innovative technologies that were expensive compared to existing technologies.

- Instead of dreaming about a system that solved all problems, researchers built the Internet to operate efficiently.

---

‡Dr. David Clark served as the Internet Architect from *1983* through *1989.*

- Researchers insisted that each part of the Internet work well in practice before they adopted it as a standard.

- Internet technology solves an important, practical problem; the problem occurs whenever an organization has multiple networks.

Summary

The Internet represents an incredible technical accomplishment. Although careful planning and attention to detail contributed to its success, agreement among researchers to demonstrate a practical, working system forced them to demonstrate ideas and eliminate weaknesses.

How People Use
The Internet

Examples of services currently available on the Internet and explanations of a few exciting applications

18

Electronic Mail

Introduction

This chapter begins a discussion of example services available on the Internet. It examines one of the most widely used services: electronic mail. Successive chapters explore other services. In each case, the text describes the service by first summarizing the basic functionality and showing a typical use. It then describes how the underlying mechanism operates. Finally the chapter summarizes the significance of the service.

Description Of Functionality

Electronic mail was originally designed to allow a pair of individuals to communicate via computer. The first electronic mail software provided only a basic facility: it allowed a person using one computer to type a message and send it across the Internet to a person using another computer.

Current electronic mail systems provide services that permit complex communication and interaction. For example, electronic mail can be used to:

- Send a single message to many recipients.
- Send a message that includes text, voice, video, or graphics.
- Send a message to a user on a network outside the Internet.
- Send a message to which a computer program responds.

To appreciate the capabilities and significance of electronic mail, one must understand a few basic facts. The next sections consider how electronic mail appears to a user. Later sections describe how electronic mail systems work and discuss the impact of electronic mail.

The Best Of All Worlds

Researchers working on early computer networks realized that networks can provide a form of communication among individuals that combines the speed of telephone communication with the permanence of postal mail. A computer can transfer small notes or large documents across a network almost instantaneously. The designers called the new form of communication *electronic mail*†, often abbreviated *e-mail*. E-mail has become extremely popular on the Internet as well as on most other computer networks.

Each User Has A Mailbox For E-mail

To receive electronic mail, a user must have a *mailbox*, a storage area, usually on disk, that holds incoming e-mail messages until the user has time to read them. In addition, the computer on which a mailbox resides must also run e-mail software. When a message arrives, e-mail software automatically stores it in the user's mailbox. An e-mail mailbox is private in the same way that postal mailboxes are private: anyone can send a message to a mailbox, but only the owner can examine mailbox contents or remove messages.

Like a post office mailbox, each e-mail mailbox has a *mailbox address*. To send e-mail to another user, one must know the recipient's mailbox address. To summarize:

> *Each individual who participates in electronic mail exchange has a mailbox identified by a unique address. Any user can send mail across the Internet to another user's mailbox if they know the mailbox address; only the owner can examine the contents of a mailbox and extract messages.*

Sending An E-mail Message

To send electronic mail across the Internet, an individual runs an e-mail application program on their local computer. The local application operates similar to a word processor – it allows a user to compose and edit a message and to specify a recipient by giving a mailbox address. Once the user finishes entering the message, e-mail software sends it across the Internet to the recipient's mailbox.

Notification That E-mail has Arrived

On most computers, when an incoming e-mail message arrives, e-mail software informs the recipient. Some computers print a text message or highlight a small graphic on the user's display (e.g., a small picture of letters in a postal mailbox). Other computers sound a tone or play a recorded message. Still other computers wait for the user

---

†The term *electronic mail* can be slightly misleading; it may be easier to think of it as a memo transfer service.

to finish using the current application before making an announcement. Most systems allows a user to suppress notification altogether, in which case the user must periodically check to see if e-mail has arrived.

Reading An E-mail Message

Once e-mail has arrived, a user can extract messages from his or her mailbox using an application program. The application allows a user to view each message, and optionally, to send a reply. Usually, when an e-mail application begins, it tells the user about the messages waiting in the mailbox. The initial summary contains one line for each e-mail message that has arrived; the line gives the sender's name, the time the message arrived, and the length of the message. After examining the summary, a user can select and view messages on the list. Each time a user selects a message from the summary, the e-mail system displays the message contents. After viewing a message, a user must choose an action. The user can send a reply to whoever sent the message, leave the message in the mailbox so it can be viewed again, save a copy of the message in a file†, or discard the message.

To summarize:

> *A computer connected to the Internet needs application software before users can send or receive electronic mail. E-mail software allows a user to compose and send a message or to read messages that have arrived. A user can send a reply to any message.*

E-mail Messages Look Like Interoffice Memos

Each electronic mail message has a form similar to the one used for a conventional interoffice memo. The message begins with a header that specifies the person who sent the memo, the person to whom the memo was sent, the date and time the memo was sent, and the subject of the memo. Following usual office conventions, information in the header appears on separate lines that begin with *From*, *To*, *Date*, and *Subject*, with each followed by appropriate information. For example, suppose on April 1, 1994 Jane sends Bob an e-mail message that contains a joke. If Jane's e-mail address is *jane@company1.com* and Bob's e-mail address is *bob@company2.com*, the message will have the following form:

---

†A user might save a copy of a message to create a permanent record of a conversation or to use the message with another application (e.g., to incorporate text from an e-mail message into a document).

```
From: jane@company1.com
To: bob@company2.com
Date: 01 Apr 1994  11:20:23 EST
Subject: some bad news

Bob,

    I heard that they've decided to cut personnel and that you
will be the first one fired.
    April Fools!

Jane
:-)
```

On the last line of the message, Jane included extra symbols to ensure that the recipient interprets the statement as humorous. The line contains three characters: a colon, minus sign, and right parenthesis. The three symbols are called a *smiley* because they resemble a smiling face turned sideways.

An e-mail header can contain items not shown in the sample message above. For example, it can contain a line labeled *Cc* that lists mailbox addresses of additional people who receive a copy of the message†.

E-mail Software Fills In Header Information

Usually, the sender only needs to supply information for the *To* and *Subject* lines in a message header because e-mail software fills in the date and the sender's mailbox address automatically. In a reply, the mail interface program automatically constructs the entire header. It uses the contents of the *From* field in the original message as the contents of the *To* field in the reply. It also copies the *Subject* field from the original message to a reply. Having software fill in header lines is convenient, and also makes it difficult to forge e-mail.

In practice, most e-mail systems supply additional header lines that help identify the sending computer, give the full name of the person who sent the message, provide a unique message identifier that can be used for auditing or accounting, and identify the type of message (e.g., text or graphics). Thus, e-mail messages can arrive with dozens of lines in the header‡. A lengthy header can be annoying to a recipient who must skip past it to find the body of a message. Software used to read e-mail can make it easier for the recipient by skipping most header lines. To summarize:

> *Although most e-mail messages contain many lines of header, software generates most of the header automatically. User-friendly software hides unnecessary header lines when displaying an e-mail message.*

---

†As in standard office memos, *Cc* stands for *carbon copy*; the term originated when typists used carbon paper to create multiple copies of a document.

‡While preparing this chapter, the author received an e-mail message with 376 lines of header!

How E-mail Works

Recall from Chapter *15* that computer communication always involves interaction between two programs called a *client* and a *server*. E-mail systems follow the client-server approach: two programs cooperate to transfer an e-mail message from the sender's computer to the recipient's mailbox (transfer requires two programs because an application running on one computer cannot store data directly in a mailbox on another computer's disk). When a user sends an e-mail message, a program on the sender's computer becomes a client. It contacts an e-mail server program on the recipient's computer and transfers a copy of the message. The server stores the message in the recipient's mailbox. Figure 18.1 illustrates the idea.

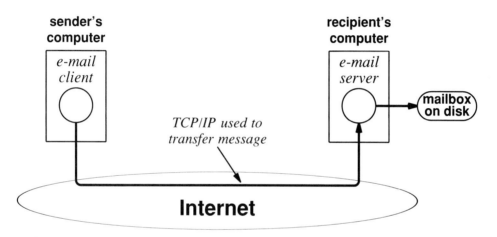

Figure 18.1 An e-mail transfer across the Internet requires two programs: a client on the sender's computer and a server on the recipient's computer.

Client software starts automatically as soon as a user finishes composing an e-mail message. The client uses the recipient's e-mail address to determine which remote computer to contact. The client uses TCP to send a copy of the e-mail message across the Internet to the server. When the server receives a message, it stores the message in the recipient's mailbox and informs the recipient that e-mail has arrived.

The interaction between a client and server is complex because at any time computers or the Internet connecting them can fail (e.g., someone can accidently turn off one of the computers). To ensure that e-mail will be delivered reliably, the client keeps a copy of the message during the transfer. After the server informs the client that the message has been received and stored on disk, the client erases its copy.

Using E-mail From A Personal Computer

A computer cannot receive e-mail unless it has an e-mail server program running. On large computers, the system administrator arranges to start the server when the system first begins, and leaves the server running at all times. The server waits for an e-mail message to arrive, stores the message in the appropriate mailbox on disk, and then waits for the next message.

A user who has a personal computer that is frequently powered down or disconnected from the Internet cannot receive e-mail while the computer is inactive. Therefore, most personal computers do not receive e-mail directly. Instead, a user arranges to have a mailbox on a large computer with a server that always remains ready to accept an e-mail message and store it in the user's mailbox. For example, a user can choose to place their mailbox on their company's main computer, even if they use a personal computer for most work. To read e-mail from a personal computer, a user must contact the main computer system and obtain a copy of their mailbox.

Mailbox Address Format

Mailbox addresses used on the Internet can be quite long, and may seem cumbersome. They consist of a string of characters separated into two parts by the *at sign* character, @. The prefix of the mailbox address identifies the user, and the suffix gives the domain name of the computer on which the user's mailbox resides. On most computers, the e-mail system uses an individual's account or login as their mailbox address. For example, the mailbox address

        jksmith@venus.engineering.somecompany.com

identifies a user who has account *jksmith* on a computer that has domain name *venus.engineering.somecompany.com*. The domain name for a computer can be difficult to remember. For example, a computer in India has the domain name

        chanakya.csa.iisc.ernet.in†

while a computer at Purdue University is named

        angwyshaunce.cs.purdue.edu

The identifier for a user can also be difficult to remember. In practice, the format for a user identifier depends on the computer system and rules the administrator establishes for assigning identifiers. Some systems use a person's first and last names plus their middle initial, with underscores separating the parts:

        Jane_K_Smith@venus.engineering.somecompany.com

---

†Computers attached to the Internet in India have names that end with *in*, the international 2-letter abbreviation for India.

To summarize:

> *Mailbox addresses used to send e-mail across the Internet consist of a text string separated into two parts by an at sign (@). The prefix of the address specifies a particular user; the suffix gives the domain name of the computer on which that user's mailbox resides.*

Abbreviations Make E-mail Friendly

Most e-mail systems allow a user to define abbreviations for mailbox addresses. Abbreviations allow a company to establish short names for each of its departments, making it possible for employees in the company to address mail without typing long suffixes. For example, if all the computers in a company understand that *eng* is an abbreviation for computer *venus.engineering.somecompany.com* in the engineering department, it is possible for an employee in the company to address an e-mail message:

```
Jane_K_Smith@eng
```

Aliases Permit Arbitrary Abbreviations

Most commercially available e-mail software also supports an *e-mail alias* facility that allows each user to define a set of abbreviations for the mailbox addresses they use frequently. Usually, alias mechanisms require the user to prepare a short list of aliases, which the mail software stores on disk. When e-mail software runs, it locates the user's list of aliases and honors them. For example, suppose a user sends e-mail to two people frequently: *John Smith* and *Mary Doe*, who have electronic mail addresses *jksmith@computer1.somecompany.com* and *mary_doe@computer2.somecollege.edu*. The user can define two aliases for the mailbox addresses:

```
john = jsmith@computer1.somecompany.com
mary = mary_doe@computer2.somecollege.edu
```

When composing an e-mail message, the user can enter *john* or *mary* in the *To* field. The e-mail software will automatically consult the user's alias list and replace the abbreviation with the full mailbox address. Thus, although the user only types the abbreviation, the outgoing mail message will contain the full mailbox address.

To summarize:

Most commercial e-mail software permits each user to define a set of abbreviations for frequently used mailbox addresses. If the user types an abbreviation when specifying a recipient, e-mail software substitutes the full mailbox address in place of the abbreviation.

Aliases Shared By All Users Of A Computer System

Because only a single individual uses a personal computer system, such systems only need one set of e-mail aliases. However, a large computer that many users share needs a more complex mechanism. In addition to a private set of abbreviations for each user, a large computer's e-mail system usually allows the system administrator to define abbreviations available to all users. When a user specifies a recipient, the mail software first examines the user's private alias list to see if the user has defined an alias for the name. If the user has not, the mail software then examines the system alias list to see if it contains an alias for the name.

Having a system-wide set of mail aliases makes it possible for all users on the system to share abbreviations. For example, suppose a system administrator decides that all reports of problems should be sent to mailbox *william* on computer *computer2.somewhere.com*. To make it convenient for users, the system administrator can choose an easily remembered abbreviation and create a system-wide mail alias. If the administrator chooses the abbreviation *trouble*, the following alias for *trouble* can be added to the system-wide list of mail aliases:

```
trouble = william@computer2.somewhere.com
```

When any user on the computer wants to report a problem, they send e-mail to *trouble*. The mail system finds the alias and sends the e-mail message to mailbox *william@computer2.somewhere.com*.

Sending To Multiple Recipients

Although e-mail was originally designed as a way for two people to communicate, most e-mail systems allow a user to send a message to multiple recipients. To do so, the sender specifies multiple mailbox addresses on the *To* line of a message. The system sends one copy of the message to each recipient. For example, the message:

```
To: bob@company2.com, jim@company3.com, susan@company2.com
From: jane@company1.com
Date: 01 Apr 1994  12:34:03 EST
Subject: some bad news

Folks,

   I heard that your corporation is about to cut personnel
and that you will be among the first ones fired.
   April fools!

Jane
:-)
```

The *To* line in the header specifies three recipients, two at *company2* and another at *company3*. Each of the three will receive a copy of the message.

Mailing List: An Alias for Multiple Recipients

One of the most useful features of e-mail arises from a simple extension of the alias mechanism: an alias that specifies multiple recipients. When the mail system expands an alias and finds multiple recipients, it sends a copy of the message to each.

Informally, people refer to an alias that specifies multiple recipients as a *mailing list*. For example, the following definition creates a mailing list named *friends* that contains three e-mail addresses:

```
friends = bob@company2.com, jim@company3.com, susan@company2.com
```

Once such an alias has been created, any message sent to *friends* will be delivered to all three recipients. The concept is straightforward:

> *A mailing list is an e-mail alias that specifies multiple recipients;
> when a message is sent to the alias, the e-mail system delivers a copy
> to each recipient on the list.*

Public Mailing Lists And Mail Exploders

System administrators can choose to establish *public mailing lists*. A public list permits a user on any computer attached to the Internet to send a message to a list of recipients. For example, suppose a computer named *comp1.somewhere.com* offers a public mailing list named *sales†*. To send an e-mail message to everyone on the list, an individual mails to address: `sales@comp1.somewhere.com`. The message can ori-

---

†The name of a mailing list can be meaningful or meaningless: *sales* can denote a group of people who work in sales, a group of customers to whom sales have been made, or a group that picked the alias to hide the purpose of the list from others.

ginate at any computer. When the e-mail message reaches the destination computer, *comp1.somewhere.com*, a program called a *mail exploder* examines the *To* field, finds the name *sales*, expands the abbreviation, and forwards a copy to each recipient on the list. Figure 18.2 illustrates the concept.

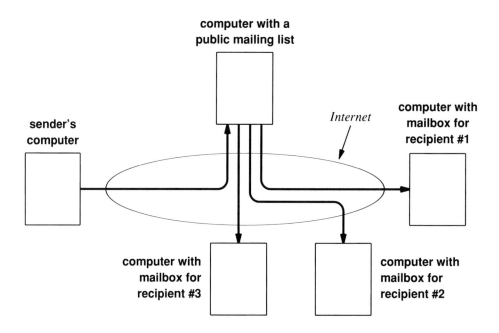

Figure 18.2 The path of a mail message sent to a public mailing list that contains three recipients. A mail exploder receives the message, and forwards a copy to each recipient on the list.

E-mail To And From Non-Internet Sites

Electronic mail on the Internet is especially useful because it reaches to other networks. For example, subscribers to commercial services such as *CompuServe* or *MCImail* can participate in electronic mail exchange. To reach a user on *CompuServe*, a user on the Internet sends e-mail to a mailbox address similar to:

```
user@company.compuserve.com
```

An intermediate computer that links CompuServe and the Internet passes e-mail between the two networks, allowing users on each network to send mail using their usual software. To an Internet user, for example, the mailbox address on *CompuServe* appears to have the same form as a conventional Internet mailbox address.

Access To Services Via E-mail

Because a computer can be programmed to respond to electronic mail automatically, any computer system attached to the Internet can provide access to its services via e-mail. More important, e-mail software on most computers has been designed to make service access easy.

As an example, consider a computer attached to the Internet that has database software running on it. Any user who logs into the computer can access the database software to search the database. Even if both computers have TCP/IP software, and both connect to the Internet, a remote user cannot access the database unless both computers have additional software: the user's computer needs a database client program and the computer with the database needs a database server program.

Client and server software can be difficult to create or expensive to purchase. However, once the server is in place, adding software that provides access to the database via electronic mail can be easy. To do so, the system administrator writes a computer program that answers incoming e-mail, passes the message to the database software, and then mails the output back to the original sender. While it sounds complex, an expert can create such a program quickly with a few lines of code. The idea is:

> *Because a computer program can answer and reply to an electronic mail message, e-mail can be used to provide access to a variety of remote services.*

Speed, Reliability, And Expectations

Internet e-mail software is efficient and dependable. An e-mail message usually takes only a few seconds to reach its destination. If the destination computer is powered down or temporarily disconnected from the Internet, e-mail software automatically retries transmission periodically. Furthermore, e-mail service is more reliable than the best postal mail systems – a message is seldom lost. If an e-mail message cannot be delivered after a fixed time (usually three days), e-mail software automatically informs the sender.

As a consequence of high-quality service, most Internet users view e-mail as a completely reliable, high-speed delivery mechanism. They send important messages via e-mail without relying on other means of communication. In particular, they do not usually send duplicate copies of messages via postal mail, nor do they use a telephone to verify that important e-mail messages arrive.

Furthermore, because messages arrive quickly, many Internet users view e-mail as an instant communication mechanism that operates more like a telephone service than a postal mail service. Users know that if they send a reply shortly after an e-mail message arrives, their reply may reach the sender while he or she is still working on the computer. Sometimes, a pair of individuals exchange a series of brief e-mail messages that resemble a short conversation. Usually such communication occurs between friends who know each other well enough to send short, abbreviated messages. Often such conversations end after a few exchanges.

However, not everyone views e-mail as a highly-reliable, instant communication mechanism – some individuals do not respond to an e-mail message for hours, days, or weeks. Such delays arise for two reasons. First, some mailboxes do not reside on a computer that always has a server available. For example, computers that do not have direct Internet access can use dial-up modems to send or receive e-mail over the telephone system. Thus, an e-mail message traveling to or from such a computer may be delayed hours until the computer's owner decides to place a telephone call.

Second, delays arise because not all individuals find e-mail convenient. Some simply do not want to be bothered; others forget to read e-mail. In particular, someone who does not work with a computer does not receive instant notification when e-mail arrives; to read e-mail, they must interrupt normal activities and find an available computer. Furthermore, because most homes do not have a computer permanently connected to the Internet, most people cannot read e-mail at home. Differences in expectations and habits among individuals can make e-mail frustrating, users learn that not everyone replies to e-mail quickly.

Impact And Significance Of Electronic Mail

The impact of e-mail is so dramatic that it is difficult to assess. For many Internet users, e-mail has become a necessity. Indeed, e-mail has replaced postal mail as their primary communication mechanism! It has changed the way they conduct their daily lives – they use e-mail to communicate with friends, colleagues, employees, customers, and family members.

To appreciate electronic mail, one must use it first hand. After extensive use, some of its benefits become apparent:

- Because e-mail provides high-speed transfer while allowing the receiver to choose when to answer, it combines the benefits of instantaneous communication with freedom from interruption.

- Because a mailing list allows an arbitrary group of individuals to exchange memos, it provides a way for a group of people who share a common interest to participate in a discussion.

- Because most computer networks offer an electronic mail service that operates with electronic mail on the Internet, it is possible to communicate with more people using electronic mail than with any other Internet service.

- Because electronic mail can include text, graphics, and voice, it can be used to transfer documents or recorded audio messages.

- Because a computer program can answer electronic mail and send a reply automatically, many services on the Internet have been constructed so a user can submit a request and receive a response using electronic mail.

In summary:

Although electronic mail was originally designed for communication between a pair of individuals, it has been extended to provide communication among a group and to provide communication with a computer program. As a result, e-mail has become one of the most widely used services on the Internet.

Joining A Mailing List

A user who wants to have their name added to a public mailing list must send an e-mail request. However, the request should not go to the list. Instead, most Internet sites that offer public mailing lists follow the convention of establishing a second mail alias that should be used for requests to join or leave a list.

To understand the problem, assume that a user named *Judy* who has mailbox address *judy@bluechip.com* hears about a mailing list named:

ballroom@athena.mit.edu

to which people send memos about ballroom dancing. If Judy sends a message to the list, everyone will receive a copy. To subscribe to a list, one sends an e-mail message to the list name followed by *-request*. Thus, to subscribe to the ballroom dancing list, Judy should send a message to:

ballroom-request@athena.mit.edu

The message will be delivered to a person who maintains the list (or to a computer program that sends further instructions). After Judy has joined the list, she will receive a copy of all memos, and can send replies.

Some sites do not establish a special alias to make requests. In such cases, a user can try sending to *postmaster*. By convention, e-mail sent to *postmaster* will be delivered to the person who maintains the e-mail system.

19

Bulletin Board Service (Network News)

Introduction

The previous chapter explains the Internet electronic mail service and shows how it can be used to exchange memos. This chapter describes an Internet service that extends the use of memos to allow an individual to join one or more discussion groups and participate in discussions with other members of the group. Electronic bulletin boards are among the most well-known services available on the Internet, and the discussions encompass a wide variety of topics. After examining how the service appears to an individual and reviewing the underlying mechanisms, the chapter provides hints about how to use bulletin boards and electronic mail.

Description Of Functionality

An electronic bulletin board service allows a person to participate in multiple discussion groups, where each group focuses on a specific topic. The bulletin board service allows an individual to:

- Select one or more discussion groups of interest.

- Periodically check to determine whether new items have appeared in a discussion and, if they have, read some or all of them.

- Post a note to the discussion group for others to read.

- Post a note that responds to an item someone else has written.

Conceptually, the Internet's electronic bulletin board service fills the same role for Internet users that conventional bulletin boards fill in everyday life – it allows individuals to post notices that others can read. In practice, the Internet provides access to thousands of electronic bulletin boards, each of which contains an ongoing discussion about a single topic. For that reason, an electronic bulletin board service is sometimes called a *computer discussion group* or a *computer conference* service.

To enable efficient discussion among an arbitrarily large group of people, an electronic bulletin board service combines features of many communication mechanisms.

- Like a conventional bulletin board, an electronic bulletin board allows anyone to post a message for others to see.

- Like a newspaper, an electronic bulletin board service distributes each message to many subscribers.

- Like a newsletter from a club or social group, the messages posted to a given electronic bulletin board focus on a single topic of interest.

- Like an electronic mail service, an electronic bulletin board service propagates copies of each message quickly.

- Like an informal discussion at a social gathering, an electronic bulletin board permits an individual to listen to a conversation, ask questions, occasionally interject small comments, or contribute lengthy statements.

Many Bulletin Boards With Diverse Topics

Internet electronic bulletin boards cover a widely diverse group of topics. For example, the Internet has bulletin boards about science, humor, politics, cooking, physical fitness, comic books, science fiction, poetry, products or services, movies, stock prices, television shows, popular music, and computers. Although many of the discussions can be understood by an average person, some require highly specialized knowledge, and some are meaningful only to someone who works at a particular company or lives in a particular country. Consequently a bulletin board can be restricted to a few computers, a single organization, or a small geographic area, or it can be distributed to sites throughout the world. For example, one bulletin board that contains a discussion of politics in Alberta, Canada is distributed only to nearby sites.

Part of the reason for the diversity of electronic bulletin boards arises from the ease with which they can be created. After a group creates an electronic bulletin board and starts a discussion, interesting side discussions inevitably arise. For example, suppose someone mentions a particular brand of cookware in a discussion of cooking. If others who read the message respond by contributing their opinions on cookware, a new discussion results. If the discussion of cookware continues to gain popularity, participants can choose to create a new bulletin board and move the cookware discussion to that bulletin board. Dividing a bulletin board is analogous to the way people form a small discussion group at a party: it allows multiple conversations to proceed without interference. The point is:

> *Because a new electronic bulletin board can be created easily and dividing discussions by topic helps focus the discussion on each bulletin board, many bulletin boards have been created.*

Network News

The major electronic bulletin board service available on the Internet is called *network news*, often abbreviated *netnews*. The netnews system uses the term *newsgroup* to refer to each individual bulletin board (i.e., each discussion group), and *article* to refer to a message that has been sent to the newsgroup for everyone to see. Each article submitted to a newsgroup resembles an electronic mail message – it can be as short as a single line of text or can contain many pages. Like an e-mail message, an article has a header that includes a *From* line to identify the sender.

Netnews originated as part of an early computer network that used dial-up modems to place telephone calls between computers and exchange information. Originally, sites exchanging network news over dial-up connections used the term *USENET* to refer to their ''network'' of computers. As networks began to grow, USENET participants invented ways to communicate network news over other technologies. As USENET sites acquired Internet access, many changed their netnews communication from the dial-up telephone system to the Internet. Although most sites that participate in network news now receive information over the Internet, those sites that do not have Internet access continue to participate in netnews using other communication networks, including BITNET and the dial-up telephone system. The term *USENET* now refers collectively to all sites that participate in the exchange of network news, regardless of the type of network they use.

Newsgroup Names

The netnews system assigns each newsgroup a unique name. Users enter a newsgroup name when they want to join the newsgroup and participate in the discussion. Each newsgroup name consists of alphabetic strings separated by periods†. The first part of a newsgroup name identifies the type of the group, while successive parts of the name identify the subject and a particular topic within that subject. For example, the newsgroup:

rec.sport.baseball

---

†Although newsgroup names resemble computer names described in Chapter *16* and IP addresses described in Chapter *11*, they are completely unrelated to either.

contains a discussion of baseball. Its name begins with *rec*, which classifies the news-group as one that contains *recreational* subjects. The second part of the name identifies the general subject as a *sport*, and the third part of the name, *baseball*, identifies a particular sport.

Figure 19.1 lists a few of the major newsgroup classifications:

Abbreviation	General category of discussions
rec	arts, hobbies, recreational activities
soc	social issues and cultures
sci	science, engineering, mathematics
comp	computer hardware and software; computer science
news	network news system itself (not current events)
talk	lengthy discussions that never seem to end
misc	topics not covered by other categories
clari	newsgroups from ClariNet†

Figure 19.1 Examples of major newsgroup classifications used by network news.

Obtaining Network News And The Software To Read Articles

Before a user can read network news, the user must have access to a computer that participates in network news and software to read articles. In most cases, an individual does not join the network news system. Instead an organization (e.g., a company) obtains a connection to the network news service. The organization receives one copy of articles that appear each day, and provides users in the organization with the software needed to join newsgroups and read articles.

A connection to the network news service, called a *newsfeed*, is not difficult to obtain. In fact, the entire network news service operates by mutual cooperation – when a new site first appears, a nearby site that already receives network news volunteers to pass on a newsfeed. Participating sites share the tacit understanding that at a later date, when additional sites appear, the new site will volunteer to pass on another newsfeed. Thus, the set of sites that exchange network news continues to grow incrementally.

A computer that connects to the network news system needs software to accept incoming news articles and store them on disk as well as application software that allows users to read articles; such software is available for most computers at no cost. For example, network news software has been written for computers manufactured by IBM, Apple, Digital Equipment Corporation, Sun Microsystems, and other vendors. Several major versions of the network news software have been created over the past thirteen years‡.

---

†A fee and license agreements are required to obtain newsgroups classified as *clari*.

‡The current version of network news software is labeled *C*; versions known as *A* news and *B* news are generally obsolete.

How Network News Appears To A User

When an individual reads an article in a newsgroup, the article appears in the same general form as an electronic mail message: it consists of a text message, separated into a header and a body by a blank line. Like the header on an e-mail message, the header on a netnews article contains a *From* line that supplies the electronic mail address of the person who posted the article, a *Date* line that gives the date and time the article was sent, and a *Subject* line that lists the topic of the article. It can also contain other lines such as a *Distribution* line that restricts dissemination of the article.

Checking For News Articles

The network news system does not notify a user when activity occurs in a newsgroup. Therefore, a user who participates in network news must check regularly for new articles in any of the newsgroups he or she is reading. Usually, a user checks network news at least once a day or whenever they log into the computer. To check news, a user runs an application program. The application scans all newsgroups the user has been reading, and reports whether any new articles have appeared.

To know exactly which articles each user has read, the news reading software maintains a record of activity. Whenever a user joins a group, the software records the name of the newsgroup. Each time a user reads an article, the software updates the saved information. When a user asks whether new items have appeared, the software uses the saved information to determine which articles the user has read. If new articles have been added to any of the newsgroups the user has been reading, the program reports them. To summarize:

> *Because the network news software does not automatically inform a user when a new article arrives in a newsgroup, a user who participates in network news must remember to check for new articles regularly. The network news software keeps information that allows it to determine which articles each user has read.*

Article Expiration

Because each article in a newsgroup occupies disk space, it cannot be kept in the computer forever. Usually, a computer system administrator instructs the network news software to erase any article after a specified number of days. For example, an administrator can choose to discard any article that becomes two weeks old.

Although automatic article expiration helps conserve disk space, it complicates checking for new articles. If a user waits too long to check the newsgroup, the article may disappear before the user has read it. To summarize:

Because most computer system administrators establish policies that cause articles to expire after a fixed time, any user who participates in network news must remember to check for new articles regularly or the local computer system may erase articles before the user has read them.

Reading Network News

Reading network news is straightforward. To read articles, a user starts an application program called a news reader; many such programs exist. Some permit a user to select items using a mouse, while others require the user to enter keystrokes. Despite minor differences in the interface, all news readers provide the same general functionality. When invoked, a news reader checks all the newsgroups that the user has joined and prints a summary of how many new articles have appeared in each. Figure 19.2 shows an example of the way one news reader formats the summary†:

```
Unread news in rec.motorcycles.harley            1 article
Unread news in rec.arts.books                     2 articles
Unread news in soc.culture.japan                  1 article
Unread news in misc.kids                          3 articles
Checking active list for new newsgroups...
```

Figure 19.2 An example of the summary a news reader presents.

The summary contains one line per newsgroup that reports how many new articles have appeared beyond those that the user has already read. If someone creates a new newsgroup, additional lines follow the summary to announce the newsgroup. The example summary lists four newsgroups that a user has been reading. Their topics are: Harley-Davidson motorcycles, books, Japan and Japanese culture, and children. The summary only lists those newsgroups that contain new articles (i.e., articles that have arrived since the user last accessed netnews).

Selecting Articles

After printing a summary of new articles, a news reader allows a user to read the new articles. Before displaying an article, it prompts the user to ask whether the user wishes to read the article or skip it. For example, a news reader that uses keyboard input prints a prompt in the following format:

```
********  1 unread article in rec.motorcycles.harley--read now? [ynq]
```

---

†The examples in this book show the format used by the *rn* (readnews) software; other news readers may use a different format.

and waits for the user to respond. The user can enter *y* (for *yes*), *n* (for *no*), or *q* to *quit* reading news at the present time.

If a user enters *n* when asked, the news reader skips the article and moves to the next one. If a user enters *y*, the news reader displays the article. The display starts with an article number followed by the contents:

```
Article 530 in rec.motorcycles.harley:


From: rick@company1.somewhere.com
Newsgroups: rec.motorcycles.harley, soc.culture.japan
Subject: Harley-Davidson in Japan
Date: 9 Feb 1994 15:35:56
Organization: Somewhere Incorporated, Fresno, California
Lines: 6
Distribution: world
NNTP-Posting-Host: nserve.company1.somewhere.com

Folks,
    A friend of mine told me that Harley-Davidson went to Japan to
sell motorcycles in 1930.  He says that H-D started the Japanese
motorcycle industry, and that the Japanese bikes eventually outsold
Harley-Davidson.  Is there any truth to the rumor?  Does anyone know
of a book that tells the story?
```

If an article is too long for the screen, the news reader displays one screenful at a time. After displaying the lines that fit on a screen, the news reader prints a message on the screen (usually the word *more*), and waits for the user to press the *space bar* before moving to the next screenful†.

After a user reads an entire article, the news reader prints another prompt. For example, the prompt can have the following format:

```
          End of article 530 (of 530) --what next? [npq]
```

The first number in the prompt repeats the article number, while the second tells how many articles are in the newsgroup. In the example, the user has just read the last article in the newsgroup (article 530 out of a possible 530). At the prompt, a user can enter *p* to move to the *previous* article, or *q* to *quit* reading the newsgroup. If more articles exist, the user can enter *n* to move on to the *next* article. In addition, a user can enter *s* followed by a filename to save a copy of an article in a file on disk.

After a user quits reading articles in a particular newsgroup, the news reader software moves to the next newsgroup that contains unread articles. The example summary in Figure 19.2 reports seven unread articles in four newsgroups. The news reader program continues though all seven articles. When a user finishes reading the last unread article in all newsgroups or instructs the news reader to quit, the program exits.

---

†Some news readers require the user to press the *enter* key, the *page down* key, or a function key to move to the next screenful.

Subscribing And Unsubscribing To Newsgroups

How does the news reader application know which newsgroups interest each user? The first time a user invokes the news reader, he or she begins with a set of newsgroups chosen by the site administrator. Often, the initial list includes local newsgroups that the organization has created to communicate with employees (e.g., a newsgroup that contains company notices). Each time a user reads netnews, the news reader provides a list of new newsgroups, and allows the user to *subscribe* if any seem interesting. A user can also *unsubscribe* from a newsgroup at any time. Whenever a user finishes reading network news, the news reader saves information about the newsgroups to which the user remains subscribed and the articles the user has read in each group. Whenever a user starts the news reader, it extracts and uses the saved subscription information. Netnews handles the subscriptions without any centralized registration:

> *Netnews software handles newsgroup subscriptions locally; the software keeps information about the newsgroups a user has joined and the articles the user has read in a file on the user's disk.*

Submitting An Article

Submitting an article to a network newsgroup is as easy as sending electronic mail. A user invokes an application that works like a word processor – it allows the user to compose and edit a message, and then send the message to one or more newsgroups. A line in the header specifies the names of newsgroups to which the message should be sent similar to the way the contents of a *To* line specifies recipients for an electronic mail message.

In addition to composing a message from scratch, a user can form a reply to an existing article. To do so in a keyboard-oriented news reader, a user types *r* at the prompt after a message. The news reader forms a header for the new message by extracting necessary information from the article to which the user is forming a reply. The news reader then invokes a word processor that allows the user to compose the reply.

Moderated Newsgroups

Many newsgroups permit anyone to submit an article. In such groups, people who submit articles range from novices to experts. More important, they range from scholars seriously interested in a topic to jokers who merely poke fun at a discussion.

To limit disruptions and compensate for differences in background, some newsgroups are *moderated*. In essence, a moderator agrees to preview all articles submitted to the newsgroup. The moderator determines whether each article is appropriate, and can choose to submit the article as received, edit the article, select and submit parts of the article, or summarize several articles. If a moderator does the job well, a newsgroup does not contain irrelevant, misleading, or disruptive comments.

Size Of Network News

Netnews has become extremely popular. By early 1994 it included over *6600* separate newsgroups divided into over *171* categories. Many of the categories belong to individual organizations, and do not represent worldwide distribution. However, thousands of newsgroups are distributed worldwide.

The daily volume of data provides another way to measure network news. As users join the Internet and more newsgroups appear, traffic continues to increase. Currently, the total size of news articles received each day exceeds *20* million characters. The consequence should be clear:

> *Because netnews contains thousands of newsgroups and the articles submitted to them each day often exceed 20 million characters, no individual can participate in all newsgroups.*

How Network News Works

The network news system attempts to optimize communication by transferring each news article once instead of fetching it on demand. To understand how the optimization works, imagine what would happen if the system obtained a copy of an article each time a user wanted to read the article. Because many users at a given location read the same article, the software would transfer many copies across the Internet. For example, if *100* people in England each requested an article that was stored on a computer in the US, their computers would each transfer a copy of the article across the Internet. The problem is significant because more than a million people read network news each day.

To avoid transferring multiple copies of each netnews article across the Internet, administrators responsible for netnews arrange the system so it distributes a copy of each new article to all sites. When a user at a given site reads netnews, the software retrieves articles from the local copy. For example, suppose companies X and Y both participate in netnews, and suppose company Y receives its newsfeed from X. Each night a computer at Y transfers a copy of all new articles to a computer at X. When someone at company X reads netnews, the news reader obtains articles from a local computer at company X; when someone at company Y reads netnews, the news reader obtains articles from a local computer at company Y.

Once a system administrator has configured network news software, transfer of news articles happens automatically without human intervention. A news transfer program starts at a scheduled time, and uses the network to contact one or more other sites as specified in its configuration. During each contact, it transfers new articles. Thus, new articles can appear in newsgroups without anyone running news transfer software manually.

Redundant Newsfeeds And Duplicate Elimination

Although transferring a copy of each new article once requires less network traffic than fetching articles on demand, using a single transfer introduces a potential problem: if hardware or software fails, one or more sites will not receive all new articles. To avoid losing articles during failures, some sites have a *backup newsfeed*. A site can receive news articles from either the primary or backup newsfeed.

Although a backup newsfeed guarantees that a site will receive new articles when its primary newsfeed does not operate, the site will receive two copies of each article when both feeds are working. To avoid storing multiple copies of an article, the netnews software automatically eliminates duplicates. Duplicate elimination requires two steps:

- Whenever a user creates a news article and submits it, the news software inserts a line in the header that identifies the article. For example, news software can number outgoing articles: *1, 2, 3*, and so on.
- Whenever a computer receives an article, the news software compares the identification line in the header to the identification line in the headers of previously received articles. If it finds a match, the software discards the duplicate copy.

To summarize:

> *To guarantee that it receives a copy of all netnews articles despite temporary network failures, a given site can have multiple newsfeeds. Users only encounter one copy of each article because the software automatically detects duplicates and stores only a single copy of each.*

More advanced versions of network news software can negotiate which articles to send across a newsfeed. Negotiating which articles should be sent saves time because the negotiation requires little time compared to the time required to transfer an article. To negotiate, the network news software at two sites exchange messages that advertise which articles each site has and which each needs. A site can advertise:

I HAVE

followed by a list of article identifiers. The other site examines the list to determine which articles it already has and which it needs and then replies:

PLEASE SEND

followed by a list of requested articles. The software then sends only the requested articles.

Relationship Between Netnews And Electronic Mail

The relationship between network news and electronic mail is more than accidental. Developers of network news decided to use electronic mail messages for news articles because it provided an easy way to integrate the two services. A person can use electronic mail to send an article to a newsgroup. When a user saves a copy of an articles from a newsgroup, the saved copy has the same format as an electronic mail message. Thus, one can use the same software to manipulate either a copy of a news article or a copy of an electronic mail message.

The most important consequence of using the same message format for news articles and e-mail arises from automatic conversion: a computer program can transfer a memo from an electronic mailing list to a newsgroup and vice versa. To understand why transfer is important, recall from Chapter *18* that the Internet contains many public mailing lists. A computer with a public mailing list can be programmed to automatically forward a copy of each mail message to a network newsgroup. Thus, whenever someone sends a message to the mailing list, everyone reading the newsgroup receives a copy. People can choose to either read a newsgroup or have their name added to its mailing list.

Impact And Significance Of Network News And Mailing Lists

The impact of bulletin boards and public mailing lists is difficult to appreciate. Internet technologies enable over a million people to participate in an electronic discussion. With that many people involved, it is difficult to imagine the diversity of topics that arise. More important, new discussions begin rapidly; a group discussing one topic can quickly shift interest to another. Many people complain that public mailing lists and newsgroups appear so quickly that they cannot possibly participate in all discussions that interest them.

Internet electronic mailing lists and bulletin board services have an interesting social effect: they provide an opportunity for people around the world to exchange views. In the past, such interactions have been limited either to people who live close enough so they can meet and talk face-to-face (e.g., a backyard discussion among neighbors), or to a few individuals who write opinions columns and editorials that appear in newspapers and magazines. Interestingly, because the Internet crosses geographic and political boundaries, it can extend discussion to a diverse set of people from many countries.

Identifiable communities develop on the Internet in exactly the same way social groups form among people in a geographic area. People discover others with common interests. Sometimes, they find others who agree with their views. Often, when a discussion diverges or strong opinions form, a newsgroup or mailing list splits in two, allowing the readership of each to form a community that shares an outlook.

Of course, interactions using network news or electronic mail differ from usual interactions. First, because memos and articles must be written, a contributor cannot use tone of voice or gestures to express emotion. Second, because the Internet can distribute memos or articles quickly, the discussion of a particular topic sometimes ends after a few days. Third, because electronic mailing lists and network news disseminate each memo or article to many people, almost any statement causes someone to respond.

To gain an appreciation of the diverse topics covered by electronic discussions, one needs to examine typical newsgroups. Appendix *1* on page 267 contains a sample of newsgroups that existed in 1994. It is not a catalog because such a catalog would be out of date before it was published. Instead, the sample provides examples of the diversity and richness that characterizes network news. The descriptions have been taken from Internet archives; some are serious and some lighthearted. For example, the description for newsgroup *alt.comics.superman* says *No one knows it is also alt.clark.kent.* Although no newsgroup exists for Clark Kent, the description is a joke that assumes every user will remember the fictional comic book hero well enough that no further explanation is needed.

The examples are not meant to be comprehensive, nor can one deduce anything about the size or activity of a given group from the specific instances selected. These are not necessarily the best, most popular, or most widely distributed newsgroups. For example, the list contains examples of newsgroups that discuss activities in an individual city or an individual country. One cannot conclude that the city or country only has the specific newsgroup mentioned because most newsgroups for each city or country have been omitted for the sake of brevity. Neither can one conclude that all cities have equivalent newsgroups; some cities have many and some cities have none.

Hints And Conventions For Participating In Discussions

Members of a society follow rules of etiquette to keep social interactions civil and to distinguish normal behavior from insults. Learning proper etiquette for Internet communication can be difficult for two reasons. First, because the Internet spans many cultures, economic backgrounds, and levels of education, it is much more likely that two people who communicate will not share a common background. Second, because the Internet is a relatively new communication medium, some people mistakenly assume that no rules of etiquette apply. Indeed, it seems that some subscribers do not adhere to the normal rules of courteous discussion.

Differences in background often become apparent in subtle ways. In some cultures, one is taught to trust what others say; in others exaggeration is accepted. Similarly, cultures do not all share the same amount of respect for a given position, rank, or title. In fact, a title in one culture or field of expertise may not be meaningful in another. A few simple guidelines help compensate for such differences†:

- When reading an electronic memo or news article, do not make assumptions about the person who wrote it. The writer may have more or less experience than you. The writer may have more or less expertise on a given topic than you. In short, assume neither that the writer is an expert nor a fool.

---

†The author compiled this particular list of suggestions from experience; apparently, a similar list of suggestions entitled *Netiquette* has been posted to some newsgroups.

- Suspect any message that appears to have been submitted by a famous person or well-known authority – the header in an electronic message can be forged, and some people seem to derive pleasure from forging them.
- When composing a submission, remember that it will be read by people whose backgrounds differ from yours. Choose words that accurately express your opinion. Provide evidence for your opinions if you have some available (e.g., a reference to a book or magazine article).
- As in any social interaction, use constraint. For example, before responding to a provocative or outrageous statement, take time to think.
- Do not take insults personally, especially when they respond to a memo you wrote. Remember that the writer does not know you and may not respect your title or position.
- Use the symbol for a smiley face, :-), to inform the reader that you mean something in a humorous way.
- Many Internet users follow the convention regarding upper and lower case: anything written in all uppercase is assumed to express screaming.
- If you are a novice, start by asking for help. In particular, some public mailing lists and newsgroups maintain a file of *Frequently Asked Questions* (*FAQ*) and answers; others maintain a summary of past discussion topics. You can submit a message that asks whether a FAQ or summary of the discussion is available online.

Summary

The major bulletin board service available on the Internet is known as Network News. News reader software allows a person to read messages that have been posted to a newsgroup or to compose and send a message to the group. The underlying mechanism makes a copy of each article available to everyone who participates in the newsgroup.

Netnews consists of thousands of individual bulletin boards on topics as diverse as education, hobbies, politics, science, entertainment, and employment opportunities. Although many newsgroups are distributed worldwide, some are restricted to a particular organization, city, country, or continent.

Network news is particularly useful because it has been integrated with electronic mail. Both netnews and electronic mail use the same format for memos. Furthermore, many electronic mailing lists and network newsgroups have been connected; a computer program automatically forwards each new article that appears in the newsgroup to the mailing list, and each new message from the mailing list to the newsgroup.

20

File Transfer (FTP)

Introduction

Previous chapters describe Internet services that transfer electronic messages. Although such services can be especially useful for sending short notes, they involve at least two people: one sends the message and another reads it.

This chapter describes the Internet service used to transfer a data file from the disk on one computer to the disk on another. File transfer services, which can copy a large volume of data efficiently, only require a single person to manage the transfer. After explaining how a file transfer service appears to a user and how the software works, the chapter provides an assessment. It explains that although file transfer accounts for many packets, the Internet file transfer service does not provide a user-friendly way to browse or locate information. Later chapters explain browsing and show why browsing services are easier to use.

Data Stored In Files

Computer systems use storage devices like disks to hold large volumes of data. From a user's point of view, the data on a disk appears to reside in named *files* which are collected together in *folders* or *directories*. Most systems have no preset limit – a file can be large or small. The file grows when the user adds data to it, and shrinks when the user erases data. For example, a word processor used to compose and edit documents usually stores each document in a separate file. A single document can consist of a few lines or hundreds of pages. The file for a document grows whenever the user places new text in the document; the file shrinks when a user removes text.

Copying A File

Soon after researchers began using the ARPANET, they realized that a network could be used to transfer a copy of a file from the disk on one computer to the disk on another. They devised software to perform the task, which they called *file transfer*. Later, researchers rewrote the software to work across the Internet. Known as the *File Transfer Protocol*, the service is usually identified by its acronym, *FTP*.

FTP Is Interactive

To use FTP, a user invokes an FTP application on their local computer. The FTP application presents the user with a prompt and accepts a series of commands interactively. During the interactive session, FTP responds to each command the user enters, and then prints the prompt when it is ready to accept another command.

A person uses FTP similar to the way one uses a telephone. After invoking the FTP application, a user identifies a remote computer and instructs FTP to establish a connection. FTP uses TCP/IP software to contact the computer. Once a connection has been established, a user interacts directly with the remote computer. For example, a user can obtain a list of files available on the remote computer or retrieve copies of one or more files. When the user finishes, he or she terminates the session. Each step of the interaction requires a user to enter a command. To summarize:

> *FTP is interactive; the FTP program accepts a sequence of commands. To interact with a remote computer, a user must identify the computer and allow FTP to establish contact; the user terminates contact when he or she finishes using the remote computer.*

Example Commands

Although most implementations of FTP include many possible commands, only a few are needed to retrieve a file. For example, although one popular version of FTP provides *58* separate commands, an average user only needs to understand the three basic commands to connect to a remote computer, retrieve a copy of a file, and exit the FTP program. Figure 20.1 lists the three basic commands along with their meanings.

command	Purpose
open	Connect to a remote computer
get	Retrieve a file from the computer
bye	Terminate the connection and leave the FTP program

Figure 20.1 The three FTP commands needed to retrieve a file.

If a command requires additional information, FTP asks the user to supply it. For example, after a user enters the *open* command, FTP asks for the name of a remote computer. After the user enters the *get* command, FTP asks for the name of the remote file to be copied as well as the name of a local file into which the copy should be written†.

A Client Can Store Or Retrieve A File

The discussion above implies that one can use FTP to obtain a copy of a file from a remote system. Indeed, most people use FTP to do just that – contact a remote computer and obtain a copy of a file. However, FTP is designed to allow a user to transfer a copy of a file to a remote computer as easily as they can retrieve a copy. Once a connection has been established, a user enters the *send* command to transfer a copy of a local file to the remote computer. Of course, FTP on the remote computer must be configured to allow file storage; few Internet sites that run FTP allow storage.

Commands For Binary And Text File Format

Although computer vendors store files in many forms, FTP only understands two basic file formats. It classifies each file as either a *text file* or a *binary file*. A text file contains a sequence of characters collected into lines. Although most computers use the ASCII encoding for text files described in Chapter 5, FTP includes commands to translate between ASCII and other character encodings (e.g., to translate between ASCII and EBCDIC). Thus, it is possible to transfer a text file between a computer that uses ASCII and one that does not.

FTP uses the classification *binary file* for all nontext files. The terminology can be confusing, because, as Chapter 4 explains, the Internet uses the binary digits to encode all data, including ASCII characters. One should interpret FTP's use of *binary* to mean *non-text*. In general, the user must specify binary for any file that contains:

- A computer program
- Audio data
- A graphic or video image
- A spreadsheet
- A document from a word processor
- A *compressed* file

The last item on the list refers to any file that has been processed to reduce its size. In general, compression means that small numbers are substituted for letters or sequences of letters; the opposite substitution must be applied to a compressed file to obtain the original. Sites that offer FTP service often compress files to reduce the total amount of disk space the files require.

---

†The file name used for the copy need not be the same as the name of the original file.

Before transferring a file, the user must tell FTP whether the file being transferred contains ASCII text or something else. One enters the command *binary* to prepare FTP to transfer a nontext file, or the command *ascii* to prepare FTP to transfer a text file. FTP remembers whether the user requested a binary or text transfer. Thus, the user only needs to enter the *binary* or *ascii* command when the type of the next file to be transferred differs from the type of the previous file. To simplify use, FTP assumes it should perform ASCII transfers unless the user enters the *binary* command.

Choosing ASCII or Binary Transfer

It is important to choose ASCII or binary transfer correctly because:

FTP does not understand the format or contents of a file. If a user requests FTP to perform a transfer using an incorrect type, the resulting copy may be malformed.

For example, suppose a user saves a spreadsheet on one computer and then uses FTP to transfer a copy to another computer. If the user fails to specify a binary transfer, the spreadsheet application may reject the copy. Some FTP software issues a warning when the file type appears to disagree with the transfer mode requested. However, one should not depend on receiving the warning because FTP may not be able to discern whether the file contains text or other data.

Choosing between binary and ASCII transfer can be difficult because most users do not understand data representations. The problem becomes especially difficult when retrieving a file from a remote computer because many such transfers involve computers and files about which the user knows little or nothing. In particular, when a user first discovers a computer on the Internet that contains a large collection of files available for transfer via FTP, the user does not usually know whether a given file contains ASCII text.

Interestingly, transferring a file in binary mode produces a correct result as long as both computers use the same representation for text files. When in doubt, one can follow a general guideline:

Choosing between binary and ASCII transfer can be difficult. When unsure about the contents of a file, enter the FTP command binary *before transferring the file.*

Commands For Authorization And Anonymous FTP

When FTP first contacts a computer, the remote system must verify that the user is authorized to access files. To do so, the remote FTP server asks the user to enter a login identifier and a password before allowing access. Like most computers that require a password, FTP turns off character display whenever a user types a password. Thus, if another person happens to look at the display, they will not see the password.

Requiring a user to enter a login and password code before allowing them to access files helps keep data secure. Unfortunately, it also restricts file access to users who have a valid account. To make files available to the general public, a system administrator can configure FTP to honor *anonymous FTP*. Anonymous FTP works like standard FTP, except that it allows anyone to access public files.

To use anonymous FTP, a user enters the login identifier *anonymous* and the password *guest*†. Anonymous login restricts access to only public files. Thus, even if the computer contains many files, a user who chooses anonymous FTP can only access those files that the system administrator has chosen to make available via anonymous FTP. To summarize,

> *A remote FTP service asks each user for authorization by prompting for a login identifier and password. To obtain access to public files, a user enters the login* anonymous *and the password* guest.

Listing The Contents Of A Remote Directory

Once FTP has established a connection to a remote machine, it permits the user to list the files that are available. To do so, the user enters the command *dir* or *ls*‡. Some FTP servers treat the two commands as synonyms and produce the same output for either; other systems provide an abbreviated listing for *ls* and a more detailed listing for *dir*.

Example Use Of FTP

An example will help clarify the use of FTP. The example shows a session in which a user invokes FTP, connects to a remote machine, lists the contents of the main directory (i.e., main folder) on that machine, lists the contents of a subdirectory, and then obtains a copy of a file. At each step, FTP prints the prompt *ftp>* and awaits a command. The user enters the *open* command to open a connection to a specified computer, the *ls* command to list a directory, and the *get* command to obtain a file. Finally, the user enters the *bye* command to exit FTP. When FTP requires additional information, it prompts the user.

---

†Some FTP servers prompt anonymous users for an electronic mail address that FTP can use to send an e-mail message in case an error occurs.

‡The *ls* command is taken from the UNIX timesharing system, which uses *ls* to list a directory.

To help the reader distinguish between text that a user enters and text that the computer generates, all text entered by the user is shown in boldface. Note that although the example contains the password *guest*, FTP does not normally display a password when the user enters it.

```
$ ftp

ftp> open
(to) ds.internic.net
Connected to ds.internic.net.
220-               InterNIC Directory and Database Services
220 ds.internic.net FTP server ready.
Name: anonymous
331 Guest login ok, send ident as password.
Password: guest
230 Guest login ok, access restrictions apply.

ftp> ls
200 PORT command successful.
150 Opening ASCII mode data connection for file list.

resources
std
ietf
isoc
internet-drafts
rfc
resource-guide
policies-procedures
fyi
internic.info
dirofdirs

226 Transfer complete.
106 bytes received in 0.02 seconds (5.2 Kbytes/s)

ftp> ls internic.info
200 PORT command successful.
150 Opening ASCII mode data connection for file list.

internic.info/access.info
internic.info/cni062593talk.ps
internic.info/dirofdirs.info
internic.info/internic.info
internic.info/ietfmar93talk.ps
internic.info/x500.person.request
```

```
internic.info/whitepages.info
internic.info/ds.status
internic.info/mailserv.info
internic.info/x500.position.paper
internic.info/database.request
internic.info/proposal
internic.info/database.info

226 Transfer complete.
remote: internic.info
377 bytes received in 0.08 seconds (4.9 Kbytes/s)

ftp> ls internic.info/mailserv.info
200 PORT command successful.
150 Opening ASCII mode data connection for file list.

internic.info/mailserv.info

226 Transfer complete.
remote: internic.info/mailserv.info
29 bytes received in 4e-06 seconds (7.1e+03 Kbytes/s)

ftp> get
(remote-file): internic.info/mailserv.info
(local-file): mserve
200 PORT command successful.
150 Opening ASCII mode data connection
226 Transfer complete.
local: mserve remote: internic.info/mailserv.info
28704 bytes received in 0.61 seconds (46 Kbytes/s)

ftp> bye
221 Goodbye.
```

The user begins by invoking the *ftp* command, which prints the prompt *ftp>*. After the user enters the *open* command, FTP asks for the name of a computer by displaying the prompt *(to)*. The user enters *ds.internic.net*†. Once FTP establishes a connection, the remote server displays the prompt *Name:* to ask the user for a login name; the user enters *anonymous*. When the remote server asks for a password, the user enters *guest*.

To obtain a list of the files available on the remote machine, the user enters command *ls*. The remote server prints a list that begins with *resources* and ends with *dirof-dirs*. Although one cannot tell from the name alone, items in the list are not files – each name refers to a directory‡ that contains many files. To see if a name refers to a file or a directory, one can use the *ls* command. When a user enters *ls internic.info* on a single line, FTP responds by displaying a list of the items contained in the *internic.info* directory. To see if the item named *internic.info/mailserv.info* is a directo-

---

† ds.internic.net is the name of a computer at the *INTERnet Network Information Center*.
‡ Recall, some computer systems use the term *folder* instead of *directory*.

ry or a file, the user again requests the *ls* command. Because *ls* only prints one line of output, the user can conclude that *internic.info/mailserv.info* is a file.

To retrieve a copy of file *internic.info/mailserv.info*, the user enters the *get* command and then supplies the name of the file to retrieve as well as the name for the local copy, *mserve*. Because the user did not enter a *binary* command, FTP assumes the file contains text.

After each data transfer, FTP prints statistics that show the number of bytes (characters) of data transferred, the time required to perform the transfer, and the average data rate. Like the implementation used for the example, most implementations of FTP provide statistics when they send a directory listing and when they send a copy of a file. All the statistics in the example came from actual transfers across the Internet. The transfers in the example illustrate that for a small request, FTP can transfer data in less than a second. As a result, FTP is extremely fast:

> *To a human user, FTP appears to provide instantaneous response for small requests.*

The example also illustrates an important disadvantage of FTP: it does not provide information about file contents. A user cannot know whether a file contains a document, graphic image, computer program or something else until the user obtains a copy of the file and examines it. To summarize:

> *Although the FTP service can transfer a file quickly, FTP is not a convenient tool for browsing directories because it does not provide helpful information or descriptions of file contents. Furthermore, the output from an FTP session can be difficult to read.*

Miscellaneous Commands

Other FTP commands handle special cases that seldom arise in casual use. For example, a user who requests a copy of a large file may need to wait many seconds for the transfer to complete. If the user anticipates a long delay, they can choose to enter either the *hash* or *bell* command. The *hash* command requests that FTP print a series of hash sign characters (''#'') on the user's screen as the transfer proceeds to reassure the user that FTP is working. The *bell* command requests that FTP sound an audible tone whenever a transfer completes. After entering the *bell* command, a user does not need to wait for a transfer to complete. Instead, they can leave FTP running and proceed with other work, knowing that the tone FTP sounds will notify them as soon as it is ready to handle another request.

How FTP Works

Like most other Internet applications, FTP uses the client-server approach. A user invokes an FTP program on the computer, instructs it to contact a remote computer, and then requests the transfer of one or more files. The local FTP program becomes a client that uses TCP to contact an FTP server program on the remote computer. Each time the user requests a file transfer, the client and server programs cooperate to send a copy of the data across the Internet. Figure 20.2 illustrates the path data follows when a user requests a copy of a file.

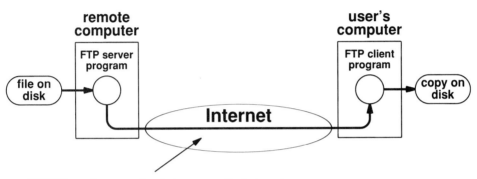

TCP/IP used to transfer data across the Internet

Figure 20.2 The path data takes when a server sends a copy of a remote file in response to a user's request. The FTP client and FTP server programs use TCP/IP to communicate.

The FTP server locates the file that the user requested, and uses TCP to send a copy of the entire contents of the file across the Internet to the client. As the client program receives data, it writes the data into a file on the user's local disk. After the file transfer completes, the client and server programs terminate the TCP connection used for the transfer.

Impact And Significance Of FTP

FTP data transfers account for a significant portion of traffic on the Internet. In fact, historically:

> *FTP data transfer has caused more traffic on the Internet than any other application.*

Why has FTP remained so popular? The answer arises from four facts. First, FTP software is widely available. In particular, FTP client software exists for most types of computers. Second, many Internet sites make files available through anonymous FTP. FTP archives contain information from computer games to scholarly research papers. The amount and diversity of information available through FTP is astonishing. Third, FTP is efficient. Because FTP does not perform complex transformations during file transfer, it can perform the transfer quickly. Fourth, because the interface has been designed so a computer program can use FTP, computer programs can invoke FTP when they need to transfer a file.

Allowing a computer program to use FTP means that a transfer can be automated. For example, a program can be devised that examines a set of files each night and transfers a copy of each file that has been changed. Running such a program enables a group of people to coordinate their activities (e.g., a program can use FTP to transfer a copy of daily sales figures from each salesperson's computer to the manager's computer; neither a salesperson nor a manager needs to initiate the transfer).

Summary

FTP permits a user to transfer a copy of a data file across the Internet from one computer to another. When using FTP, a user establishes communication with a remote computer and obtains authorization by sending a login and a password. The user can list the files available on the remote computer, request a copy of a particular file, or send a copy of a local file.

Although an FTP program usually offers many commands, the user only needs a few to perform most transfers. Two of the commands enable the user to specify whether the file being transferred consists of ASCII text or non-text data; when FTP begins it assumes files will contain ASCII text.

On the Internet, most computers that offer files for access via FTP support anonymous FTP. Anonymous FTP allows any user on an arbitrary computer to access public files; the user does not need a valid login to retrieve a public file.

Although FTP accounts for many packets on the Internet and can handle large transfers efficiently, it does not provide a user-friendly service to browse information. The output is difficult to understand, and FTP does not describe the contents of a file.

21

Remote Login (TELNET)

Introduction

Previous chapters describe Internet services used to transfer electronic mail, news articles, or files among computers. In each case, the information being transferred remains static – it must be prepared and stored on one computer before being transferred to others.

This chapter begins a discussion of services that provide dynamic interactions between a user at one location and a computer at another. It considers an important Internet service that permits a user to run programs on a remote computer. Succeeding chapters extend the idea of remote program execution to show how the Internet can provide a variety of interactive services.

The Internet's remote login service is an extension of the login facility used on a conventional timesharing computer. Thus, to understand remote login, one must first understand conventional login. The next sections provide the necessary background. They review how a large timesharing computer operates and discuss why such a system requires login. Later sections describe how the Internet's remote login service extends the idea to allow login on a remote computer.

Users Access A Timesharing System Through Terminals

Unlike a small personal computer that is usually dedicated to a single individual, a large computer system allows many people to use the computer simultaneously. To support multiple users, a large computer needs sophisticated software known as a *timesharing system*. An individual user usually interacts with a timesharing computer through a terminal that includes a keyboard, display, and possibly a mouse. Multiple terminals attach to a timesharing computer, allowing one user at each terminal to interact with the computer. The timesharing software switches the computer among the users quickly to ensure that each user's computation proceeds.

From an individual's point of view, a timesharing computer appears to operate the same as a personal computer – the software gives each user the illusion of an independent computer. A user can choose an application program and decide when to run it. For example, one user can run a spreadsheet application while another runs a word processor. The timesharing system partitions the computer's memory into separate parts, and devotes one part to each user. In addition, the timesharing system allocates each user disk space that can be used to save files. Like a personal computer, a timesharing system appears to respond to input instantly. For example, the timesharing system displays characters or moves the cursor as fast as a user presses keys or moves a mouse. In fact, many timesharing systems operate so efficiently that a user does not usually know whether other users are working on the same computer unless they attempt to use a shared resource simultaneously (e.g., when two users attempt to use a printer at the same time, one of them must wait until the other finishes printing).

A Timesharing System Requires Accounting Information

Because multiple users can interact with a timesharing computer, the system requires each user to identify themselves for accounting purposes. For example, a timesharing system permits all users to store files on disk. To protect files from unauthorized access and to account for storage, the system keeps ownership information with each file. Whenever a user attempts to access a file, the system verifies that the user has permission to access the file (e.g., the user owns the file). The system also keeps a record of the disk space each user allocates to prevent a single user from allocating all the space.

Before an individual can use the timesharing system, he or she must be assigned an account. The account has a unique name called a *login identifier* that the system uses to identify the user. In addition, each user is assigned a *password* that the user must keep secret to prevent others from accessing their account. Whenever a user begins interacting with a timesharing computer, the system software requests their login identifier and password. Computer professionals refer to the procedure as *logging in* or *login*.

For example, a computer might print the following on the display:

```
login:
```

After a user has entered their login identifier, the system prints another prompt that requests them to enter their secret password:

```
password:
```

To help keep passwords secure, the timesharing system turns off character display while the user enters a password. Thus, although the computer accepts the password as the user types it, nothing appears on the screen.

After successfully logging into a timesharing system, a user can enter commands or invoke application programs. When a user finishes using a timesharing computer, he or she informs the system by *logging out*. After a user logs out, the system displays the login prompt on the terminal and waits for another user to log in.

To summarize:

> *A timesharing computer system permits multiple users to run programs simultaneously. Each user is assigned a login identifier and secret password; a user must enter the login identifier and password to use a terminal connected to the timesharing computer.*

Remote Login Resembles Conventional Login

The Internet remote login service allows a user to log into a remote timesharing computer system as if the user's keyboard and display attach directly to the remote computer. To use the login service, a user invokes an application program on the local computer and specifies the name of a remote computer. The local application program uses the Internet to make a connection to the remote computer. Once a connection has been established, the remote computer takes over the user's display, and issues the *login* prompt exactly as it does on any terminal that connects directly to it. After the user enters a correct login identifier, the remote system prompts for the user's password. The remote computer turns off character display while the user types a password exactly as it does on a conventional terminal.

Remote Login Provides General Access

After a user enters a valid login, the remote computer permits the user to interact by typing on the keyboard or using the mouse. The user can run any command or invoke any application program that he or she could run from a conventional terminal on the timesharing system. In essence, a timesharing computer accessed by remote login reacts exactly the same way it does when a user enters the same input on one of its terminals.

After a user finishes using the remote machine, he or she logs out as usual. When a user logs out, the remote computer breaks the Internet connection, the local remote login program exits, and control of the keyboard and display return to the user's local computer.

Generality Makes Remote Login Powerful

The power of remote login arises because it provides general access to the programs on a computer without requiring modifications to the programs themselves. Once remote login software has been installed, users can run conventional applications from remote locations. An example will help clarify the idea.

Consider a hypothetical company that uses a database to store information about the company's products, prices, and current inventory. Assume that the database software runs on a conventional timesharing computer, and that the company's sales personnel use the database to determine product prices and availability.

Suppose the company decides to make the information from the database accessible to potential customers through the Internet. Unfortunately, the database software is not designed to use the Internet or to be accessed from a remote location. More important, because the company invested money acquiring the existing database system and training employees to use it, they cannot afford to replace the database with new software that has been designed to work with the Internet.

Remote login solves the company's problem easily. The company adds remote login software to the timesharing computer without changing the database software. The company then issues accounts and passwords to remote users so they can log in and access the database. The company can choose, for example, to create a single public account that provides access to the database system. Alternatively, the company can choose to issue each customer a separate account to simplify access control.

Remote Login Accommodates Multiple Types Of Computers

The Internet's remote login service solves an important problem: it permits arbitrary brands of computers to communicate. For example, suppose a company's database software only works on computers manufacturered by IBM Corporation, and suppose that sales personnel who needed to access the database use computers manufacturered by other vendors including Apple Corporation. Remote login software permits an employee using an Apple computer to contact an IBM computer and run the database software.

To summarize:

> *A remote login service allows a user at one site to interact with application programs that run on a computer at another site. The power of remote login arises because it allows remote access to application programs without requiring any changes to the programs themselves.*

How Remote Login Works

Remote login follows the client-server paradigm discussed in Chapter *15*. When a user on a local computer decides to log into a remote system, the user invokes a local application program for the remote login service, and enters the name of a remote computer to contact. The application becomes a client that uses TCP/IP to connect across the Internet to a server on the remote computer. The server sends exactly the same login prompt used for conventional terminals. Figure 21.1 illustrates the idea.

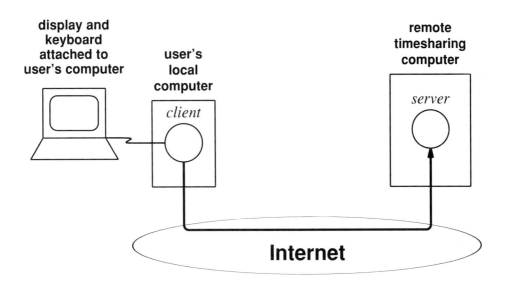

Figure 21.1 Remote login across the Internet uses two programs. The user invokes an application on the local computer. The local application connects the user's keyboard and display to the remote timesharing system.

Once a connection has been established between the client and server, the software allows the user to interact directly with the remote computer. When the user presses a key on the keyboard or moves the mouse, the client application sends the data across the connection to the remote machine. When the application program on the remote computer produces output, the server sends it back to the client.

After a user logs out of the remote computer, control of the keyboard and display return to the local computer. In practice, when a user logs out of the remote machine, the server on the remote computer terminates the Internet connection. When the client program is informed of the termination, it exits and control of the local machine returns to the underlying command interpreter or desktop the local machine uses.

Escaping From Remote Login

Although a remote login client usually passes each keystroke to the remote computer, client software provides a way for a user to *escape* and communicate with the local client. To understand why such a facility is needed, one must understand two facts:

1. During remote login, two programs run simultaneously – the application on
   the remote computer and the remote login client on the local computer.

2 One of the keys on the keyboard can be used to abort a running program.

Aborting a program is not a normal activity. However, if an application mis-
behaves or freezes, it may be necessary to abort it and regain control. Normally, a remote login client sends all keystrokes to the remote computer. Thus, when a user
presses the special key used to abort a program, the client sends it to the application
running on the remote system. However, the user may also need to abort the local
client program. To do so, the user must enter a sequence of two keys: one key that
''escapes'' from the remote application followed by the abort key†. In essence, the escape key means, ''Please stop communication with the remote system, and allow communication with the local client program.

Displays And Windows

In most cases, when a user runs a remote login application, the application takes
over the entire display. On a computer system that has a window system, however, a
remote login client can use a separate, rectangular region of the screen called a *window*.
From the remote system's point of view, the window used by a client acts as a single
terminal. Any output that the remote computer emits appears in the window, and the
remote computer receives input typed on the keyboard when the window is active.
Thus, remote login from a window operates exactly as if the window is a small terminal
screen.

Internet Remote Login Is Called TELNET

The Internet standard for remote login service is found in a protocol known as
TELNET; its specification is part of the TCP/IP documentation. The TELNET protocol
specifies exactly how a remote login client and a remote login server interact. The standard specifies, for example, how the client contacts the server, how the client encodes
keystrokes for transmission to the server, and how the server encodes output for
transmission to the client.

Because both the TELNET client and server programs adhere to the same specification, they agree on communication details. For example, although most computers interpret one of the keys on a keyboard as a request to *abort* the running program, not all

---

†Although the key labeled *ESCAPE* was originally intended to be used as described here, so many programs use *ESCAPE* for other purposes that Internet remote login programs use *CONTROL-*] as an escape key.

computer systems use the same key. Some computers use a key labeled *ATTN*, while others use a key labeled *DEL*. TELNET specifies the sequence of bits a client uses to represent an *abort* key. When a user presses the abort key on a local keyboard, the TELNET client program translates the key into the special sequence. Thus, TELNET allows a user to press the same key to abort a remote program as they press to abort a local one, even if the local and remote computers usually require different keys.

Using TELNET To Access Other Internet Services

To understand why TELNET is especially popular on the Internet, consider how an organization can use TELNET to provide Internet access. Assume that the organization has a timesharing computer connected to the Internet as well as many other computers on workers' desks. The organization obtains one copy of the software needed to access Internet services, and places the copy on the timesharing computer. To use the Internet, a worker in the organization runs TELNET software to connect to the timesharing computer, and then runs software that accesses Internet services. That is, a worker always uses TELNET to reach a computer inside the organization, and then runs software that uses the Internet to reach a remote computer.

From a user's point of view, using TELNET to connect to a local computer before accessing the Internet introduces extra overhead. From the organization's point of view, the strategy can save time and expense. Keeping a single copy of each Internet access program simplifies the task of acquiring and maintaining software because it means the organization only needs to maintain one copy of the software. Using TELNET to access a timesharing system also eliminates problems with incompatibilities among computers because it means the organization does not need to acquire Internet access software for each type of computer. Furthermore, a user does not need to acquire a copy of access software before they can use new Internet services – most computers in the organization only need TELNET software that permits them to connect to a timesharing system. More important, TELNET allows any computer in the organization to access any Internet service from the organization's timesharing computer. The organization can install a new timesharing computer or new software that provides access to additional services without changing the TELNET software on the users' personal computers.

Assessment Of Remote Login

The Internet remote login service is significant for three reasons. First, remote login is fundamentally different than services discussed earlier because it allows a user to interact with a program that runs on a remote computer. Instead of sending a data file or a message from one computer to another, remote login allows a program running on a remote computer to accept input, react to it, and send output back to a user on a distant computer.

Second, remote login is significant because of its generality. After a user logs into a remote computer, the user can execute any application program available on that computer. In particular, although a given program may run on one brand of computer, remote login permits users on other brands of computers to use it.

Third, remote login is significant because many people use it. For example, users who have small personal computers or workstations on their desks often rely on remote login for much of their work. They create a window for remote login, and connect to a large timesharing system. They leave the window on the screen and move to it whenever they need to perform a significant or specialized computation. Indeed, many users do the majority of their computing via remote login; computers and networks operate so quickly that one cannot perceive differences between local and remote computations.

Summary

A remote login facility permits a user who is using one computer to interact with a program on another computer. The service extends the login concept used by conventional timesharing computer systems to permit access to a remote timesharing system.

The Internet's remote login service is called *TELNET*. To use the service, one must invoke a local application program and specify a remote machine. The local program becomes a client, which forms a connection to a server on the remote computer. The client passes keystrokes and mouse movements to the remote machine, and displays output from the remote machine on the user's display screen.

Remote login is significant because it shows how the Internet can provide interactive services. Unlike services described in previous chapters, remote login does not merely transfer static data. Instead, remote login permits a user to interact with a program that runs on a remote computer. The remote program can respond to input from the user, and the user can respond to output the remote program displays.

22

Information Browsing (Gopher)

Introduction

Previous chapters discuss basic Internet services used to transfer files and log into a remote computer. This chapter begins to explore dynamic services that allow a user to browse information on remote computers. It describes how a browsing service operates, gives an example of one particular browsing service, and shows why such services are especially popular among nontechnical users. Later chapters explore alternative browsing facilities.

Description Of Functionality

An *information browsing service* allows an individual to locate and evaluate information stored on remote computers. Most information browsing services operate interactively – they permit one to search through information on remote computers without retrieving individual files or reading their contents. In particular, browsing services:

- Locate remote computers that contain information of interest.
- Display information from a remote computer interactively.
- Read descriptions of the files stored on a remote computer.
- Retrieve or print a copy of selected information.
- Follow a reference found on one remote computer to related information stored on another remote computer.

Searching For Information

Finding information on the Internet can be difficult. Because the Internet connects over a million computers, an exhaustive examination of all information on all computers is impractical. Surprisingly, an exhaustive examination of the information found on a single computer can also be impractical – a computer can store so much information that it would take a human weeks to browse through it.

To understand the problem, think of a large public library. When one enters the library, they discover thousands of books on shelves that extend through many rooms. Although the books contain significant amounts of information, an individual cannot search through all books to find an item of interest. More important, an individual cannot read all the titles. Similarly, one cannot read the names of all files stored on the Internet.

Tools To Aid Searching

In a traditional library, one uses clues and tools to help locate information. For example, one can consult a card catalog to obtain an initial list of books on a given topic. Alternatively, one can begin with a set of references obtained outside the library (e.g., recommendations from friends or a magazine article). Librarians place closely related books together on the shelves, making it possible to search for additional related books by scanning the nearby shelves when retrieving a book.

Although scanning shelves or a card catalog sometimes helps uncover a pertinent book, little can be deduced from the book titles alone. One can usually obtain better results by using information found inside selected books to guide a search. In particular, in addition to information about a given topic, a book often contains references to related works. Thus, one can start with an initial set of books on a subject, and follow references in them to a second set of books. Those will contain references to a third set, and so on.

Searching The Internet

An individual also uses clues and tools to search for information on the Internet. One begins with a topic and tools to locate relevant information, and then follows references to other information.

Of course, it is possible to search the Internet using a retrieval tool like the FTP file transfer service described in Chapter *20*. However, FTP only provides basic retrieval; one must know the name of the computer on which information has been stored and the name of the file on that computer in which the information can be found. Furthermore, although FTP allows one to list the names of the files available on a given computer, it does not provide any information about file contents. In summary,

Although FTP handles file transfer efficiently, it does not help a user understand file contents or locate information.

Information browsing services help users locate information in two ways. First, an information browsing service allows an individual to find computers that contain items of interest. Second, an information browsing service allows an individual to read descriptions of information before obtaining a copy. The former is important because the Internet contains so many computers that one cannot hope to find information by randomly searching. The latter is important because discarding unwanted information after transferring it across the Internet wastes Internet resources.

To summarize:

An information browsing service permits an individual to locate and evaluate information on remote computers. Browsing differs from information retrieval because browsing does not require a user to retrieve files of data to determine their contents.

An Example Information Browsing Service

The Internet offers several information browsing services. For example, the *gopher* service provides access to information at many Internet sites. Gopher is especially popular among novices and nontechnical users because it is intuitive and easy to use. Indeed, one can use gopher after only a few minutes of training.

The name *gopher* may seem unusual for an Internet information access service. However, many Internet users have enjoyed the name and perpetuated jokes about it†. The inventors offer at least two justifications for the name. First, the software was invented at the University of Minnesota, which is known locally as the home of the *golden gophers*. Second, the nickname *gofer* is sometimes used to describe a person who is assigned to run errands because they must "go for" things – one uses the gopher service to "go for" information.

Gopher Is Menu-Driven

The gopher service is an interactive menu-driven browser. When gopher runs, it displays a *menu* of choices. The choices usually consist of short, self-explanatory phrases in English.

Conceptually, each item on a gopher menu denotes a file of information or a reference to another menu. The user scans the list of items on the menu and selects one of them. If the selected item corresponds to a file of information, the gopher software retrieves the file and displays its contents; if the selected item corresponds to another

---

†The popular press has used phrases such as *tunneling through the internet* and *rodents on the information superhighway.*

menu, the gopher system retrieves the new menu and allows the user to select an item from it. The point is:

> *The gopher information browsing system is menu-driven. By selecting an item from a menu, a user can retrieve information or find another menu.*

A Menu Item Can Point To Another Computer

The power of information browsing systems like gopher arises from their ability to span computer systems: an item in a gopher menu on one computer can refer to a gopher menu on another computer. More important, a user does not need to take any special actions to follow a link to another computer. At any given time, the gopher software on a user's computer is in contact with a specific remote computer. When a user selects an item, the gopher software automatically determines the computer on which the item resides. If the selected item resides on a different remote computer than the remote computer being used, the gopher software automatically contacts the new computer and retrieves the item. Gopher does not inform the user when it contacts a different remote computer – it fetches the new item efficiently without a long delay. Thus, from the perspective of a user:

> *Gopher hides computer boundaries completely, and makes information on a large set of computers appear to be part of a single, integrated system of menus. A gopher user can jump from computer to computer without knowing or caring about which computers are being used.*

How Gopher Works

Understanding a few basics about how the gopher service operates is essential to understanding how to use it. Like other Internet services, gopher uses client-server interaction described in Chapter *15*. Figure 22.1 illustrates the idea.

A user invokes *gopher client* software on the local computer. The user interacts with the gopher client to select menu items and control the search for information. The gopher client contacts gopher servers one at a time. Over one thousand computers attached to the Internet run *gopher server* software that provides information to any client that requests it. The servers remain ready to be contacted at all times.

Whenever a user selects a menu item, the gopher client uses the Internet to retrieve the information and display it. A selected item can reside on the same computer as the menu or on a different computer. The gopher client automatically contacts the correct computer and retrieves the selected item without notifying the user. Thus, browsing through a set of menu items can cause the local gopher client software to contact many other computers. However, the client only needs to contact one computer at any time.

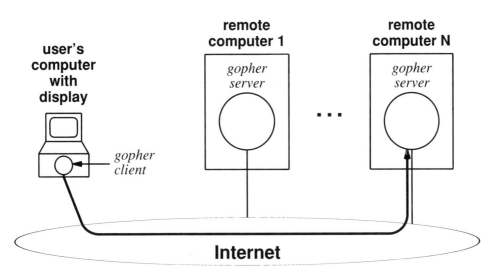

Figure 22.1 The gopher service uses client-server interaction. Multiple servers run continuously; a client on the user's computer contacts one server at a time.

Gopher Has Two User Interfaces

Although several implementations of gopher software exist, most use one of two basic styles. The two styles have arisen to accommodate the two basic varieties of user interface hardware on computers. Some computers include a pointing device called a mouse and a high-resolution screen on which the software can display graphic images (e.g., a small cursor). Other computers or terminals do not include a mouse. Such systems can only display typewriter-like characters on the screen and have only a keyboard for input.

Gopher's Point-And-Click Interface

On a computer that has a mouse and high-resolution display, gopher software uses a *point-and-click* style of interaction. That is, the software permits a user to navigate through menus using only the mouse; one does not need to type on the keyboard. The mouse can be used, for example, to choose an item from a menu, return to the previous menu, or quit using gopher.

Figure 22.2 shows how the screen might appear to someone who is using gopher's point-and-click interface.

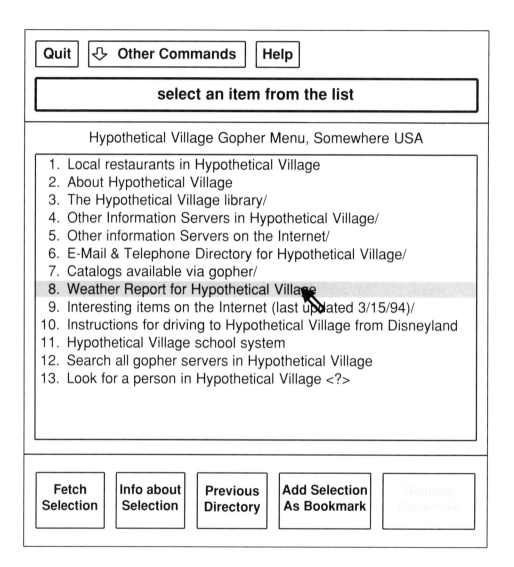

Figure 22.2 An example of the way gopher presents information on a computer that has a mouse. In this example, the cursor is an arrow that moves as the user moves the mouse.

The screen is divided into three main areas. The top area contains boxes that can be used to perform general operations (e.g., to quit the gopher program or to obtain help using gopher). In addition, the top area contains a line that tells the user what action gopher expects next. The center area contains the most important information – a title for the menu and a list of items that the user can select. Finally, the bottom area contains a set of specific operations that the user can perform.

A user can only choose among some of the operations at any time. To help the user determine which operations are valid, the gopher interface displays valid operations in black and invalid operations in grey. In Figure 22.2, for example, the operation labeled *Remove Bookmark* is grey because the user cannot invoke that operation at the present time. As the user interacts with gopher, the set of valid operations changes and gopher changes the display accordingly.

The center area in Figure 22.2 contains a title that declares the menu to be from a hypothetical village and a list of thirteen items from which the user can select. In the list, some lines end with a slash (/) or question mark in brackets <?>, and others do not have any punctuation. As the example shows, some gopher software displays a slash at the end of each item that leads to another menu, a question mark at the end of each item that corresponds to a program that the user can invoke, and no punctuation after an item that corresponds to a file of information. For example, in Figure 22.2, items numbered 1, 2, 8, 10, 11, and 12 all correspond to files of information, while item 13 corresponds to a program that a user can invoke. Each of the other items leads to another menu.

To select a menu item with a mouse, a user slides the mouse across the desktop. As the user moves the mouse, the computer moves the cursor, shown as an arrow, across the screen. When the user presses the mouse button, gopher highlights the item under the cursor, and waits for the user to select an operation. For example, Figure 22.2 shows the display immediately after a user has positioned the cursor over item number *8* and pressed the mouse button. If the user chooses to follow the highlighted menu item, he or she must move the mouse to the box labeled *Fetch Selection* and press the mouse button again†.

Gopher's Textual Interface

On a computer that does not have a graphic display or a mouse, gopher client software displays all output in the form of characters, and uses keystrokes to move the cursor and select items. For example, Figure 22.3 shows how a gopher client displays output on a character-oriented screen.

---

†Like most software for a mouse, gopher allows a user to fetch a selection by *double-clicking* (i.e., pressing the mouse button twice in quick succession).

```
               Hypothetical Village Gopher Menu, Somewhere USA

      1. Local restaurants in Hypothetical Village
      2. About Hypothetical Village
      3. The Hypothetical Village library/
      4. Other Information Servers in Hypothetical Village/
      5. Other information Servers on the Internet/
      6. E-Mail & Telephone Directory for Hypothetical Village/
      7. Catalogs available via gopher/
 -->8. Weather Report for Hypothetical Village
      9. Interesting items on the Internet (last updated 3/15/94)/
     10. Instructions for driving to Hypothetical Village from Disneyland
     11. Hypothetical Village school system
     12. Search all gopher servers in Hypothetical Village
     13. Look for a person in Hypothetical Village <?>




 Press ? for Help, q to Quit, u to go up a menu            Page: 1/1
```

Figure 22.3 An example of the way a gopher client displays output on a character-oriented display such as an ASCII terminal. The user must press keys to move the cursor and select an item.

As Figure 22.3 illustrates, gopher displays the characters `-->` to denote a cursor when it uses a character-oriented display. The figure shows how gopher displays the menu immediately after the user has moved the cursor to item number *8*. To control the cursor or perform an operation, the user types single-letter commands on the keyboard. The letters themselves do not appear on the screen – gopher merely performs the operation associated with the key. Four contiguous keys handle most operations†. Pressing the *j* key moves the cursor down one line, while pressing the *k* key moves the cursor up one line. Pressing the *l* key selects the item to which the cursor points, and pressing the *h* key moves to the previous menu.

Figure 22.3 illustrates that gopher can display the same menu information using a character-oriented interface as with a point-and-click interface. Thus,

---

†Some keyboards use arrow keys to move the cursor.

Despite differences in the two ways users can interact with gopher, all interfaces provide access to the same set of menus.

An Example Trip Through Gopher

To understand how gopher makes it possible to browse information and why it has become popular, one must use the service. The information accessible includes such diverse items as descriptions of university courses, satellite weather maps, computer programs, lists of books offered for sale, and telephone directories. This section contains a simple example of browsing through the Internet gopher service in 1994. Although a single example cannot capture gopher's size and diversity, it will help illustrate the general idea of browsing, and show a small sample of the information one can encounter.

Whenever a user starts gopher client software running on a local computer, the software automatically determines an initial remote computer to contact. Usually, gopher clients are programmed to contact a server run by the user's organization. However, to illustrate the gopher system, our example starts by contacting a gopher server on a computer at the University of Minnesota where gopher was invented. The computer is named:

gopher.micro.umn.edu†

When a user invokes gopher, the software contacts the initial remote server and displays the main menu page from that server. The menu page begins with a line that identifies the menu followed by a list of items from which the user can select. The initial menu contains the following list of items:

```
                    Univ of MN Gopher server (Mama gopher)

---> 1.   Information About Gopher/
     2.   Computer Information/
     3.   Discussion Groups/
     4.   Fun & Games/
     5.   Internet file server (ftp) sites/
     6.   Libraries/
     7.   News/
     8.   Other Gopher and Information Servers/
     9.   Phone Books/
    10.   Search Gopher Titles at the University of Minnesota <?>
    11.   Search lots of places at the University of Minnesota <?>
    12.   University of Minnesota Campus Information/
```

---

†Although the example name contains the term *gopher*, most gopher servers run on computers that do not have *gopher* in their names.

The particular gopher server the user has chosen was created to provide information to students and faculty at the University of Minnesota. Consequently, the general public will not find most of the menu items relevant. However, item number eight refers to information about other gopher servers.

Assume whoever is browsing decides to investigate other gopher servers, and selects item number *8* from the menu. In response, the gopher client retrieves a new menu and displays it:

```
                Other Gopher and Information Servers

---> 1.  All the Gopher Servers in the World/
     2.  Search titles in Gopherspace using veronica/
     3.  Africa/
     4.  Asia/
     5.  Europe/
     6.  International Organizations/
     7.  Middle East/
     8.  North America/
     9.  Pacific/
    10.  South America/
    11.  Terminal Based Information/
    12.  WAIS Based Information/
```

Given the topic of the menu, *Other Gopher and Information Servers*, most of the items make sense. By scanning the list quickly, for example, almost anyone can guess that the information has been divided by geographic region. Such guesses are an important part of browsing – at each step, the user scans a menu and guesses how the information has been organized and which, if any, of the items will be interesting. A correct guess can save time by eliminating useless searches.

Guessing can be difficult, however, because gopher does not provide guidelines or conventions to make gopher servers consistent – each organization that runs a gopher server chooses information to place in the server and the menus used to access that information. Thus, not all items make sense to all users, and a user cannot know exactly what an item will contain until the item has been selected. For example, in the above menu, the terms *veronica* and *WAIS* will not make sense to an average person (both are technical terms defined later in this book). Furthermore, menu items *1*, *2*, *6*, *11* and *12* are not the names of geographic regions.

To determine whether a menu item leads to information being sought, a user must select the item. If the user finds the result of a selection uninteresting, gopher can reverse the decision with a single mouse movement or keystroke. Thus, exploring costs little and has no permanent consequences. In short:

Trial and error is the essence of browsing – after one guesses which items in a list contain interesting information, the user must explore each item to determine what it contains.

To continue our example use of gopher, suppose whoever is browsing selects item number *8* with the label *North America*. The gopher client contacts the remote server to obtain the new menu, and displays the following:

North America

```
---> 1.  Canada/
     2.  Costa Rica/
     3.  Mexico/
     4.  USA/
```

The title *North America* does not explain the full purpose of the menu. Recall that the previous menu was entitled *Other Gopher and Information Servers*. Thus, the menu being considered only contains information about other gopher and information servers in North America. The point is:

The title on a gopher menu does not specify its complete purpose. To interpret a title, a user must remember the context of the search.

To continue exploration, assume that the user selects item number *4* with the label *USA*. The user's client retrieves the next menu and displays:

USA

```
--->  1.  All/
      2.  General/
      3.  alabama/
      4.  arizona/
      5.  california/
      6.  colorado/
      7.  connecticut/
      8.  delaware/
      9.  florida/
     10.  georgia/
     11.  hawaii/
     12.  idaho/
     13.  illinois/
     14.  indiana/
     15.  iowa/
     16.  kansas/
     17.  kentucky/
     18.  louisiana/
```

In fact, the list of all gopher sites in the USA contains more items than the menu shows. However, gopher only displays the part of a menu that fits on the screen – it keeps the remainder of the menu hidden until the user requests it. If the user requests that the cursor move downward beyond item number *18*, gopher will automatically display the next piece of the menu†.

Suppose the user selects menu item *14* labeled *indiana*. The user's client contacts a server to obtain the next menu, which lists sites in the state of Indiana that have a gopher or other information server. The following menu appears:

```
                              indiana

---> 1. BMEnet Whitaker Biomedical Engineering Information Resource/
     2. Ball State University (root) gopher server/
     3. Butler University Gopher/
     4. Cell-Relay (ATM) Archives (Indiana University)/
     5. Earlham College Gopher Server/
     6. Hanover College/
     7. INDnet Gopher/
     8. IUBio Biology Archive, Indiana University (experimental)/
     9. IUPUI Integrated Technologies/
    10. Indiana State University gopher server/
    11. Indiana University Bloomington Gopher/
    12. Indiana University Honors Division/
    13. Indiana University School of Medicine Ruth Lilly Medical Library/
    14. Indiana University Stat/Math Center/
    15. Indiana University, Center for Innovative Computer Applications/
    16. Indiana University, Laboratory for Spectrochemistry (experiment)/
    17. Indiana University-Bloomington Libraries/
    18. Indiana University-Purdue University at Indianapolis/
```

The menu illustrates a fundamental point:

> *Universities and colleges have been enthusiastic about gopher. Consequently, many gopher servers operate on college campuses.*

Because the menu contains more items than fit on the screen, gopher only displays the first part of the menu. To see remaining items, the user must move the cursor down beyond item number *18*. When the cursor moves down, gopher displays additional items in the menu:

```
                              indiana

--->19. Purdue Cooperative Extension/
    20. Purdue University Computer Sciences Department, West Lafayette/
    21. Purdue University Libraries, West Lafayette, Indiana/
    22. Purdue University News/
    23. Purdue University SSINFO Gopher/
    24. Saint Joseph's College Gopher Server (Collegeville, IN)/
```

---

†To move to the next page when using gopher's point-and-click interface, one uses the mouse and a conventional scroll bar along the side of the window.

        25. The Bonzo Gopher server at Indiana University/
        26. University of Indianapolis/
        27. University of Notre Dame/
        28. Vincennes University/

Item *21* describes a gopher server for the libraries at Purdue University in West Lafayette, Indiana. If the user moves the cursor down and selects item *21*, the local gopher client software contacts the gopher server on a computer at Purdue University to obtain the next menu. From the user's point of view, the selection proceeds like any other – gopher manages the transition from the remote computer at Minnesota to the remote computer in Indiana automatically. After gopher contacts the computer at Purdue, it displays the following menu:

            Purdue University Libraries, West Lafayette, Indiana

---> 1. About Purdue University.
      2. About THOR+ the Purdue University Libraries Gopher Site.
      3. Other Information Servers at Purdue University/
      4. Other information Servers on the Internet/
      5. Thor+ Suggestion Form <TEL>
      6. Administrivia/
      7. E-Mail & Telephone Directory for Purdue & World Wide/
      8. Library Catalogs and Gophers/
      9. Purdue University Libraries/
     10. Weather Reports and Maps/
     11. Interesting items on the Net (1/5/94)/
     12. Current Contents On Diskette/
     13. Instructions for searching Directories of all Purdue Gophers.
     14. Search Directories of all Purdue Gophers (experimental) <?>
     15. Scholarly Databases (Experimental)/

Item *10* may appear interesting. If the user moves the cursor and selects item *10*, gopher displays another menu:

                         Weather Reports and Maps

---> 1. About Weather.
      2. W. Lafayette Weather (Dept. of Computer Science).
      3. Satellite Surface Map (from Purdue E&AS Dept.) <Picture>
      4. LATEST Satellite Weather Image (U. of Illinois) <Picture>
      5. LATEST Weather Map (from U. of Illinois) <Picture>
      6. Current Weather Map (from Kansas State) <Picture>
      7. Weather (from U. of Michigan)/

The weather menu lists six files of data about weather and one item (number *7*) that points to another menu related to weather at the University of Michigan. If a user selects any of the first six items, gopher retrieves the requested item and displays it.

For example, requesting item number *2* produces output similar to the following:

```
BENTON-BLACKFORD-BOONE-CARROLL-CASS-CLINTON-DELAWARE-FOUNTAIN-GRANT-
HAMILTON-HOWARD-JASPER-JAY-MADISON-MIAMI-MONTGOMERY-NEWTON-RANDOLPH-
TIPPECANOE-TIPTON-WARREN-WHITE-
INCLUDING THE CITIES OF...LOGANSPORT...MUNCIE...MARION...KOKOMO...
RENSSELAER...CRAWFORDSVILLE...LAFAYETTE
1030 AM EST MON MAR 21 1994

THIS AFTERNOON...PARTLY SUNNY. NOT AS COLD. HIGH IN THE MIDDLE TO
UPPER 30S. SOUTHWEST WIND 10 MPH.
TONIGHT...CLOUDY. LOW IN THE LOWER 30S. SOUTH WIND 10 MPH.
TUESDAY...CLOUDY AND WARMER WITH PATCHY FOG. HIGH IN THE MIDDLE TO
UPPER 40S.
```

The selection is not a menu – the example journey has finally uncovered information. In this case, the information is a weather report for the region in which Purdue University is located. Although the first few lines of output may not be meaningful to an average person, someone who lives in Indiana will recognize them as a list of Indiana counties covered by the report.

Interestingly, in this particular case, gopher obtains the weather information from a different computer than the menu. However, an average user does not know or care which computer contains the information.

The important point is:

> *Gopher menus can point to information as well as other menus, and the information can reside on the same computer as the menu or on another computer. When a user selects an item that corresponds to information, gopher displays the information and allows the user to read it.*

Of course, the user's computer hardware determines how gopher can present information. If selected text cannot fit on the user's screen, gopher displays one piece at a time, and asks the user to press a key or move the mouse before it scrolls to the next piece. If the computer does not have the hardware needed for display, gopher prints an error message. For example, the previous menu contained several items labeled as a *Picture*. If the user's computer has a high-resolution display, gopher can display a picture. However, if a user attempts to select a picture while using a computer that does not have the hardware capability to display a picture, gopher reports the problem. Similarly, gopher cannot play sounds on a computer that does not have hardware for audio.

Once a user finishes reading information, he or she can save a copy on disk, print a copy, or continue browsing. The user can return to view the same information again later, or can browse new information.

Backing Out Of A Browsing Session

A user can choose to terminate browsing at any time by selecting gopher's *Quit* option. However, a user may also decide to return to a previous menu. In our example, once a user finishes reading the weather report, gopher returns them to the last menu from which a selection was made. When displaying a menu from which a selection has been made, gopher leaves the cursor positioned at the last item selected:

```
                    Weather Reports and Maps


       1. About Weather.
---> 2. W. Lafayette Weather (Dept. of Computer Science).
       3. Satellite Surface Map (from Purdue E&AS Dept.) <Picture>
       4. LATEST Satellite Weather Image (U. of Illinois) <Picture>
       5. LATEST Weather Map (from U. of Illinois) <Picture>
       6. Current Weather Map (from Kansas State) <Picture>
       7. Weather (from U. of Michigan)/
```

At any time, a user can enter *u* to move "up" to the previous menu. For example, if a user enters *u*, gopher will display the Purdue Library menu with the cursor positioned at the weather map selection:

```
         Purdue University Libraries, West Lafayette, Indiana

       1. About Purdue University.
       2. About THOR+ the Purdue University Libraries Gopher Site.
       3. Other Information Servers at Purdue University/
       4. Other information Servers on the Internet/
       5. Thor+ Suggestion Form <TEL>
       6. Administrivia/
       7. E-Mail & Telephone Directory for Purdue & World Wide/
       8. Library Catalogs and Gophers/
       9. Purdue University Libraries/
--->10. Weather Reports and Maps/
      11. Interesting items on the Net (1/5/94)/
      12. Current Contents On Diskette/
      13. Instructions for searching Directories of all Purdue Gophers.
      14. Search Directories of all Purdue Gophers (experimental) <?>
      15. Scholarly Databases (Experimental)/
```

It is possible to encounter the same menu twice on a trip through gopher. In the Purdue University Libraries menu, for example, item *4* leads to the gopher server at the University of Minnesota where our example search started†. Thus, the menus form a cycle: the initial menu in the University of Minnesota gopher server eventually leads to a menu in the Purdue University server, which leads back to the initial menu at the University of Minnesota.

---

†One cannot determine where the menu leads from the printed text; it is necessary to request that gopher display information about the selection to learn which computer stores the item.

Finding a cycle among gopher menus is not a problem because a gopher client remembers the sequence of menus a user visits. When a user requests gopher to return to a *previous* menu, gopher consults its memory to determine the item the user had selected to arrive at the current menu. Thus, if a user visits a particular menu twice, gopher remembers and ''unwinds'' the path in exactly the opposite order.

The important idea is:

> *Gopher allows items in menus to lead a user to a cycle that returns to the same menu. To make it possible to back out of a cycle, local client software on the user's computer remembers the path that the user selected when exploring the menus.*

Remembering A Menu

A user cannot always afford to browse to locate information. For example, suppose one wanted to consult the gopher server at Purdue University each day to obtain a daily weather report. Starting with the gopher server at the University of Minnesota and selecting the same menu items each day would become tiresome.

To allow a user to jump directly to a given piece of information, gopher provides a way to record the location of a menu. At any time while browsing, a user can request gopher to remember the current menu selection. Later, the user can ask gopher to display the set of all selections the user has saved, choose one, and move to it directly. For example, a user can search through gopher menus once to find the weather selection, and then ask gopher to remember its location. The next day, when the user wants to obtain a weather report, he or she can use gopher to recall the location of the weather item directly without searching the menus.

Gopher Remembers Locations In Bookmarks

Gopher uses the term *bookmark* to refer to the stored location of an item. The terminology makes sense because, like a conventional bookmark, a gopher bookmark permits one to locate a place quickly.

Each user can save a set of bookmarks; gopher stores the bookmarks on the user's disk. While browsing, a user can add the current menu item to his or her set of bookmarks by clicking a mouse button or pressing a key. At any time, a user can ask gopher to display the list of all bookmarks the user has saved. Gopher displays the bookmark list in the same way it displays a conventional menu; a user moves through the set of bookmarks and selects one

The advantage of bookmarks should be clear:

> *Gopher's bookmarks eliminate tedious repetition by allowing a user to record the locations of interesting menu items and return to those locations later without following a long search through many menus.*

Summary

Information browsing services differ from basic information retrieval services because they permit a user to discover information without retrieving a copy. Most information browsing services operate interactively. Software on the user's computer permits the user to contact a remote computer and examine the information it contains.

Gopher is a specific information browsing service available on the Internet. A user interacts with the gopher client software on his or her local computer, which contacts gopher servers running on remote computers as needed.

From the user's point of view, gopher consists of a large set of menus that span many computers. Each item in a gopher menu represents a file of information, a computer program, or a pointer to another menu. When the user selects an item, gopher either displays the information, runs the computer program, or fetches and displays the new menu. An item in a menu can reference information on a different computer. Whenever a user selects such an item, the gopher software contacts the new computer automatically. Because gopher keeps the exact location of computers hidden from the user, it provides the illusion of a single, large set of interconnected menus.

To make it easy for a user to return to a menu item, gopher permits the user to record the item's location in a bookmark. A user can follow a bookmark directly to a particular item without searching the menu system.

23

Advanced Browsing (WWW, Mosaic)

Introduction

The previous chapter introduces information browsing and discusses a simple browsing service in which menu items consist of textual descriptions. This chapter extends the concept of interactive information browsing, and describes an advanced browsing service. It shows how a single service can provide uniform access to many sources of information, how a browsing service can display graphic images as well as text, and how menu items can be integrated with information.

Description Of Functionality

An advanced information browsing service allows an individual to:

- Locate and access information on remote computers interactively.
- Display text, graphics, or photographic images from a remote computer.
- Play sounds or display videos from recordings stored on a remote computer.
- Access information from several Internet browsing and retrieval services using a single, uniform mechanism.

Menus Can Be Embedded In Text

The gopher system discussed in the previous chapter keeps menus separate from information. While a user is running a gopher client program, the display either contains a menu of items that the user can select or it contains information that the user can read. In essence, a user browses through menus until discovering information of interest. When a user selects information, the menu disappears from the screen and a document replaces it. Similarly, when a user finishes viewing the information and chooses to browse again, the menu reappears and replaces the document.

A browsing service that keeps menu items separate from other information makes it easy to recognize the type of display; there is seldom any ambiguity about whether the screen contains a menu or other information. However, such browsing services often limit a menu item to a short phrase that can fit on a single line of text. Thus, a given menu item can be difficult to understand because it does not provide much detail. For example, a short menu item does not include descriptive prose, pictures, or other information.

Advanced browsing services take a fundamentally different approach. Instead of separating menus from other information, they embed menu items directly in the text. Embedded menu items can make selection easier because the surrounding prose gives context to an item. To understand integration, consider the following example paragraph which is shown as it might appear when displayed by a browsing system that provides embedded menu items.

> The New York Stock Exchange is a world-renown center of business activity. Located on Wall Street in downtown New York City, the stock exchange allows stock brokers to buy or sell shares of stock. At the end of each day, the average price per share of stock as well as the total number of shares traded are computed and used as a measure of activity. Many newspapers list the closing stock prices each day in their business section.

The example contains a short narrative about the stock exchange in New York City. It provides facts such as the location of the exchange, and has been written to inform the reader. In addition to the narrative, the paragraph contains several terms that have been highlighted with an underscore. The highlighted terms are items that a reader can select, analogous to menu items in a menu-oriented browser.

When the browsing service displays a paragraph, the user can choose to read all the information or scan for highlighted terms. A user who already knows basic information about the topic and is searching for details can choose to look at highlighted terms; he or she only needs to read the surrounding text when the meaning of a term is not clear.

Because highlighted terms catch a reader's eye, looking at embedded terms can be as fast and easy as looking through a menu. For example, one can scan the previous page in this book and locate the highlighted terms in a few seconds; it is not necessary to read the entire text.

Once a user selects a highlighted term, an advanced information browsing service responds similar to the way gopher responds to a menu selection. For example, if a user selects the item *average price per share*, the browsing service displays information related to the average cost of shares of stock. If a user selects the item labeled *Wall Street*, the browsing service displays details about Wall Street in New York City.

The Importance Of Integrated Menus

Although the example paragraph is small, it illustrates that menu items can be embedded in other information. An integrated menu system helps a user in two ways.

- First, displaying information and menu items on the screen simultaneously explains a topic in more detail and makes it easier to understand highlighted items. Often, for example, the context around a menu item helps clarify its purpose and eliminates ambiguities.

- Second, having menu items embedded in information encourages a user to explore items as they are encountered. The browsing service helps further because it remembers where a user was reading when an item was selected, so the browser can return to the same place after the user finishes reading about the item.

One way to think about using an integrated browsing service is to imagine reading a book. A reader who reaches an unknown word or phrase can stop reading and consult a dictionary. If the dictionary's definition contains additional terms that the reader does not understand, the search may continue further. Eventually, after mastering the terminology, the reader returns to the book and continues reading. An information browsing service that embeds menu selections in information encourages the same behavior – a user can begin to examine a document, pause to obtain information about an embedded item, and then return to the original document.

In summary,

> *Advanced browsing services can embed menu items in other information, eliminating ambiguities and making it easier to understand each item. In addition, combining menu items with information encourages a user to explore items when they are encountered.*

Menus Embedded In Text Are Called Hypertext

The concept of embedding selectable menu items in text is called *hypertext*. Hypertext did not originate with Internet browsing services – it has been used with conventional computer programs for several years. For example, one computer manufacturer uses a hypertext system to display documents that describe how to use the computer and the programs it contains. A user begins by asking the system to display a document that describes the computer. The user can read the display like an ordinary piece of prose, or can select any term in the document. When a user selects a word or phrase, the hypertext software looks up the term and displays information related to it.

To understand hypertext documents stored in a computer system, imagine a set of paper documents laid on a desktop with the items in each document that refer to other documents highlighted. The diagram in Figure 23.1 shows an example of six documents with references to other documents indicated by arrows.

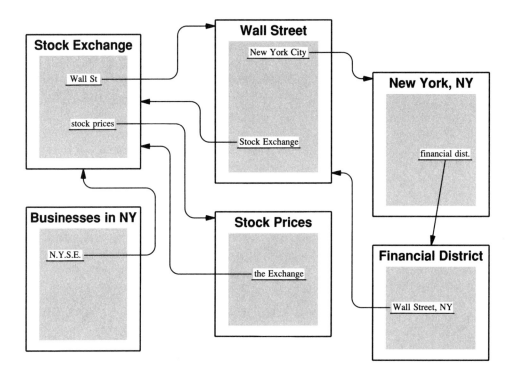

Figure 23.1 An illustration of six documents with text obscured except for the title and references to other documents. An arrow has been drawn between a word or phrase and the document it references.

In the figure, the document labeled *Wall Street* contains two references: one to *New York City* and another to *Stock Exchange*. The reference labeled *New York City* points to a document titled *New York, NY*, which contains a reference to the *financial district*.

When viewed as a collection of documents two points become clear:

- A reference does not need to be the same as the title of the document to which it refers. For example, although the document that has title *Stock Prices* contains a reference to *the Exchange*, the document to which it refers has the title *Stock Exchange*. The designers of a hypertext document specify the connection between each item and the document to which it refers.

- Not all documents contain the same number of references. A document can contain many references or only a few.

Of course, when using a hypertext system, a user does not see a graphic illustration of the links between documents. Instead, one document appears on the screen at a time, and the user must follow a reference to determine where it leads.

In summary,

> *Although documents in a hypertext system can contain a complex maze of references, the complexity may not be obvious to a user who can view only one document at a time.*

The power of hypertext arises from its combination of generality and instant reference – each document can contain text or embedded menu items that point to other documents. A user can choose to read an entire document, stop at any time to select a word that leads to a new document, or return to a previous document and continue reading. Because a conventional hypertext system keeps documents in a single computer, hypertext software can follow a reference from one document to another instantly.

Some Computers Have Multimedia Capabilities

To understand how Internet browsing services extend hypertext, it is necessary to understand computer hardware. Although early computers could only display output using typewriter-like characters that each occupy the same width, most modern computers have sophisticated hardware that can display graphic images or play sounds. Such computers use the graphics hardware to display text using proportional spacing – the space allocated for each character is proportional to the character's width†. Using advanced technology, modern computers can also display multiple colors, geometric shapes or diagrams, and still or moving pictures. In addition, sophisticated computers can emit audio and reproduce the sound of human speech or music. A computer capable of playing audio and displaying video has *multiple media* output; such computers are often called *multimedia* computers.

---

†For example, in proportional text, the letter *i* occupies less width than the letter *w*.

Video And Audio References Can Be Embedded In Text

Multimedia computers make it possible to access additional forms of information. For example, consider the following paragraph.

> Several <u>city tours</u> include visits to the New York Stock Exchange. During a typical working day, many people crowd onto the floor of the exchange. Visitors can <u>hear the sounds</u> of traders bidding and <u>view the sights</u> of trading activity recorded by cameras that look down on the scene.

The paragraph describes a day at the New York Stock Exchange and the activity that a visitor can encounter. As in the earlier examples, phrases that can be selected are highlighted by an underscore. Unlike earlier examples, however, some highlighted phrases do not correspond to textual information. Instead ''view the sights'' and ''hear the sounds'' refer to available video and audio information.

When a hypertext system contains references to nontextual information, it is called a *hypermedia* system. Figure 23.2 illustrates the conceptual organization of a hypermedia document that contains references to nontextual information.

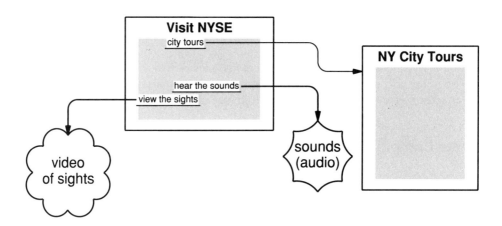

Figure 23.2 The conceptual organization of a hypermedia document. When a user selects *hear the sounds*, the computer plays stored audio. When a user selects *view the sights*, the computer displays the stored images.

Inside a computer, nontextual data must be stored in digital form. For example, a computer stores sound as a sequence of numbers, similar to the way music is stored on a compact disc. A computer also uses numbers to store graphics or other video images. A user who plays the audio or displays the video never sees the underlying sequence of numbers.

To summarize:

> *A hypermedia system can embed references to nontextual information as well as references to textual information in a document. If the user selects a reference to a document, the hypermedia system displays the document; if the user selects a nontextual reference, the hypermedia system plays the audio or displays the images.*

The World Wide Web

The Internet offers an advanced browsing service that extends the concept of hypermedia to include many computers. Known as the *World Wide Web†* (*WWW*), the service is a mechanism that links together information stored on many computers. In essence, WWW allows the references in a document on one computer to refer to textual or nontextual information stored in other computers. For example, a World Wide Web document on a computer in the United States can contain a reference to a stored video image on a computer in Switzerland.

A user browses the World Wide Web in the same way that one browses hypermedia documents on a single computer. At any time, the user's display shows a document that contains highlighted references. When the user selects an item, the system follows the reference, obtains the referenced item, and either plays the sound or displays the document. Thus, a user can browse through the World Wide Web without knowing where information resides.

Although it can be difficult to understand how a hypermedia service works, its ability to present information visually makes it appealing. As a result, the World Wide Web has become an incredibly popular Internet service‡. In summary,

> *In addition to displaying textual information, an advanced Internet browsing service can play sounds and display images. To display nontextual information, a computer must have multimedia hardware.*

Mosaic Software Used To Access WWW

Although software exists to allow WWW access from a character-oriented terminal, such software cannot display images or play sounds. Instead, such software displays text in a typewriter-like font, and inserts [IMAGE] each place a graphic image should appear. Most users who access WWW choose software built at the National

---

†The World Wide Web was developed to allow physicists around the world to share information.
‡Between the summers of 1993 and 1994, for example, use of WWW tripled.

Center for Supercomputer Applications (NCSA) that can display audio, video, text, and graphics. Called *Mosaic*, the software controls the user's display and permits the user to browse multimedia information using a mouse.

When a document appears on the screen, Mosaic highlights the embedded menu items. To select an item, a user moves the mouse until the cursor has been positioned over the item, and presses the mouse button to request Mosaic to follow the reference. If the item refers to a prerecorded sound, Mosaic plays the sound. If the item refers to a drawing or photograph, Mosaic displays the graphic on the user's screen. If the item refers to a video of a moving image, Mosaic can retrieve the video and display it like a television picture.

More important, Mosaic does not restrict documents to text. It permits references to be embedded in graphic images. For example, Mosaic can display information that includes graphics as well as text, and allows the user to make a selection from highlighted text or parts of the graphic design. In short,

> *The Mosaic program provides access to the World Wide Web. Mosaic can display a hypermedia document, and allows the user to select items with a mouse.*

An Example Hypermedia Display

A simple example will illustrate how Mosaic appears to a user. Assume that a user is exploring the World Wide Web and reaches the information for a company called the *Hypothetical Rocker Company*. Figure 23.3 illustrates how the Hypothetical Rocker Company's WWW entry might appear when displayed by Mosaic.

As the example shows, Mosaic divides the screen into three areas: a section at the top is used to identify the entry, a series of rectangles across the bottom each contain the name of an operation that a user can perform, and a large region in the center of the screen is used to display information. The example information illustrates two ideas about the Mosaic interface. First, a company can arrange its WWW entry to display text in various sizes and styles along with graphic images. In particular, some words have been italicized and others appear in boldface. Second, an embedded menu item can refer to information outside the company. In the example, the highlighted phrase *The Bakery* refers to an establishment located across the street from the Hypothetical Rocker Company. Presumably, The Bakery has either agreed to provide a reference to the Hypothetical Rocker Company in its WWW entry or has paid the Hypothetical Rocker Company a fee for advertising.

File	*Options*	*Navigate*	*Annotate*	*Help*

Document Title: Hypothetical Rocker Company

Document URL: http : / / www . hrocker . com /

Welcome to Hypothetical Rocker. Our showroom is located on Main Street across from The Bakery in downtown Hypothetical Village, USA. Stop in to meet the cheerful staff and try our chairs.

HR

Our corporate logo: select it to return to this page

We aim to please!

◁●▷ **SEE FOR YOURSELF**

- Video catalog of our products
- Choose a sales representative
- Employee of the month
- Types of rocking chairs

HOURS: M - F   9:00 am to 5:00 pm
              Sa   8:00 am to 6:00 pm

SPECIAL SALE: This month 50% off outdoor rockers.

E-mail: service@hrocker.com   Phone: 201-555-4991

Back	Forward	Home	Reload	Open	Save as	Clone	New Window	Close Window

Figure 23.3 A hypothetical example of WWW information displayed by Mosaic. Highlighted text or graphic symbols can be used as menu selections.

The example in Figure 23.3 shows one possible visual effect produced by a WWW page that intermixes multiple text sizes and styles as well as graphics. The variety of presentation and lack of uniformity gives the information a cluttered appearance and makes it difficult to read.

WWW pages do not need to be complicated or cluttered. Indeed, the best entries organize information and present it simply. For example, consider the item labeled *Types of rocking chairs*. The Hypothetical Rocker Company has stored information describing its rockers. For each rocker, the information could be a picture, audio sounds, or a document similar to the one shown. If a user selects *Types of rocking chairs*, Mosaic will retrieve and display the associated information. For example, Figure 23.4 shows one possible way to organize the available information as a simple list.

Recording The Location Of Information

Suppose you have been using Mosaic to wander through the World Wide Web, and happen to reach the page of information shown in Figure 23.4. You might want to tell a friend about the page or record its location so that you could return to it later. Because a path through a set of hypermedia documents can be long and complex, it can be difficult to remember the entire series of selections that led to a given page.

To make it possible for an individual to tell others the location of information, the World Wide Web assigns each page of information a unique identifier. The identifier consists of a string of characters that can be recorded in a computer file, written on a piece of paper, or sent to another person. Given the identifier, an interface like Mosaic can return to the page of information instantly – the user does not need to search through menus or select items.

An identifier used to specify a particular page of WWW information is called a *Uniform Resource Locator* (*URL*). When Mosaic displays a page of information, it also displays the URL for the page. Thus, a user can easily save and remember a URL. For example, the box near the top of the screen in Figure 23.4 labeled *Document URL* contains the example URL†:

http://www.hrocker.com/types

A URL may seem like a nonsensical collection of letters and punctuation. However, the precise syntax conveys meaning that computer programs like Mosaic can use to retrieve information.

> *A Uniform Resource Locator consists of a short character string that identifies a particular multimedia document. Given a valid URL, a program like Mosaic can quickly retrieve the page of information to which it refers.*

---

†Like the company in the example, this URL is hypothetical.

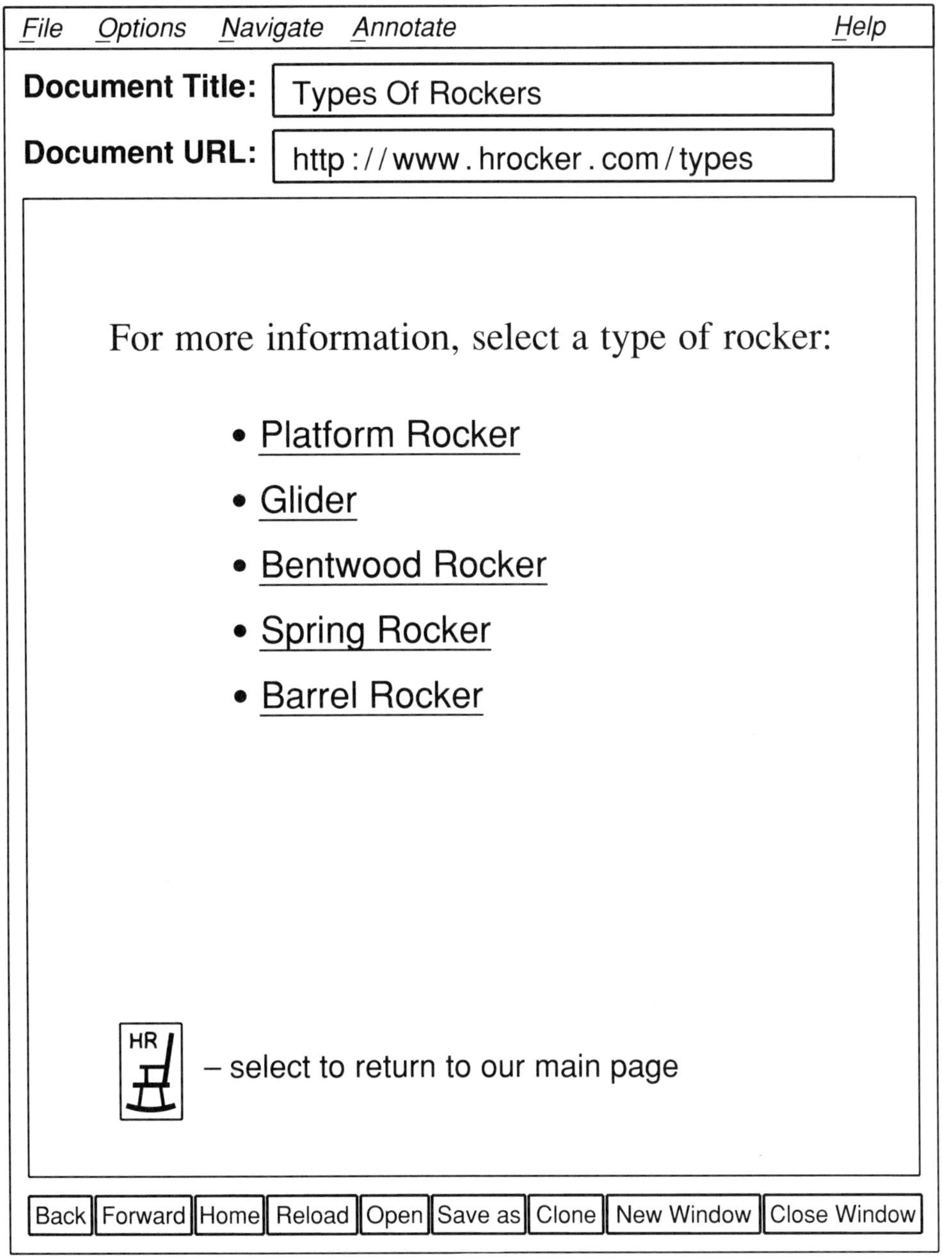

| *File* | *Options* | *Navigate* | *Annotate* | *Help* |

Document Title: | Types Of Rockers

Document URL: | http : / / www . hrocker . com / types

For more information, select a type of rocker:

- Platform Rocker
- Glider
- Bentwood Rocker
- Spring Rocker
- Barrel Rocker

– select to return to our main page

| Back | Forward | Home | Reload | Open | Save as | Clone | New Window | Close Window |

Figure 23.4 An example display that corresponds to the selection in Figure 23.3 labeled *Types of rocking chairs.*

How The World Wide Web Works

Like other services, the World Wide Web uses client-server interaction. A user initiates interaction by invoking the Mosaic program and entering a URL. The Mosaic program becomes a client that uses the Internet to contact a remote server and obtain a copy of the information referenced by the URL. The server on the remote system returns a copy of the page to display along with additional information that describes the contents.

The additional information a WWW server returns tells Mosaic two important things. First, it describes how to display the information. Second it gives a URL for each item on the page that the user can select.

When Mosaic receives a page from a remote server, it displays the page, and then waits for the user to select one of the highlighted items. Once a user makes a selection, Mosaic consults the additional information associated with the page to find the URL for the selection. Mosaic then uses the Internet to obtain the newly selected page of information. Thus, at any given instant, the Mosaic client is either waiting for the user to select an item, or is contacting a remote server to obtain the information corresponding to the user's selection. Figure 23.5 illustrates the interaction.

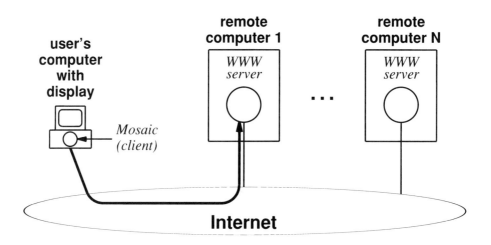

Figure 23.5 When a user selects an item, Mosaic becomes a client that contacts the remote server to obtain a copy of the corresponding page of information. Mosaic only contacts one remote server at any time.

A URL Tells Mosaic Which Computer To Contact

How does Mosaic determine which remote computer contains a given page of information? The URL tells it. Each URL contains, among other information, the domain name of a remote computer. In a sense, a URL is like a telephone number – it is a short string that identifies a specific point of contact. When given a URL, Mosaic extracts the computer's name, and then uses the Internet to contact a server on that computer.

A URL Tells Mosaic Which Server To Contact

In addition to the name of a remote computer, a URL describes a particular server and a page of information available from that server. After contacting the server on the remote computer, Mosaic asks the server for a copy of the specified page of information.

> *Each URL uniquely identifies a page of information by giving the name of a remote computer, a server on that computer, and a specific page of information available from the server.*

Composing A Page Of Multimedia Information

A person who designs a page of multimedia information for the World Wide Web must specify exactly how the page should appear. For example, the person must specify the style and size of lettering, the items that should be highlighted, the graphics to be included, and the colors to use when displaying each item. When Mosaic obtains a copy of the information for a page, it produces a form suitable for the computer's display hardware. For example, if the computer has color capability, Mosaic displays the page using the colors that were specified originally. If the computer cannot display color, Mosaic shows the page in black and white, using shades of gray in place of colors. In essence, Mosaic attempts to create a representation that provides the best display on the available hardware.

Mosaic Provides Access To Multiple Services

In addition to providing access to multimedia documents, the World Wide Web extends Internet browsing services in another significant way: it provides access to multiple services through a single, advanced browsing service. For example, Mosaic understands how to access information stored in a gopher browsing system or in a file accessible through the FTP file transfer service. Furthermore, references to such information can be associated with a menu item in a multimedia document.

The key to understanding WWW's generality lies in realizing that the URL mechanism contains an identifier for a service as well as the name of a computer on which the service operates. A URL that begins with the string *http* refers to the WWW service that clients use when they retrieve a hypermedia document. A URL that begins with the string *ftp* refers to a file accessible through the FTP service.

People often employ the same technique as WWW to encode a type of service with an address. For example, a business card often contains strings such as:

> Telephone: 315-555-7895
> Fax: 315-555-7802

The initial string specifies whether the number can be used to place a voice telephone call or send a FAX. That is, a prefix like *Fax:* tells one the exact access mechanism to use.

Conceptually, a user can think of Mosaic as a giant program that has several other client programs built in. Given a URL, Mosaic examines the part that specifies a service and chooses the appropriate client to access that service. Figure 25.6 illustrates the concept and explains why the program can be thought of as having a "mosaic" design.

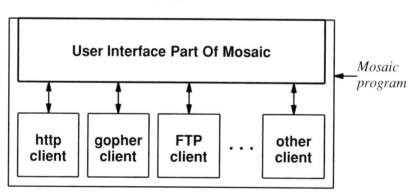

Figure 23.6 Internal organization of the Mosaic program. A user interacts with a single, uniform interface that uses information in the URL to choose one of the built-in client programs to access information on the Internet.

For example, Mosaic understands the FTP file transfer protocol. If a URL specifies that a file can be obtained via FTP, Mosaic uses the FTP service to retrieve the file. From the user's point of view, the selection of an appropriate access mechanism is automatic – the user browses through the World Wide Web making selections to request information.

> *Mosaic's novelty and power arises because it integrates access to multiple Internet services into a single, seamless browsing system. Mosaic uses information in the URL to automatically select an access mechanism from among such services as remote login, file transfer, and gopher.*

Hotlists And Private WWW Documents

The URL for a document provides an easy and quick way to locate information. Like the bookmark system available in gopher, Mosaic provides an easy way to store a URL on disk so it can be used later. The storage mechanism is known as a *hotlist*. Suppose, for example, a user encounters an interesting document while browsing, but does not have time to read it. The user can record the document's URL on a hotlist, and postpone reading it. To do so, a user selects the *Navigate* menu located near the top of the screen, and requests Mosaic to save the URL on the hotlist. Later, when the user starts Mosaic, the hotlist becomes available and any item on the hotlist can be selected.

WWW is more flexible than gopher because it permits each user to create a private multimedia document that contains references the user has found interesting. A user's private page of information is known as a *homepage*; the term also applies to the main page of information for a particular company. Technical users often spend much time arranging their homepages to use multiple fonts and contain graphic images. To share something with a friend or colleague, they simply pass a URL for their homepage, and tell the person which reference to follow. Given a URL for a user's homepage, Mosaic accesses and displays the homepage; the user can select a reference from a private homepage in the same way they select a reference from any other page of information in WWW.

Getting Started With Mosaic

Using Mosaic for the first time is not difficult. When a user runs Mosaic software, Mosaic contacts a WWW server and displays an initial hypermedia document. If the local site does not have a server, Mosaic usually is programmed to contact a server at the National Center For Supercomputer Applications in Champaign, Illinois.

The user can proceed to investigate the Internet by selecting items on the initial page or using Mosaic commands. The user can position the cursor over the *Navigate* menu and press a mouse button to see a list of commands. Selecting the menu item labeled *Internet Starting Points* produces a description of interesting and informative documents available on the World Wide Web.

Summary

Advanced Internet browsing services enhance information access in two significant ways. First, such services use a technique known as hypertext to integrate menu items and information. Second, such services allow text, graphics, audio, and video to be combined to form multimedia documents. The result is known as a hypermedia system in which a given multimedia document can contain references to other multimedia documents. To display output from a multimedia document, a computer must have hardware that can display images and reproduce sounds.

The World Wide Web of information is an advanced browsing service available on the Internet. One can think of the WWW as a large set of hypermedia documents stored on computers throughout the Internet. A given WWW document can contain embedded menu items that refer to WWW documents stored on various other computers.

The most popular software used to access the World Wide Web is named Mosaic. Mosaic allows a user to browse information using a mouse. After Mosaic displays a particular multimedia document, the user selects one of the embedded menu items and requests Mosaic to obtain and display the document to which it refers. Thus, from a user's point of view, the location of information is irrelevant – the World Wide Web appears to be a seamless interconnection of documents each of which can be accessed directly.

To make it possible to record the location of a particular piece of information, each WWW document is assigned a Uniform Resource Locator (URL). A document's URL is a string of characters that identifies the type of document and its location in the Internet. Given the URL for a document, Mosaic software can determine the computer on which the document resides, the service on that computer used to access the document, and the location of the specific document. Because Mosaic can use a variety of mechanisms including gopher and FTP to retrieve documents, it provides a uniform, seamless way to access information on the Internet.

An Observation About Hypermedia Browsing

Many people find the World Wide Web fascinating. In only a few minutes, one can learn how to make a selection and move from one page of information to another. In a short time, novices find that they have examined documents on a myriad of topics located on a variety of computers at Internet sites around the world. For example, one professor at a midwest university was amazed to find pictures of Hawaii, while a colleague was equally astounded by information on high-energy physics obtained from a site in Europe.

The maze of interconnected WWW documents is neverending. Because the World Wide Web is growing at an incredible rate, the information that comprises the Web keeps changing, enticing one to browse again. As a result, browsing WWW can become addictive and time-consuming.

24

Automated Title Search (Archie, Veronica)

Introduction

The previous chapters describe Internet services that permit one to explore information interactively. Interactive services require a user to make decisions (e.g., to choose items from menus). The process is informally called *navigating*.

This chapter discusses automated search services that do not require human interaction during the search. Such services can find information on remote computers without requiring a user to browse through menus. The chapter explores two examples that illustrate how search services appear to a user and how such services can be accessed in several ways.

Description Of Functionality

An *automated search service* allows an individual to find specified information on remote computers. Automated searching differs from browsing and retrieval because automated search uses a computer program instead of a human to navigate through a set of remote computers. In particular, automated search services allow one to automatically locate:

- Remote computers that contain a particular file.
- Remote computers that contain a particular computer program or package of programs.
- A specific gopher directory or a specific page in WWW.

Automated search services also allow one to save the names of remote computers found as the result of a search or to pass the names to software that can access the information.

Browsing Vs. Automated Searching

Although browsing can be enjoyable, the size of the Internet makes it impossible to find information by searching one computer at a time. In fact, the continual growth makes such searches futile – new computers appear on the Internet faster than a human can browse through the information stored in them.

To keep up with Internet growth, automated searching is needed. That is, one needs a computer program that can automatically contact other computers on the Internet, search for specified information, and report the results. Such a program is called an Internet *search tool*, and the service it provides is an *automated search service*.

Tools for automated search are important for two reasons. First, when a user decides to explore a topic, a search tool can answer the question, ''where does one begin to look?'' Second, automated search tools can also help when a user accidentally loses the location of information. To understand why loss occurs and how search tools help recovery, imagine a user who spends many hours searching the Internet to find a particular computer program (a game, perhaps). Suppose that after the user discovers the game in an FTP directory, the power on the user's computer fails briefly, causing the computer to restart†. When the computer restarts, the user cannot obtain a new copy of the game without either specifying the name of the remote computer on which the program resides or searching the Internet to find it. The problem of loss also occurs if power fails while one is using a browsing service like gopher. When the gopher software restarts, the user must enter the name of a remote server. In summary,

> To find information on a large and growing Internet, one needs a tool that automatically searches for information. Such tools help when looking for new information or when recovering the location of an item after loss.

Automated Searching Proceeds By Name or Description

In general, automated search mechanisms fall into one of two broad categories. Some tools search for items that have a specified name, and others search for documents that contain a specified content. Both types of search can be useful. When a user knows the exact name of a program or file, a tool that searches names can provide a precise answer about the file's location. When a user knows about the contents of a file but not the exact name, a tool that searches contents can find the file.

---

†Loss does not require power failure; users can accidentally erase a program or data file.

The Archie Directory Service

This chapter considers two examples of Internet search services that illustrate the concept of automated searching by name. It shows how such services appear to a user and describes how they operate. The first example, *archie*, was developed at McGill University in Montreal, Canada. Archie searches the directories of files available via the File Transfer Protocol, FTP.

Recall from Chapter 20 that FTP allows one to obtain a list of the files on a remote computer. To do so, a user invokes the FTP program, and specifies the name of a remote computer. The FTP program becomes a client that forms a connection to a server on the specified remote computer. Once a connection has been established, the *ls* command provides a listing. In essence, a user who enters *ls* is asking FTP, "What files are available on the computer to which I am connected?"

Archie solves a broader problem – it lists all the files with a given name on all computers:

> When someone using archie enters a file name, they are asking archie to, "please find all the files with the specified name on computers that offer the FTP service."

Multiple Archie Servers Handle The Load

Archie does not limit its answers to local computers or even to nearby computers. When archie answers a user's question, it lists all occurrences of the specified file on computers throughout the Internet. Thus, a user in Japan and a user in England both receive the same answer from archie when they make a request. The list of computers in the answer may include computers in Japan, computers in England, or computers in other countries.

In theory, one archie server would suffice for the entire Internet because all users receive the same answer to a given question. In practice, however, so many users around the world access archie that a single computer cannot handle the load. To prevent the service from becoming overloaded, two dozen sites around the world have volunteered to run an archie server. Figure 24.1 lists the names and IP addresses of computers that offered the archie service in 1994.

Although all servers return the same result, Figure 24.1 lists the country in which each server resides. There are two reasons the country is relevant. First, users who pay for Internet access may be charged less when they access services in their home country. Second, if one knows the country in which each server resides, it may be possible to avoid contacting that server during working hours when the demand reaches a peak†.

---

†All servers listed for the USA are in the Eastern Time Zone, except for *archie.unl.edu*, which is in the Central Time Zone.

Name of Computer	Address of Computer	Country
archie.ac.il	132.65.20.254	Israel
archie.ans.net	147.225.1.10	USA
archie.au	139.130.4.6	Australia
archie.doc.ic.ac.uk	146.169.11.3	United Kingdom
archie.edvz.uni-linz.ac.at	140.78.3.8	Austria
archie.funet.fi	128.214.6.102	Finland
archie.internic.net	198.49.45.10	USA
archie.kr	128.134.1.1	Korea
archie.kuis.kyoto-u.ac.jp	130.54.20.1	Japan
archie.luth.se	130.240.18.4	Sweden
archie.ncu.edu.tw	140.115.19.24	Taiwan
archie.nz	130.195.9.4	New Zealand
archie.rediris.es	130.206.1.2	Spain
archie.rutgers.edu	128.6.18.15	USA
archie.sogang.ac.kr	163.239.1.11	Korea
archie.sura.net	128.167.254.195	USA
archie.switch.ch	130.59.1.40	Switzerland
archie.th-darmstadt.de	130.83.22.60	Germany
archie.unipi.it	131.114.21.10	Italy
archie.univie.ac.at	131.130.1.23	Austria
archie.unl.edu	129.93.1.14	USA
archie.uqam.ca	132.208.250.10	Canada
archie.wide.ad.jp	133.4.3.6	Japan

Figure 24.1 A list of archie servers available in 1994. Each server returns the same answer as others; multiple copies exist to avoid the problem of overloading.

In summary,

> *Multiple archie servers exist because a single computer cannot handle all requests. Each user can choose a server that gives best performance; users often choose the geographically closest server.*

How Archie Appears To A User

Archie is interesting because it illustrates an Internet service that can be accessed multiple ways. In particular, one can choose one of four ways to access archie. One can:

- Run a command that forms a single request, sends it to an archie server, and displays the answer.

- Send a request to an archie server in an electronic mail message and receive a reply via electronic mail.
- Use TELNET software to form a connection to archie, interactively type search requests, and receive the answers on the display screen.
- Run a program that locates a file using archie, forms a connection to the computer on which the file resides, and allows the user to move through the list of all files on that machine using a mouse.

The variety of ways to use the archie service makes it extremely flexible because it allows each person to use the access mechanism that is fastest, most reliable, or least expensive. For example, someone who has electronic mail software but does not have TELNET software can send a request in an e-mail message. Similarly, a user who does not have a mouse can use software that requires a keyboard instead of a mouse. In summary,

Archie illustrates how a user can access a given service in several ways. The variety of access mechanisms makes it possible for each user to choose a method appropriate for their situation.

Archie Can Be Accessed Using A One-Line Command

When using a command-line interface for the archie service, a user must enter a new command for each request. For example, suppose a user wishes to find the locations of all files that contain the string *color*. The user must choose a server from the list in Figure 24.1, and invoke the *archie* command. If the user chooses server *archie.sura.net*, the command is†:

archie –server archie.sura.net color

The presence of *–server* on the command line means that the next item on the command line (*archie.sura.net*) is the name of the archie server to contact. When the command runs, archie produces a list of files that satisfy the request and displays it on the screen.

A user can choose to add other keywords that tell archie how to conduct a search. Normally, when a user specifies a search string, archie prints a list of all files that have the search string in their name. For example, when a user specifies the string *color*, archie finds all files that have a name in which those five letters appear in sequence. Thus, because file names such as *color.print*, *colorwheel*, and *image.without.color* all contain the string *color*, archie will declare that they match the request and report them to the user.

Although archie's method of finding a match works well in most cases, it may generate excessive output. To specify that archie should only report files with a name that exactly matches the search string, a user can add the keyword *–exact* to the command line. For example, the command:

_____

†The details of command access may vary among computer systems.

archie −server archie.sura.net −exact color

requests that archie find all files named *color*, but exclude files that have names such as *colorwheel* or *color.picture*.

The keyword *–nocase* can be used with or without exact matching. It tells archie to treat upper and lower case letters identically when comparing file names. Thus if a user specifies *-nocase*, archie reports that files named *Color*, *color*, and *CoLoR* all match *color*. Ignoring case differences can be important in an Internet that contains many types of computers because some computer systems allow file names to contain lower and upper case while others restrict names to one case.

Although archie's command-line access mechanism allows a user to pose an arbitrary request, it can be awkward. The syntax can be difficult to remember and enter correctly. Furthermore, entering a complete command for each request becomes tedious because one must repeatedly enter information such as the server name. As a result, many users prefer other access mechanisms.

Archie Can Be Accessed Using E-Mail

Sites that offer the archie service also provide access to the service through electronic mail. To access archie through e-mail, a user must compose an e-mail message that contains valid commands and send it to the address:

archie @ *server*

where *server* is one of the archie servers listed in Figure 24.1. The simplest valid command consists of the word *help* starting in column 1 (all commands in e-mail to archie must start in column 1). When archie receives a request for help, it returns additional information on how to use archie through e-mail, including details about other commands.

An e-mail message that contains the command *find* followed by a search string causes archie to search for files with the specified name. For example, a user named *henry* could send archie the following e-mail message to request a list of all files with the string *color* in their name†:

```
From: henry@company.somewhere.com
To: archie@archie.sura.net
Subject:
Date: April 15, 1994

find color
```

Using e-mail to access an Internet service can take longer than a more direct method; users who can use other access mechanisms seldom send archie e-mail messages. However, at times e-mail can be quite useful because a busy server can accept

---

†Note: because archie's e-mail access mechanism also examines the *Subject* line in an e-mail message for commands, a user can send *help* as the subject of the e-mail message instead of the body.

e-mail and store the request on its disk. When a server becomes too busy to handle all requests for direct connections, a user can compose an e-mail message that contains a request. Later, when the demand decreases, the server handles requests that have arrived in e-mail messages. Thus, users who find an archie server too busy to handle a direct connection can use e-mail to guarantee that the server will automatically handle the request as soon as it has time. The user does not need to try to contact the server repeatedly.

Archie Can Be Accessed Using TELNET

Recall from Chapter 21 that TELNET is a remote login service that connects a user's computer to a remote computer. The computers listed in Figure 24.1 allow users to log in and run archie interactively. To use archie interactively, one invokes a TELNET client program and specifies the computer on which the server operates:

telnet *server*

When the computer prompts for a login name, the user enters *archie* (no password is needed). For example, the sequence:

```
telnet archie.sura.net
login: archie

prog color
```

initiates an interactive archie session on the computer *archie.sura.net* and requests that archie search for all files with names that contain *color*. After the login, the archie server prints messages about the service and then accepts search commands from the user. A user can enter *help* for information about possible commands, or *prog*† followed by a string to request a search.

Archie's interactive access mechanism can be more convenient than a one-line command for two reasons. First, the interactive interface eliminates retyping the server name when making a series of requests (e.g., with various search keys). Second, when accessed interactively, archie provides status information that tells the user how the search is proceeding. While the server is searching, archie displays a single line on the screen that shows how many file names have matched the user's request and what percentage of all files have been searched. Thus, if a long delay occurs, a user can tell that the server is operating and whether archie has found any names that match the search string.

---

†Some servers use the command *find*; to determine how to interact with a server, read the instructions that the server prints after a connection has been established.

Archie Can Be Accessed With A Mouse

In addition to the access mechanisms described above, a user who has a mouse and a window system can obtain software that provides a point-and-click interface for archie. The user enters a search string and requests that archie retrieve names that match. Archie displays the output and allows the user to select a file from the list with a mouse.

Figure 24.2 illustrates how the screen initially appears to someone using a point-and-click interface for archie. The top of the screen contains a series of command menus, the bottom contains space for information about a selected file, and the middle contains two areas used to display search information and to select a file.

To search for a file, a user moves the mouse to the box labeled *Search Term* and enters a string. In response, archie produces a list of all computers that contain files matching the term. The list appears in the left panel of the center area of the screen†. The user then moves the mouse to the list of computer names and selects one. In response, archie uses the right panel to display the list of files on the selected computer that match the search term. If a user moves the mouse to the list of file names and selects a specific file, archie displays detailed information about that file in the boxes at the bottom of the screen.

The user can change any part of the selection using the mouse; archie responds to a change instantly. If the user selects a different file, the information at the bottom of the screen changes. If the user selects a different computer, the list of files changes to show the files on the newly selected computer. The point is,

> *Software that provides a point-and-click interface to archie allows a user to select a computer and examine the list of pertinent files on that computer with a mouse. Such software provides the most convenient way to use archie.*

How Archie Works

In theory, when a user enters a search string, archie must search all computers on the Internet to find files with names that match the specified string. In practice, however, searching through the files of all computers on the Internet takes many hours, much longer than someone is willing to wait. How can archie answer requests quickly if searches take a long time?

To understand how archie responds quickly to a request, think of a telephone book. To make telephone number lookup efficient, the phone company collects a list of each customer's name and number, sorts the list into alphabetical order, and prints a telephone book. When someone wants to find everyone named *Jones* in a given city, they do not need to search door-to-door. Instead, they look under *J* in the telephone book.

---

†Some versions of the software divide the center area into three panels.

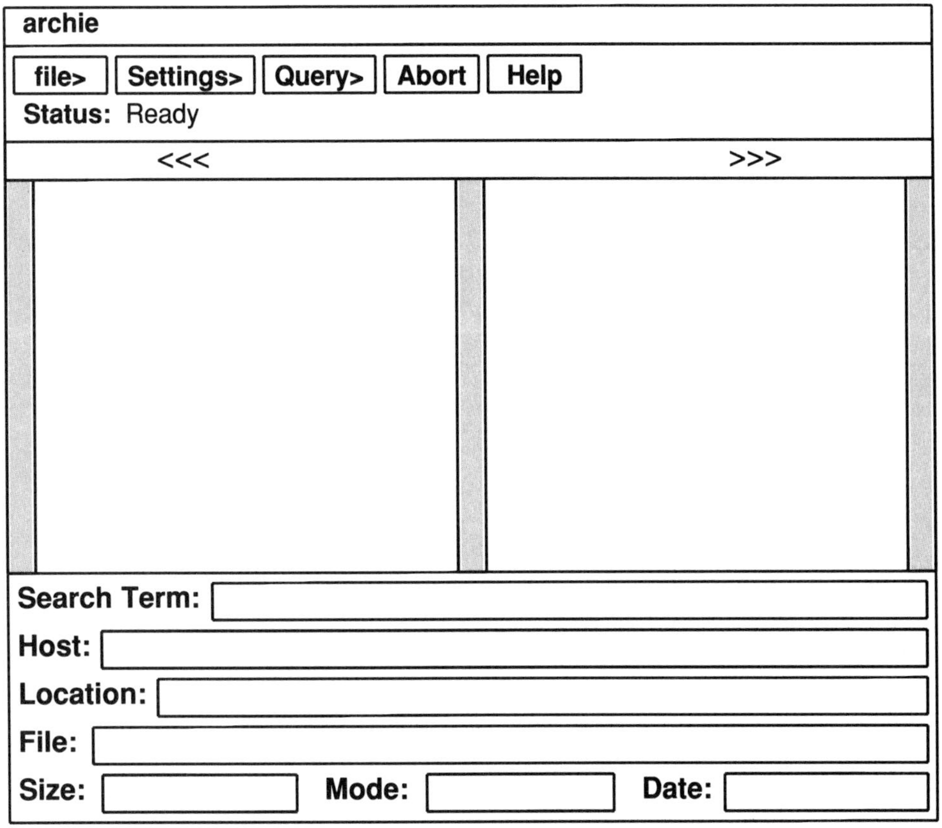

```
┌──────────────────────────────────────────────────────────────┐
│ archie                                                         │
├──────────────────────────────────────────────────────────────┤
│ ┌──────┐┌──────────┐┌────────┐┌───────┐┌──────┐               │
│ │ file>││ Settings>││ Query> ││ Abort ││ Help │               │
│ └──────┘└──────────┘└────────┘└───────┘└──────┘               │
│ Status: Ready                                                  │
├──────────────────────────────────────────────────────────────┤
│            <<<                              >>>                 │
├──────────────────────────────────────────────────────────────┤
│ ┌─┐┌───────────────────┐  ┌─┐┌───────────────────────────┐    │
│ │ ││                   │  │ ││                           │    │
│ │ ││                   │  │ ││                           │    │
│ │ ││                   │  │ ││                           │    │
│ │ ││                   │  │ ││                           │    │
│ │ ││                   │  │ ││                           │    │
│ │ ││                   │  │ ││                           │    │
│ └─┘└───────────────────┘  └─┘└───────────────────────────┘    │
├──────────────────────────────────────────────────────────────┤
│ Search Term: ┌────────────────────────────────────────────┐   │
│              └────────────────────────────────────────────┘   │
│ Host: ┌──────────────────────────────────────────────────┐    │
│       └──────────────────────────────────────────────────┘    │
│ Location: ┌──────────────────────────────────────────────┐    │
│           └──────────────────────────────────────────────┘    │
│ File: ┌──────────────────────────────────────────────────┐    │
│       └──────────────────────────────────────────────────┘    │
│ Size: ┌───────────┐  Mode: ┌───────────┐  Date: ┌─────────┐   │
│       └───────────┘        └───────────┘        └─────────┘   │
└──────────────────────────────────────────────────────────────┘
```

Figure 24.2 An illustration of the initial screen that appears when one uses a
point-and-click program to access archie.

An archie server uses a similar trick to enable it to reply quickly. A computer program contacts computers on the Internet, gathers the names of available files, sorts the list, and then stores the result on a disk at each archie server. When a client program sends a search string to an archie server, the server does not contact other computers on the Internet – it searches for the answer in the list of file names on its local disk.

Gathering information makes lookup fast, but has a disadvantage – the information can become incorrect if changes occur. Telephone companies solve the problem of change by producing a new telephone book periodically, usually once each year. Archie uses a similar technique. Periodically, usually once each day, software in an archie server automatically contacts computers on the Internet and gathers a new list of file names. After obtaining a new list, the software writes the list on disk for the archie server to use when answering questions. Figure 24.3 illustrates the process.

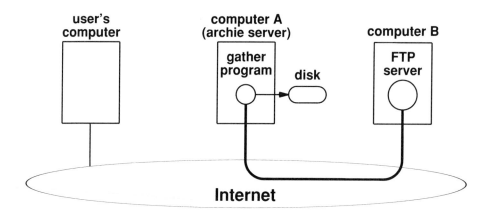

(a)

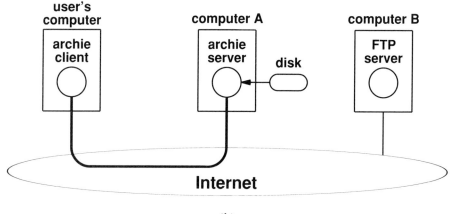

(b)

Figure 24.3 Archie uses a 2-step process. (a) Approximately once each day, an archie server automatically contacts all computers that run FTP servers and stores a list of file names on disk. (b) When a client program contacts an archie server to search for a file name, the server uses the list on its disk to form a reply.

In the figure, computer *A* runs an archie server. Periodically, a program on computer *A* uses FTP to contact other computers one at a time (e.g., computer *B*) and request a list of files. The program stores the list on *A*'s local disk.

Later, when a user makes an archie request, a client program on the user's computer contacts the archie server on computer *A*. The client sends a search string. The server examines the list of file names stored on its local disk and returns the answer. In the example, the archie server on computer *A* can tell the client about files on computer *B*; the server responds to the user without contacting computer *B*. The important idea is:

> *Because each archie server gathers file name information and stores it on a local disk, the server does not need to search computers on the Internet for each request a user sends.*

A Second Search Tool Example

Archie was among the first services for automated search on the Internet. Others have also appeared. One particular service named *veronica* illustrates how automated search can be integrated into browsing systems.

Veronica searches gopher menus on computers across the Internet analogous to the way archie searches for files available via FTP. That is, veronica does not help a user navigate a particular menu or find something on a particular computer. Instead, veronica searches menus on many gopher servers.

Like archie, veronica requires the user to enter a search string. It then searches for occurrences of the string on all computers that have gopher servers. Entering a search string is equivalent to initiating an Internet search:

> *When someone using veronica enters a search string, they are asking veronica to, "please find all the gopher menu items on all computers that contain the string."*

How Veronica Appears To A User

A user encounters veronica as a menu option inside gopher. For example, the menu item might say:

Search gopherspace using Veronica

When a user selects the item, gopher displays a menu of computers that have a veronica server, and waits for the user to select one. As with archie, although all servers produce the same data, a server may be busy at certain times of the day. If one server is busy, the user can either choose another server or wait until the server can respond.

After a user has selected a veronica server, gopher prints a prompt on the screen that asks the user to enter a search string. Gopher sends the search string to the veronica server, which finds all gopher menu items that contain the string. For example, if the user types *color*, veronica finds all gopher menu items that contain *color*.

Veronica Displays Results As A Menu

The way veronica responds to a search request is interesting: veronica displays the results of a search as a gopher menu! From the user's point of view, the new menu appears on the screen exactly like any other gopher menu. The user can page through the menu or select an item using the same commands used for other menus. That is:

> *Veronica is integrated into gopher – a user accesses veronica by selecting a gopher menu item, and the results of a search appear as a gopher menu.*

Remember that veronica creates a menu by extracting individual items from gopher menus on many machines all across the Internet. As a result, the output may not make much sense. For example, in response to the search string *this*, veronica will find menu items such as:

Information about this company.

Such items may make perfect sense in a normal gopher display because they are surrounded by other menu items that give the company name. When veronica extracts the item, however, the company name does not appear. More important, if a dozen companies happen to have the same phrase in their gopher menus, veronica will find all of them.

Complex Search Patterns

To help users extract more meaningful menu items, veronica allows a user to specify more than a simple search string. For example, the search string:

color not wheel

specifies that veronica should find all menu items that contain the phrase *color* but do not contain the phrase *wheel*. A user can insert *–t0* in a request to restrict the search to those menu items that correspond to a data file, or *–t1* to restrict the search to menu items that lead to other menus. For example, the search string:

–t0 goose not mother

requests a list of all menu items that contain the term *goose* but not the term *mother* and which, if selected, produce a file of data.

How Veronica Works

The set of computers that contain gopher menus is too large to search each time a user enters a veronica request. To avoid long delays, a computer that offers the veronica service works like archie. Periodically, a veronica server contacts computers on the Internet and gathers a list of all gopher menus. It stores the list on a disk. When a user selects veronica, the user's gopher program contacts a veronica server and sends the search request. The veronica server searches the list of menu items on its disk to produce an answer, and then sends the answer back in the form of a single menu.

Summary

Because the Internet is large and growing rapidly, a human does not have sufficient time to browse through all available information interactively. Instead, one must use automated search services to locate information. Such tools are useful when initiating a search for new information or when location information has been lost.

Two examples illustrate how automated search services appear to a user and how they operate. The archie service locates files accessible via FTP. When using archie, a user enters a search string, and archie responds with a list of all files on all computers that contain the string in their name. The veronica service finds gopher menu items. When using veronica, a user enters a search string, and veronica responds with a list of all gopher menu items that contain the specified string.

Because searching computers on the Internet takes hours, an automated search service cannot perform a search each time it receives a request. To guarantee quick response, automated search services periodically gather the data needed to answer requests and store it on disk. When a user enters a request, the server extracts the answer from the data on disk without contacting other computers.

The archie system illustrates how an Internet service can be accessed in a variety of ways. In particular, a user can enter a one-line command, send an electronic mail message, use a remote login program like TELNET, or invoke a program that uses windows and a mouse to provide a point-and-click interface.

The veronica system illustrates how an Internet service can be integrated into a menu system. A user invokes veronica by selecting an item in a gopher menu, and the output appears as another gopher menu.

A Comic Strip and A Joke

When a name was needed for the gopher menu-searching service, its inventors made a humorous choice when they selected *veronica*. The humor arises because a well-known comic strip features teenagers named *Archie* and *Veronica*. Internet users can joke, ''archie and veronica go together – archie searches file names and veronica searches menu items.'' As might be expected, other groups have extended the analogy. For example, one Internet tool (much less well-known than archie and veronica) is called *jughead*, after another character in the comic strip. Ironically, Internet users who are well-informed, know that the name *archie* has nothing to do with the comic strip character; it is short for *archive*. After the veronica service had been built and named, an acronym was contrived to go with the name. As a result, *veronica* stands for:

Very Easy Rodent-Oriented Network-wide Index to Computerized Archives

25

Automated Contents Search (WAIS)

Introduction

The previous chapter introduces automated searching. It shows how an automated search service can help a user find information without requiring the user to know the names of remote computers on which the information resides. The example automated search services considered in the previous chapter, archie and veronica, use titles to search for information. Archie searches for files names and veronica searches for gopher menu items that contain a specified string.

This chapter considers an alternative approach to automated search services that examines the contents of a document instead of the document title. It discusses the motivation for searching contents, and shows how such searches appear to a user.

Names Vs. Contents

Recall from the previous chapter that automated search services fall into two broad categories. Services like archie belong in the first category because they use titles as search keys. When an archie user enters the search string *forest*, for example, the user is asking archie to, "please find all files with *forest* in their name." A service that searches entire documents belongs in the second category. In such services, a user who enters the search string *forest* is asking the service, "please find all documents that contain the word *forest*."

The advantage of searches that use titles lies in speed. To understand how using names makes searching proceed quickly, imagine being given several boxes of books, and asked to search for the term *flower*. If you are asked to find all books with *flower* in the title, you must look at the title on each book. If you are asked to find all books that contain the word *flower*, you must look at the words in each book until you encounter the word *flower* or reach the end of the book, a time-consuming task. The same idea holds for an Internet search service: a search that examines document contents requires significantly more computation than a search that examines titles.

Although searching titles can proceed quickly, the method has a disadvantage. The disadvantage arises because a document's title does not always accurately describe the contents. Consider searching books. On one hand, words can appear in the title of literature that have little to do with the contents. For example, the search string *cat* matches titles like *Cat On A Hot Tin Roof*, a story about personal relationships. On the other hand, a title may not contain words that do describe the subject. For example, although *Gone With The Wind* is a well-known novel about the south during the U.S. Civil War, neither the string *south* nor the string *civil war* appears in the title.

In summary,

> *An automated search service that examines titles requires less computation than an automated search service that examines document contents. Because a document title does not always describe its contents, searches that use titles can report unrelated information or fail to find all information on a topic.*

Reading Vs. Scanning

When a human reads a document, he or she translates words into ideas. The translation can be quite complex, and involves much more than understanding the meanings of words separately. The simple statement:

> *The warm climate encouraged growth, resulting in food for the entire family.*

asserts that the weather helped plants grow, and that the resulting crop was used to feed a family. Although the statement:

> *The economic climate was adequate for growth.*

contains similar words, it has nothing to do with the weather or plants. (It asserts that the economy was doing well.) Similarly, the question:

> *Do you see what I mean?*

does not really have to do with eyesight (it asks if the reader understands what has been stated).

Because computers cannot easily parse language or understand the meaning of a document, most computer programs do not attempt to read documents the way a human does. Instead, they treat a document as a long list of words, and simply scan for a particular term. In essence, when given a word, the computer compares it to the words in a document without trying to understand their meaning. If it finds a match, the computer declares that the document satisfies the request.

Document Scanning Does Not Suffice

The documents selected by scanning for matching strings can be surprising. As the examples above show, when scanning for the string *climate*, a computer can select a document on economics as well as a document on weather. In addition, scanning can produce other unwanted selections. For example, suppose the following sentence appears in a document:

This document has absolutely nothing whatsoever to do with a bicycle, India, or fishing.

A human who interprets the meaning of the sentence knows that the document does not pertain to bicycles. However, if a computer scans the document looking for the string *bicycle*, it will find a match†. In general,

> *Because a computer cannot read and understand a document as easily as humans, most automated search services scan documents for a given word or phrase. Incorrect selections can result because a document usually contains many words that are irrelevant to its topic.*

Automated Document Search Is Not New

Several years ago, librarians realized that a computer can help find documents on a particular topic. Researchers have investigated how computers can automate and expedite retrieval in libraries. Although their work concentrates on document retrieval in a single computer instead of a network of computers, their observations and approaches to the retrieval problem have been used for document retrieval on the Internet. Researchers have found, for example, that scanning for specific words or phrases does not usually extract the documents pertinent to a topic. Instead, they use a two-step process:

1. Ask a user to enter search terms, and then scan all documents to look for the specified terms. Present the user with a (usually long) list of documents that contain the terms.
2. Ask the user to examine documents on the list and select a few documents that contain information they desire. Then, instruct the computer to analyze the words in the sample documents and start searching all documents again to find documents that are "similar."

---

†Interestingly, a computer scan of this book found *bicycle* as well as many other terms unrelated to the topic of computer networks, including *phonograph*, *motorcycle*, *China*, *planets*, and *muppets*.

Because a computer cannot easily understand the meaning of printed language, it does not attempt to read or understand the content of the samples. Instead, a computer counts the occurrences of words and uses a mathematical formula to evaluate whether two documents are "similar." In general, if the sample documents that a user selects repeatedly use the same words, the computer will look for additional documents that contain those words. Although the computer cannot guarantee that mathematically similar documents will contain related information, the idea works well in practice.

To understand how selection proceeds, suppose a user is interested in finding information on antique automobiles. The user can begin by instructing the computer to:

"find documents about automobiles or antiques"

In response, the computer produces a list of all documents that contain the term *automobile* or *antique*. The computer presents the list to the user, and allows the user to browse, either by reading the titles of documents or by obtaining a copy of each individual document. The user chooses documents that contain information on antique automobiles, and instructs the computer to:

"find more documents like these"

The computer analyzes the chosen documents to determine common words and phrases. For example, the terms *carriage*, *wheel* or the phrase *classic car* might occur in many of the sample documents about antique automobiles. After extracting a list of common words and phrases, the computer uses the list to search for additional documents that contain the same words. In general,

> *When a user enters a search request, a retrieval system scans for documents that contain the specified words. The system asks the user to select examples from the list, and searches for additional documents that contain similar words or phrases.*

The Wide Area Information Service

The Internet offers an automated search service that examines document contents. Called the *Wide Area Information Server*† (*WAIS*), the service was invented in a cooperative effort among several companies. In particular, Thinking Machines Corporation participated because WAIS demonstrates the capabilities of their computers. Later, an independent company, WAIS Inc., was formed to build and sell WAIS.

Like the document retrieval software on a single computer, WAIS can locate a set of documents that contains a given term or phrase. Also like a conventional document retrieval system, WAIS permits a user to identify sample documents and uses them to find additional documents that are similar. In summary,

---

†The name is slightly misleading; think of WAIS as the Wide Area Information *Service* instead.

WAIS is an automated search service available on the Internet. Un-like the search services described in previous chapters, WAIS exam-ines document contents.

Despite many similarities, WAIS differs from conventional document retrieval sys-tems in two significant ways. First, WAIS is accessible via the Internet and can include sets of documents from many computers. Second, WAIS divides documents into groups to help eliminate irrelevant information.

How WAIS Appears To A User

Like most Internet services, WAIS provides several ways to access the service. For example, a user can form a TELNET connection to the computer *quake.think.com*, log in with userid *wais*, and begin interacting directly with the WAIS service. Alterna-tively, a user can run a WAIS client program that forms a connection to a WAIS server and permits a user to interact. Client software is available for a computer that has a standard keyboard and character-oriented display, as well as a computer that has a mouse and a graphics display. Finally, a user can access WAIS through the Mosaic program described in Chapter 23.

Although the details of how WAIS appears and how one interacts with the service differ among the various methods of access, they follow the same general pattern.

1. A user begins by choosing a collection of documents to scan. WAIS calls each collection a *source*; over 500 sources currently exist.
2. The user enters a question, which consists of a sequence of words. WAIS responds by finding documents in the specified collection that contain words from the question.
3. The user selects a few sample documents and asks WAIS to, ''find additional documents like these.''

A Question Can Be Written in English

When a WAIS user enters a question, the question can be phrased in English. For example, in response to the question:

Tell me about documents related to France or England.

WAIS will find documents that pertain to France and England. Despite the appearance, however, WAIS does not understand English. Instead, it merely extracts individual words from the question and uses them to scan documents in the specified collection. WAIS ignores common words like *to* that appear in most documents, and uses words like *France* that only appear in a few. In fact, a user can omit unnecessary words and enter only the words to be used in the search:

France England

WAIS does not care whether the sentence makes sense because it does not interpret the meaning.

A User Chooses Among Collections Of Documents

WAIS divides all documents into collections called *sources*. Before entering a question, a user must specify which sources of documents to use for the search. Limiting a search to specified collections of documents helps WAIS retrieve only documents of interest to the user. For example, suppose that a user intends to travel to France and wants to search for information regarding travel to foreign countries. A search using the term *France* might produce documents on topics as diverse as French literature, the economy in France, or French cuisine. However, limiting the search to documents from a source that provides travel information helps ensure that the documents retrieved will pertain to travel.

Before asking WAIS to search for documents, a user must decide which document collections to use as sources. How can a user choose sources? Incredibly, one uses WAIS to conduct the search!

Using WAIS to search for sources makes the service somewhat awkward for beginners. However, the idea is not complex. When a user first contacts WAIS, the system begins with a special source called a *directory of servers* that is not a conventional collection of documents. Instead, it contains descriptions of the document collections available to WAIS. When a user poses a question using the directory of servers source, the result is a list of document collections.

To search the description of sources, a user enters a sentence or search terms. WAIS looks through the directory of servers, and lists all pertinent items. Each item on the list describes one collection of documents. The user can then select one or more items and specify that WAIS use them for subsequent searches. The example in the next sections illustrates how a user selects a source, and then searches the source for documents.

Using A Mouse To Access WAIS

Several programs are available that provide a point-and-click interface for WAIS. Figure 25.1 illustrates how the screen might appear when running such a program. The software begins by listing the *directory of servers* source and waiting for the user to enter a question.

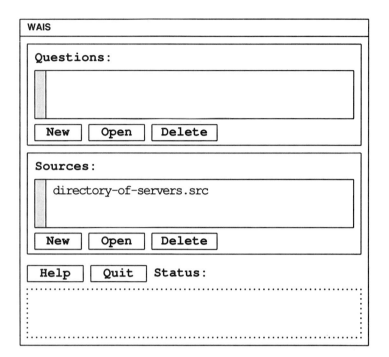

Figure 25.1 An illustration of the way WAIS first appears to someone who is
using a point-and-click interface.

As the figure shows, WAIS displays a small window that is divided into three
areas. The top area contains questions, the middle area contains a list of sources, and
the bottom displays status information. Each area includes operations (e.g., *New* and
Help) that the user can select. The operation labeled *Help* displays information on how
to use WAIS; the operation labeled *Quit* terminates the program.

Selecting Among Sources

To request a search, the user moves the mouse to position the cursor over operation
New in the *Questions* section, and presses a mouse button to select the operation.
WAIS displays a second window labeled *WAIS New Question* that can be used to enter
the search information. Figure 25.2 illustrates the format.

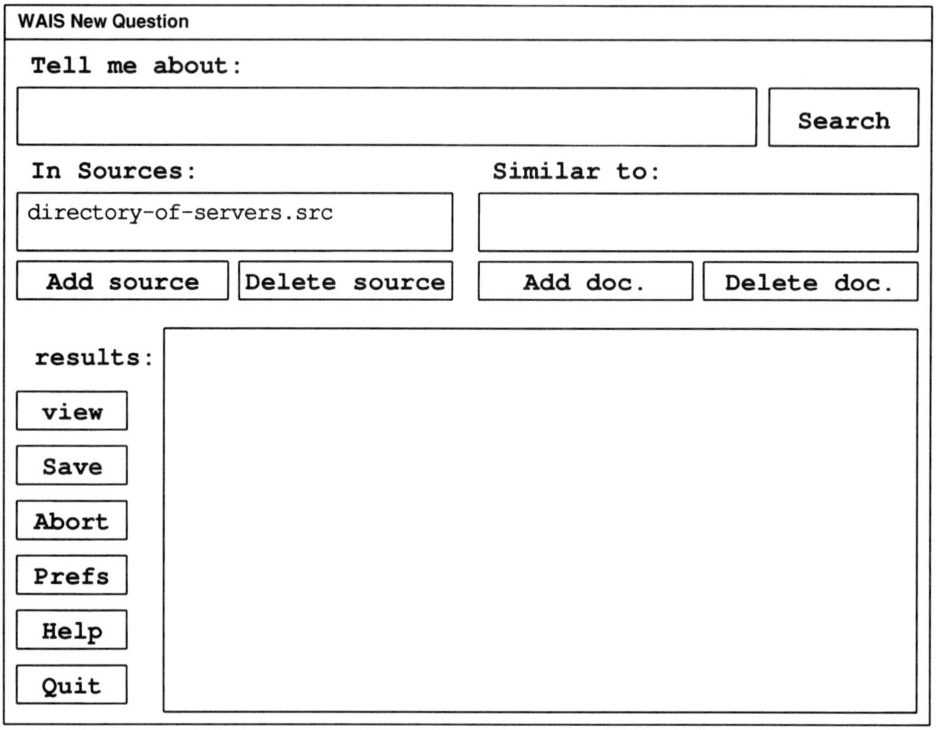

```
┌──────────────────────────────────────────────────────────────────────┐
│ WAIS New Question                                                      │
├──────────────────────────────────────────────────────────────────────┤
│                                                                        │
│   Tell me about:                                                       │
│   ┌────────────────────────────────────────────────┐  ┌────────────┐ │
│   │                                                  │  │            │ │
│   │                                                  │  │  Search    │ │
│   └────────────────────────────────────────────────┘  └────────────┘ │
│                                                                        │
│   In Sources:                      Similar to:                         │
│   ┌──────────────────────────────┐ ┌──────────────────────────────┐  │
│   │ directory-of-servers.src     │ │                              │  │
│   │                              │ │                              │  │
│   └──────────────────────────────┘ └──────────────────────────────┘  │
│   ┌──────────────┐ ┌──────────────┐ ┌──────────────┐ ┌─────────────┐ │
│   │ Add source   │ │Delete source │ │ Add doc.     │ │ Delete doc. │ │
│   └──────────────┘ └──────────────┘ └──────────────┘ └─────────────┘ │
│                                                                        │
│   results:   ┌──────────────────────────────────────────────────────┐│
│   ┌───────┐  │                                                      ││
│   │ view  │  │                                                      ││
│   └───────┘  │                                                      ││
│   ┌───────┐  │                                                      ││
│   │ Save  │  │                                                      ││
│   └───────┘  │                                                      ││
│   ┌───────┐  │                                                      ││
│   │ Abort │  │                                                      ││
│   └───────┘  │                                                      ││
│   ┌───────┐  │                                                      ││
│   │ Prefs │  │                                                      ││
│   └───────┘  │                                                      ││
│   ┌───────┐  │                                                      ││
│   │ Help  │  │                                                      ││
│   └───────┘  │                                                      ││
│   ┌───────┐  │                                                      ││
│   │ Quit  │  │                                                      ││
│   └───────┘  └──────────────────────────────────────────────────────┘│
└──────────────────────────────────────────────────────────────────────┘
```

Figure 25.2 The window that appears when a user clicks on the *New* operation under the *Questions* section of a WAIS window.

The window contains several areas. Near the top, a box labeled *Tell me about* allows the user to enter a sentence or words to be used in the search. The second section of the window contains two areas, one labeled *In Sources* and the other labeled *Similar to*. The box for sources lists the sources WAIS will consult when the user asks it to search. The box contains only the name *directory-of-servers.src* because the user has not yet selected other sources.

To enter a search string, a user moves the cursor to the box labeled *Tell me about*, types a sentence or a sequence of words, and clicks on the *Search* command to request that WAIS perform the search. WAIS consults the directory-of-servers source, and displays the output from the search in the large box labeled *results*. For example, suppose a user is interested in information on travel. The user enters the search key *travel* to request that WAIS find collections of documents that pertain to travel. Note that the initial search does not produce documents themselves – the user is using WAIS to find collections of documents. WAIS responds to the question in a few seconds by filling in fields of the *results* area as Figure 25.3 shows.

```
┌──────────────────────────────────────────────────────────────────────────┐
│ WAIS New Question                                                          │
│ ┌────────────────────────────────────────────────────────────────────────┐│
│ │ Tell me about:                                                         │ │
│ │ ┌────────────────────────────────────────────────┐  ┌────────────────┐ │ │
│ │ │ travel                                         │  │    Search      │ │ │
│ │ └────────────────────────────────────────────────┘  └────────────────┘ │ │
│ │ In Sources:                          Similar to:                       │ │
│ │ ┌──────────────────────────────────┐ ┌───────────────────────────────┐ │ │
│ │ │ directory-of-servers.src         │ │                               │ │ │
│ │ └──────────────────────────────────┘ └───────────────────────────────┘ │ │
│ │ ┌──────────────┐ ┌────────────────┐  ┌─────────────┐ ┌───────────────┐ │ │
│ │ │ Add source   │ │ Delete source  │  │  Add doc.   │ │  Delete doc.  │ │ │
│ │ └──────────────┘ └────────────────┘  └─────────────┘ └───────────────┘ │ │
│ │                 ┌──────────────────────────────────────────────────────┐│ │
│ │  results:       │ 1000 (02/02/94) US-State-Department-Travel-Advisories.src││
│ │ ┌──────────┐    │  259 (05/02/94) Omni-Cultural-Academic-resources.src  ││ │
│ │ │  view    │    │  222 (12/12/93) ANU-SSDA-Australian-Census.src        ││ │
│ │ └──────────┘    │  222 (06/18/94) ANU-SSDA-Australian-Opinion.src       ││ │
│ │ ┌──────────┐    │                                                       ││ │
│ │ │  Save    │    │                                                       ││ │
│ │ └──────────┘    │                                                       ││ │
│ │ ┌──────────┐    │                                                       ││ │
│ │ │  Abort   │    │                                                       ││ │
│ │ └──────────┘    │                                                       ││ │
│ │ ┌──────────┐    │                                                       ││ │
│ │ │  Prefs   │    │                                                       ││ │
│ │ └──────────┘    │                                                       ││ │
│ │ ┌──────────┐    │                                                       ││ │
│ │ │  Help    │    │                                                       ││ │
│ │ └──────────┘    │                                                       ││ │
│ │ ┌──────────┐    │                                                       ││ │
│ │ │  Quit    │    │                                                       ││ │
│ │ └──────────┘    └───────────────────────────────────────────────────────┘│
│ └────────────────────────────────────────────────────────────────────────┘│
└──────────────────────────────────────────────────────────────────────────┘
```

Figure 25.3 An illustration of how WAIS might respond when a user types the request *travel* to the directory-of-servers source.

The output may seem cryptic. Each line in the *results* section corresponds to a collection of documents that has something to do with travel. A line contains a ranking number that tells how well the collection matches the description, the date that the information was last changed, and a name for the collection. Although a user may have trouble understanding what each line means, one can guess that the collection labeled:

US-State-Department-Travel-Advisories.src

corresponds to a source that contains documents issued by the U.S. State Department. Some of the other lines mention Australia, but the text does not explain the purpose of the sources or the documents found in them.

After WAIS displays the results of an initial search, the user must decide whether to modify the question and search again or to choose among the sources listed. To do the former, the user repositions the cursor in the box labeled *Tell me about*, replaces the search key, and clicks on the operation labeled *Search*.

If a user decides to search for documents within one or more of the sources, the user must select a source. To do so, the user moves the cursor to a line in the *results* section that names a source, and clicks to highlight the line. WAIS changes the selected line to reverse video. Figure 25.4 shows how the window appears after a user has selected a source.

```
┌──────────────────────────────────────────────────────────────────────┐
│ WAIS New Question                                                      │
│ ┌──────────────────────────────────────────────────────────────────┐ │
│ │ Tell me about:                                                     │ │
│ │ ┌────────────────────────────────────────────────┐  ┌───────────┐ │ │
│ │ │ travel                                         │  │  Search   │ │ │
│ │ └────────────────────────────────────────────────┘  └───────────┘ │ │
│ │ In Sources:                     Similar to:                        │ │
│ │ ┌──────────────────────────────┐ ┌──────────────────────────────┐ │ │
│ │ │ directory-of-servers.src     │ │                              │ │ │
│ │ └──────────────────────────────┘ └──────────────────────────────┘ │ │
│ │ ┌────────────┐ ┌──────────────┐  ┌────────────┐ ┌──────────────┐  │ │
│ │ │ Add source │ │ Delete source│  │  Add doc.  │ │ Delete doc.  │  │ │
│ │ └────────────┘ └──────────────┘  └────────────┘ └──────────────┘  │ │
│ │  results: ┌────────────────────────────────────────────────────┐ │ │
│ │           │ 1000 (02/02/94) US-State-Department-Travel-Advisories.src│ │
│ │  ┌──────┐  │  259 (05/02/94) Omni-Cultural-Academic-resources.src│ │ │
│ │  │ view │  │  222 (12/12/93) ANU-SSDA-Australian-Census.src      │ │ │
│ │  └──────┘  │  222 (06/18/94) ANU-SSDA-Australian-Opinion.src     │ │ │
│ │  ┌──────┐  │                                                     │ │ │
│ │  │ Save │  │                                                     │ │ │
│ │  └──────┘  │                                                     │ │ │
│ │  ┌──────┐  │                                                     │ │ │
│ │  │ Abort│  │                                                     │ │ │
│ │  └──────┘  │                                                     │ │ │
│ │  ┌──────┐  │                                                     │ │ │
│ │  │ Prefs│  │                                                     │ │ │
│ │  └──────┘  │                                                     │ │ │
│ │  ┌──────┐  │                                                     │ │ │
│ │  │ Help │  │                                                     │ │ │
│ │  └──────┘  │                                                     │ │ │
│ │  ┌──────┐  │                                                     │ │ │
│ │  │ Quit │  └────────────────────────────────────────────────────┘ │ │
│ │  └──────┘                                                          │ │
│ └──────────────────────────────────────────────────────────────────┘ │
└──────────────────────────────────────────────────────────────────────┘
```

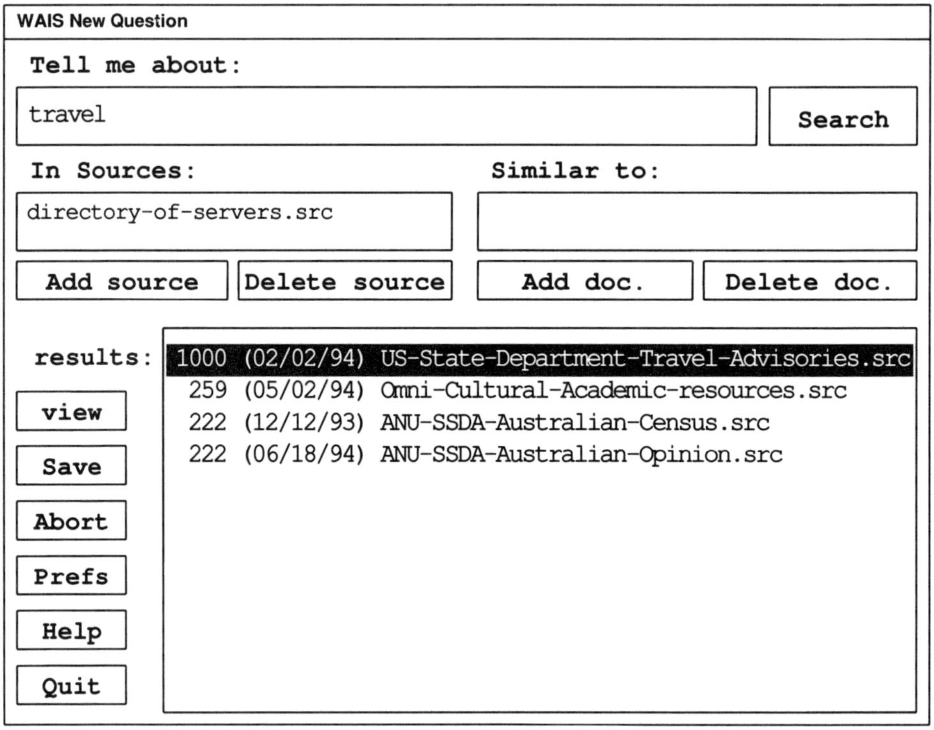

Figure 25.4 An illustration that shows how a WAIS window appears after a user selects a line in the *results* section.

After a user highlights a line in the *results* section, the user can select an operation from the list on the lower left side of the window. The *view* operation provides additional information about the highlighted line. For a source, the information includes details about the computer WAIS must contact to access the source and the amount of money, if any, the owner charges for access. After a user views information about the source, the user can select the *Save* operation to store information about the source on disk.

Once a user has selected a source and stored it on disk, WAIS automatically includes the source whenever the user accesses the WAIS service; a user can delete the source if it is not relevant to a search. In summary,

*A WAIS user must select among collections of documents before using
WAIS to search. Although the selection requires several steps, a user
can save the information on disk to avoid repeating the selection.*

Posing A Question To WAIS

Using WAIS becomes easier after a user has selected sources and saved them on
disk. Whenever a user invokes WAIS, it automatically retrieves the set of saved
sources from the user's disk and makes them available to use for searches. For example, suppose a user has chosen to search in the U.S. State Department Travel Advisory
collection, created a question window, and entered the search string *France or Europe*.
Figure 25.5 shows how the screen might appear when WAIS responds to the search.

```
┌────────────────────────────────────────────────────────────────────────┐
│ WAIS  New Question                                                       │
│ ┌────────────────────────────────────────────────────────────────────┐ │
│  Tell me about:                                                          │
│ ┌──────────────────────────────────────────────────┐  ┌──────────────┐ │
│ │ france or europe                                 │  │              │ │
│ │                                                  │  │   Search     │ │
│ └──────────────────────────────────────────────────┘  └──────────────┘ │
│   In Sources:                       Similar to:                          │
│ ┌──────────────────────────────────┐  ┌──────────────────────────────┐ │
│ │ US-State-Department-Travel-Adviso│  │                              │ │
│ └──────────────────────────────────┘  └──────────────────────────────┘ │
│ ┌────────────────┐┌────────────────┐  ┌──────────────┐ ┌──────────────┐│
│ │  Add source    ││ Delete source  │  │   Add doc.   │ │  Delete doc. ││
│ └────────────────┘└────────────────┘  └──────────────┘ └──────────────┘│
│                                                                          │
│   results:  │ 911  france /var/spool/Internet Resources/US-State-Depart │
│  ┌────────┐ │ 312  albania /var/spool/Internet Resources/US-State-Depar │
│  │  view  │ │ 266  french-west-indies /var/spool/Internet Resource/US-S │
│  └────────┘ │ 266  andorra /var/spool/Internet Resources/US-State-Depar │
│  ┌────────┐ │ 266  monaco  /var/spool/Internet Resources/US-State-Depar │
│  │  Save  │ │ 177  hungary /var/spool/Internet Resources/US-State-Depar │
│  └────────┘ │ 177  czech-republic /var/spool/Internet Resources/US-Stat │
│  ┌────────┐ │ 155  russia /var/spool/Internet Resources/US-State-Depar  │
│  │ Abort  │ │ 155  slovak-republic /var/spool/Internet Resources/US-St  │
│  └────────┘ │ 133  malta /var/spool/Internet Resources/US-State-Departm │
│  ┌────────┐ │ 101  albania /var/spool/Internet Resources/US-State-Depar │
│  │ Prefs  │ │                                                           │
│  └────────┘                                                              │
│  ┌────────┐                                                              │
│  │  Help  │                                                              │
│  └────────┘                                                              │
│  ┌────────┐                                                              │
│  │  Quit  │                                                              │
│  └────────┘                                                              │
└────────────────────────────────────────────────────────────────────────┘
```

Figure 25.5 An example of the display a WAIS user encounters when searching for documents within a collection. WAIS uses the same
form of display whether a user searches for sources or for documents within selected sources.

WAIS retrieves the documents that contain words from the search string and displays a list in the *results* section. WAIS counts the times the search words occur in each document, and orders the list by decreasing count. In the example, the first document on the list contains more occurrences of the search words *france* and *europe* than any other document on the list. The point is:

> *A user often finds the documents WAIS places at the top of the list most relevant to a search because those documents contain more occurrences of the search words than other documents in the list.*

Retrieving A Document With WAIS

A user can use the mouse to select a line in the *results* list, and then click on the *view* operation to view the document. WAIS retrieves the document and displays it on the screen. For example, Figure 25.6 shows how the screen appears if a user retrieves the first document from the list shown on the previous page.

```
                 STATE DEPARTMENT TRAVEL INFORMATION - France
                 = = = = = = = = = = = = = = = = = = = = = = = =
    France - Consular Information Sheet
    April 30, 1994

    Country Description:  France is a highly developed and stable
    democracy in Europe with a modern economy.  Tourist facilities
    are widely available.

    Entry Requirements:  A passport is required.  A visa is not
    required for tourist or business up to three months.  For
    further information concerning entry requirements for France,
    travelers can contact the Embassy of France at 4101 Reservoir Road
    N.W. Washington, DC 20007,  Tel: (202) 944-6000, or the nearest
    French Consulate General in Boston, Chicago, Detroit, Honolulu,
    Houston, Los Angeles, Miami, New Orleans, New York, San Francisco,
    or San Juan.

    Medical Facilities:  Medical care is widely available.  U.S.
    medical insurance is not always valid outside the United States.
    Travelers have found that in some cases, supplemental medical
    insurance with specific overseas coverage has proved useful.
    Further information on health matters can be obtained from the
```
| Find Key | Save To File | Done | |

Figure 25.6 An illustration of the way WAIS displays a document.

As the figure shows, WAIS divides the output window into two areas. The text of the document appears in the large, central section of the window, and a small set of operations appears at the bottom of the window. If a user selects the *Save To File* operation, WAIS stores a copy of the document on disk. When a user selects the *Done* operation, WAIS removes the document from the display and allows the user to view another document.

Only part of a document is visible at any time. A user can move to other parts in two ways. As with most window displays, a user can page through the document by pressing a mouse button while the cursor is positioned on the scroll bar at the left side of the window. In addition, WAIS can locate occurrences of search words.

Whenever one of the search words appears in the document, WAIS highlights the word by displaying it in bold type. In the example, the terms *France* and *Europe* appear highlighted because both are search words. WAIS provides the operation labeled *Find Key* to allow a user to move forward in the document to the next occurrence of a search word. If the next occurrence appears later in the document, WAIS repositions the window so the search word appears on the display. Thus, when a user selects the *Find Key* operation, WAIS may skip arbitrary amounts of text before it stops to display information in the window.

How WAIS Works

Like other Internet services, WAIS uses the client-server approach. A user invokes client software that contacts a WAIS server when the user requests a search. Each source corresponds to a specific server. When a user first encounters a source and saves it on disk for later use, WAIS records the location of the server along with the name of the source. Whenever the user specifies a source to search, the client software automatically consults the information on disk to determine which server offers that source.

Like the Internet search services discussed in the previous chapter, WAIS does not need to scan all documents in a given collection each time a user enters a question. Instead, computer programs scan documents, and make lists of all words in each. When a user poses a question, a server compares the words in the question to the list of words in the document. Similarly, when a user selects a document and requests WAIS to find other documents that are similar, WAIS can compare the words in the selected document to words in other documents.

Special Computers Make WAIS Efficient

Extracting words from a document does not guarantee that a computer will search quickly. Because large documents can contain thousands of different words, searching a collection of documents can take slow computers many seconds. In most cases, however, WAIS can answer a question quickly.

The secret to quick response lies in the computers chosen to run WAIS. Instead of small, slow personal computers, WAIS servers usually run on special-purpose computers that are large and fast. For example, although an average computer contains only one processor, some of the computers used to answer WAIS questions each contain several processors that can all work on questions simultaneously.

Summary

Automated search services can examine the contents of documents as well as titles. Most retrieval systems use a two-step process. In the first step, a user specifies keywords, and the system finds a list of documents that contain the keywords. In the second step, the user selects documents from the list and requests the system to find additional documents that are similar. Because searching content requires more computation, such searches take longer than searching titles and require special high-speed computers for efficiency.

The Internet offers a service known as the Wide Area Information Server that can search document content. WAIS uses the same two-step process as a conventional document retrieval system A user can request WAIS to search for specific words, or can identify a set of documents and request WAIS to find documents that are similar.

WAIS divides all documents into collections called sources. When a user requests a search, the user must identify one or more collections of documents in which WAIS should search. Interestingly, a user can use WAIS to identify appropriate collections. To do so, the user requests a search on a special collection called a *directory of servers*. Because information about collections of documents can be saved on disk, a user only needs to find a source once.

26

Audio And Video Communication

Introduction

Previous chapters describe a wide variety of Internet services that allow users to send memos, read messages on a bulletin board, transfer data files, browse menus, or perform automated searches. In all cases, the information must be recorded. This chapter examines Internet services that allow people to communicate directly. It describes services that permit a user to send sounds, video, or images directly to others without recording the information, and explains how such services make it possible for people to work together in new ways.

Description Of Functionality

Internet audio and video services make it possible to:

- Send voice to another person or a group of people.
- Send a live television image to a single person or to a group of people.
- Broadcast audio or video information throughout the Internet.
- Allow a group of people to see and edit a document.

Audio And Video Require Special Hardware

Before a user can participate in audio or video services, their connection to the Internet must have sufficient capacity and their computer must have special hardware. Technically, the capacity of a network is known as its *bandwidth*. An inexpensive, low-bandwidth connection† suffices for electronic mail, file transfer, or browsing. Although a user must wait longer for the data to arrive over a low bandwidth connection, the data eventually arrives.

Live video or audio requires high bandwidth because audio and video packets are generated rapidly. If the network has insufficient bandwidth (i.e., capacity) for video and audio, the picture and sound appear to freeze, and then jump ahead. Because moving pictures require approximately *100* times more bandwidth than continuous sound, a connection can have sufficient bandwidth for audio but insufficient bandwidth for video.

In addition to a high-bandwidth Internet connection, audio and video services require a computer with:

- A *microphone* to capture sounds. A typical microphone is about one-half as large as a credit card and thinner than a person's finger. A microphone can be mounted on the front of the computer with adhesive or pinned to the user's clothes. A cable attaches the microphone to the computer.

- A *speaker* to reproduce sounds; two speakers are required to reproduce stereo. Speakers can be hidden inside a computer or can be separate. Some computers provide an inexpensive internal speaker, but also permit the user to plug in an external speaker when higher quality sound is desired. As an alternative, some users prefer to wear earphones which allow the user to hear clearly without annoying others. Earphones are also helpful when using a microphone because they prevent sounds played on the speaker from interfering with other sounds in the room.

- A *camera* to record images. A camera, which resembles a small flashlight, is usually mounted on the top of the computer and pointed toward the user's face. The least expensive cameras cannot capture colors, and the images they send are somewhat blurry. A cable connects the camera to the computer.

- A *high-speed processor* to manipulate video and audio without introducing delay. Older or inexpensive computers may not have sufficient computing power to operate a microphone, camera, speaker, and display without losing some of the picture or sound.

To understand how computers use such hardware, it is important to understand that the computer controls all the devices electronically. For example, a computer can start or stop a camera and raise or lower the volume of sound without requiring the user to physically turn dials and switches. Software allows a user to control devices with keystrokes or mouse movements.

---

†As might be expected a high bandwidth connection to the Internet costs more than a lower bandwidth connection.

Radio Programs On The Internet

One of the experimental audio services available on the Internet operates like a radio station. A single site has equipment that converts an audio signal to digital form, places the result in packets, and sends the packets across the Internet. A user who wants to listen to an Internet radio broadcast runs software that extracts the packets, converts them back to sound, and plays the sound through a speaker or earphones.

Known as the *Internet Multicasting Service*†, the Internet radio service transmits a mixture of conventional radio programs (e.g., speeches by political leaders) and discussions of interest to people who work with computers and computer networks. For example, one can listen to speeches presented at National Press Club Luncheons or to talks given by networking experts at technical conferences.

Interestingly, the Internet Multicasting Service has found that many users do not listen to live audio. Instead, such users prefer to have the information recorded in a file so they can access it later. To accommodate such users, the Internet Multicasting Service stores sound in files and makes the files available via gopher or World Wide Web. A user can browse though listings of prerecorded programs, extract a file, and play the sound in the same way that one selects and plays prerecorded music.

Like many other Internet services, more information about the Internet Multicasting Service can be obtained using the Internet. For example, the WWW homepage for the Internet Multicasting Service is available with the following URL:

http://www.town.hall.org/

and a gopher menu can be obtained from the URL:

gopher://gopher.town.hall.org/

Finally, information can be obtained by WAIS from the computer:

wais.town.hall.org

Audio Teleconferencing

Another Internet service permits a group of users to hold audio discussions similar to telephone ''conference calls.'' Each discussion is known as an *audio teleconference*. To create a teleconference, a user runs software that organizes and controls the discussion. The software requests the names of the participants, and then attempts to contact each of them. The software either displays a message on each participant's screen or otherwise notifies them that a teleconference exists. The notification is analogous to a telephone call – a user can choose to answer the request and join the teleconference, or ignore the message and let the teleconference proceed without them.

To join a teleconference, a user must run a program that handles audio reception and transmission. The program monitors the user's microphone, converts the signal to digital form, and sends a copy to other users in the teleconference. The program also receives messages, converts the messages back into sound, and plays the results for the

---

†The term *multicasting* refers to the mechanism the Internet uses to send audio and video information to many computers.

user to hear. All participants hear the conversation similar to a conference telephone call.

Audio teleconferencing is significant because it allows participants to convey and understand emotion. Unlike written communication, voice carries inflection that tells the listener whether the speaker is excited, tired, angry, or joking.

A Cooperative Document Markup Service

While audio can simplify interaction among people, a written document is usually needed to guarantee that all participants agree on details. Imagine, for example, a committee of people trying to write a joint report. Initially, the committee can use audio to hold a general discussion and generate ideas. However, audio communication does not provide an effective way to handle details or edit wording. In such cases a written document is needed.

Software exists that permits a group of Internet users to examine and edit a single document. Figure 26.1 shows how the screen might appear when a user creates a shared document session.

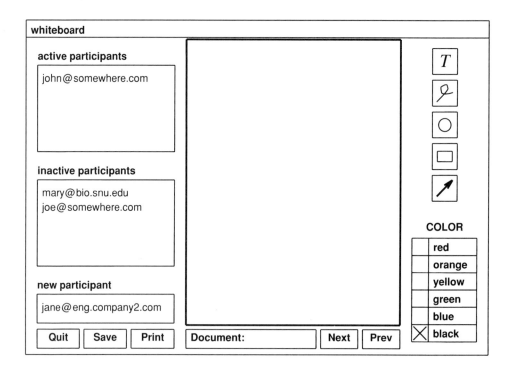

Figure 26.1 An illustration of how the screen might appear as a user creates a shared document session.

A shared document service is called a *whiteboard service*. As Figure 26.1 illustrates, the whiteboard service lists the names of all participants on the left side of the screen. A user named *John* working on computer *somewhere.com* has created the session and is adding participants. To add a participant, John types their login identifier and computer name in the box labeled *new participant*. The system sends a message to each person and moves their name to the *inactive participants* box until they respond. When a person responds and joins the session, their name appears in the *active participants* box.

To display a document, one of the users must move to the box labeled *Document* and enter the name of a document on disk. The whiteboard service obtains a copy of the document and displays it on all participants' screens. Figure 26.2 illustrates how the session appears when two more participants have joined and a document has been specified.

The *inactive participants* box shows that Joe has been invited to participate, but has not yet responded to the invitation. Recall that a user can only join the session if one of the participants enters their name in the *new participant* box. Any participant can choose to leave the session at any time; when a user leaves, the whiteboard software moves their name to the *inactive participants* box.

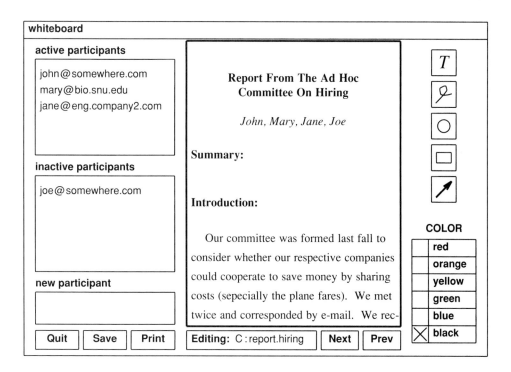

Figure 26.2 Illustration of a document displayed by a whiteboard service. All participants see the same display.

Marking A Document

A participant uses a mouse to control interaction with a whiteboard service. For example, any user can page through the document by selecting the *Next* and *Prev* commands. In addition, a user can draw or type on the document at any time. When a participant moves to the next or previous page or changes the document, all other participants see the change on their screen. In fact,

> *A whiteboard service is similar to a sheet of paper that all participants can see. Whenever a participant makes a change, all other participants see the change immediately.*

Figure 26.2 illustrates how a user controls a whiteboard session. The right side of the display contains a set of boxes that specify a drawing mode. A user selects the box labeled *T* to type *text*, the second box to draw an arbitrary line, the third to draw a circle, the fourth to draw a rectangle, and the last to draw an arrow.

In addition to the drawing mode, a user must select a color from the list on the lower right side of the screen. Modifications a user draws or types on the document appear in the color the user has selected.

The Participants Discuss And Mark A Document

Usually, participants in a whiteboard session also engage in an audio teleconference at the same time. Thus, they can hear each other and see the document on the screen. For example, suppose the participants who view the document shown in Figure 26.2 decide that the committee members' names should be changed to full names. Also assume that in the discussion, Mary agrees to supply a summary and someone notices the misspelling of *especially*. Any of the participants can draw on the document or take notes from the discussion. Jane might notice the misspelling and draw a circle around it, and Joe might decide to make a note about the names. As the discussion proceeds and the participants add items, the document appears as Figure 26.3 shows. The additions do not become part of the document – they only appear on the whiteboard. Later, one of the participants will need to use a word processor to change the original document.

Users who have a color display can use colors to enhance their drawing and comments. On a document with black text, for example, red notation stands out. Furthermore, if each participant chooses a different color, the colors show which participant creates a given message. Alternatively, the group may agree to use one color for questions and proposed changes, and reserve another color for final decisions. For example, in Figure 26.3, the circle around the spelling change could be red because the change is mandatory, while the note *USE FULL NAMES* might be in blue until Joe agrees to adopt the change.

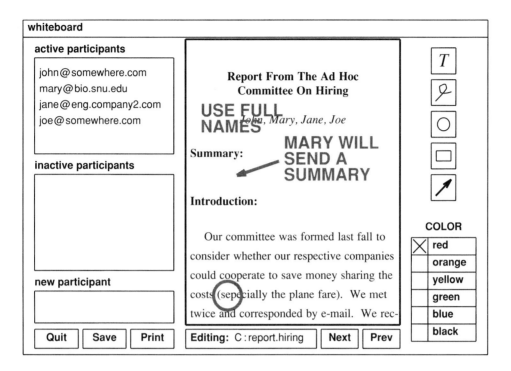

Figure 26.3 A sample whiteboard that illustrates how participants mark a document. The whiteboard service saves the session on disk so it
can be reviewed later.

Video Teleconferencing

Audio teleconferencing and shared whiteboard services provide a way for people to
work together. Such services can be especially helpful when preparing or reviewing a
document. However, face-to-face interactions usually work better when a group needs
to generate ideas or discuss a topic because facial expressions can show surprise or
agreement without requiring words.

To enable face-to-face interaction, the Internet offers *video teleconferencing* services. A video teleconference begins the same as a whiteboard session: a user runs a
program that starts a video session. The software allows the user to enter information
about other participants, and contacts each of them. When a new participant joins the
teleconference, an image from the camera on their computer appears in a small window
on everyone's screen. The pictures are similar to an ordinary television picture†. When
a participant smiles or frowns, everyone sees their expression.

---

†Of course, the picture produced by an inexpensive camera is not as clear as the picture produced by professional television equipment. The picture may flicker or jump if a user's connection to the Internet does not
operate at high speed.

Of course, video alone does not help people communicate. Therefore, most video teleconferencing services incorporate both video and audio into a single teleconference session. When a participant joins the teleconference, they hear as well as see all other participants.

Video Teleconference Among Groups Of People

A video teleconference works well when used with a few people. Each user's display shows the pictures of other participants. However, when more than a few pictures appear on a display, it becomes difficult to watch all of them.

When many people participate in a video teleconference, the screen cannot hold individual images from cameras on the participants' computers. Instead, people must gather in smaller groups in rooms that each have a camera and a large-screen computer display. In essence, the entire room becomes a single participant in the teleconference. The camera sends a picture of the room to all other participants where it is projected on a display large enough for everyone to see. Instead of small rectangles that each contain an individual's face, the display contains rectangles that each show a view of a remote room.

Sending audio for an entire room can be difficult. A single microphone may not be sensitive enough to detect sounds in all parts of the room. Multiple microphones sometimes detect background noise such as papers rustling. To handle the problem, rooms equipped for a video teleconference sometimes have portable microphones that can be passed to whoever needs to speak.

A Combined Audio, Video, And Whiteboard Service

Audio and video teleconferences become more interesting when combined with a whiteboard service. To understand the effect, imagine that each user's computer has a display as large as a typical television screen. Small rectangles around the edge of the screen each display the video image from the camera of one remote participant, usually a close-up of their face. A whiteboard occupies the center of the screen.

The combination of audio, video, and whiteboard makes it possible for everyone to see and hear one another as well as view a common document. When the participants need to discuss an idea, they can use audio and video communication. When they need to specify a precise document modification, they can rely on whiteboard communication. In fact,

> *Because experience has shown that combining a whiteboard service with an audio and video teleconference provides the most flexibility, many teleconference services include all three.*

Summary

The Internet offers audio and video services that permit two or more people to interact. The Internet Multicasting Service transmits audio programs like a radio station; anyone can listen. In addition, one can obtain a stored copy of a sound file and play it at any time.

An audio teleconference service works like a multi-way telephone call. Two or more people establish a teleconference and begin talking to one another. The group can designate other users and allow them to participate in the conversation. A video teleconference service operates like an audio teleconference except that it sends a motion picture from the camera attached to each participant's computer. To display video from other participants, a computer divides the screen into rectangles, and displays the video from one camera in each rectangle. When many people participate in a video teleconference, they gather in rooms that have a camera and microphone. Each room acts as one participant.

A whiteboard service permits a group of people to interactively review and mark a document. One person creates the whiteboard session by designating a list of participants. Each participant receives an invitation to join the session, and can leave at any time. The whiteboard service shows each active participant a copy of the shared document, and allows them to choose a color and then modify the document by drawing or entering text. All other participants see the results.

A Personal Note

Although a teleconference provides exciting possibilities, it uses more network resources than other services. Unlike data transfers which simply slow down or stop temporarily when the Internet becomes overloaded, video and audio transmission must continue or the picture and sound will be lost. As a result, a teleconference can overload slow Internet connections.

Recently, I was engaged in an audio teleconference and whiteboard session in which one of the participants used a low-speed Internet connection. Every so often, our colleague was cut off from the conversation for a short period of time. Eventually, my friend, who is a computer scientist, measured the network traffic and found the problem – our teleconference was completely saturating our friend's connection to the Internet. When the teleconference began again, we discussed ways to reduce the traffic. We decided that if we wanted to stay in contact, we would all have to talk less!

27

The Global Digital Library

Introduction

Previous chapters examine the services available on the Internet and show how each can be useful. More important, each chapter explains a basic concept such as hypermedia browsing or automated search, and shows how the concept is used in Internet services.

This chapter summarizes the discussion. It explains the digital library concept, and shows how Internet services provide a global digital library. In addition, the chapter provides perspective about Internet services, explains how each service can use others, and discusses the changes that can be expected.

A Cornucopia Of Services

Previous chapters explain many of the basic concepts that provide the foundation for Internet services. The concepts include menu browsing, used by *gopher*; hypermedia browsing, used by the *World Wide Web*; automated searching, used by *archie*, *veronica*, and *WAIS*; file transfer, used by *FTP*, and memo communication, used by *electronic mail* and *network news*. Although the list of example services seems diverse, it does not include all available Internet facilities or services. In fact, so many services exist that an individual would need months of effort to learn about all of them†. In summary:

---

†Appendix 2 contains a short summary of over a dozen additional services.

*The Internet contains many services that permit an individual to
search for information, transfer information, and interact with other
users. Internet services handle diverse forms of information, including text, sound, graphic images, real-time video, and multimedia combinations.*

New Services Appear Regularly

Although many services exist, the Internet continues to evolve. Programmers and
researchers continually devise and implement new services. Some of the most exciting
services have existed for only a short time (e.g., World Wide Web).

One cannot appreciate the Internet without understanding that:

*The Internet is still in its infancy. Internet researchers continue to
find new ways to store, communicate, reference, and access information.*

The continual change in available services and facilities has two important consequences. First, continual change means that any printed list of services becomes out-
of-date quickly. Second, continual change means that an Internet user always has an
opportunity to learn about new facilities.

Flexibility Permits Change

Why has the Internet been able to support such diverse services when other communication systems have not? The answer is simple: the basic technology the Internet
uses is more flexible than other technologies.

All the services described in this book communicate using the TCP/IP protocols
described in Chapters 11 through 17. TCP/IP allows computers to exchange pictures or
sound as easily as electronic mail. In fact, large computers that allow many users to run
programs simultaneously usually only have one copy of TCP/IP software that all services use. More important, many of the computers and Internet services that use
TCP/IP have been invented after TCP/IP; the design is flexible enough to accommodate
change. To summarize,

*The basic communication technology used in the Internet is extremely
flexible. It supports a wide variety of computers and services that had
not been invented when the technology was being developed.*

A Digital Library

The term *digital library* has been used to characterize a large storehouse of digital information accessible through computers. Like a traditional library, a digital library serves as an archive of knowledge that spans many topics. Like a newsstand, a digital library provides information that changes quickly. Like a telephone or television, a digital library provides access to events as they occur.

Because information can be stored in many forms, a digital library can contain text, sounds, graphic images, still and moving pictures, and conversations. In addition, a digital library can access information live as it occurs; the information need not be recorded. For example, a digital library can provide access to services that show the changes in a user's face, sample the current weather conditions at a given geographic location, measure current traffic on a highway, or find the current delay at an airport.

Card Catalogs And Search Tools

Although many libraries now use computers, traditional libraries used a file of small cards to record the names of books and periodicals. Known as a *card catalog*, the file contained two sets of cards, one ordered by author and the other ordered by title.

A library's card catalog served as its primary index mechanism. One could use the card catalog to find books or periodicals without searching the entire library. Furthermore, one could locate an item either from the title or from the name of the author.

A digital library has a much richer and varied set of index and search mechanisms. Computers make it possible to construct a system of menus that refer to files of information. Alternatively, a reference to a piece of information can be embedded in a hypermedia document. In addition, computers can search document contents. The point is:

> *Unlike a traditional library that used a card catalog, a digital library contains many index mechanisms and provides services that use the mechanisms to search for information. As a result, a given piece of information can be located several ways.*

Internet Services Can Be Integrated

The search mechanisms in a digital library can be combined and integrated to form a cross-reference between services. In fact, many of the services discussed in preceding chapters have been integrated, allowing one service to reference information available in another. For example, a user can access the archie service via TELNET, or can reach veronica through gopher. A World Wide Web document can contain a reference to a gopher menu. If a user selects an item that corresponds to a gopher menu, the software temporarily leaves WWW and uses gopher to present the menu. When the user finishes with gopher, the software returns to the WWW hypermedia document.

FTP directories can be integrated into gopher in the same way gopher menus are integrated into WWW. Once a particular FTP directory has been integrated, one can use gopher to list and retrieve the files. To a gopher user, the list of files appears as a gopher menu.

In another example of service integration, several sites provide FTP access via e-mail. To invoke the service, a user sends an e-mail message to a special address. The e-mail message contains the name of a file the user wishes to retrieve. When the message reaches the special address, a program uses FTP to retrieve the requested file, and sends the results back to the user in a second e-mail message. For example, sending the e-mail message *help* to:

ftpmail@dec.com

provides information on how one can access FTP from e-mail.

Such facilities are especially helpful for users who can send e-mail but do not have access to FTP. The idea is fundamental:

> *Although each Internet service has been designed independently, services can be combined in interesting ways. A given service can access information available from other services.*

Mr. Dewey, Where Are You?

For centuries, librarians struggled to organize archives of the world's knowledge. Should books be ordered by title, author, or subject? Should a library mix works of fiction and nonfiction, or keep them separate?

Melvil Dewey proposed a solution to the problem of organizing a library. He invented a universal numbering scheme, known as the *Dewey Decimal System*, that allows librarians to organize books by topic. The scheme was successful in standardizing the organization of libraries.

The Internet digital library desperately needs an analogous organization scheme. Although many tools have been developed, information is still organized in random ways. For example, consider gopher menus. In most organizations, individuals or small groups can decide to run a gopher server. Each group can choose the information to include and decide how menus will appear in its server; there is little uniformity. The result is chaos – the menus in one gopher server do not resemble the menus in another. After a user learns to navigate the menu system at one company, they must learn a new menu system when they contact another company. Similarly, the menu system at one university does not resemble the menu system at another. In short,

> *Because each computer on the Internet that offers a service can organize information however it chooses, there is little similarity among servers.*

Information In The Digital Library

We have focused on the services used to locate and access information in the digital library without considering details of the information itself. One might wonder, "exactly what information is available?" Or one might ask, "where are the servers that contain the most interesting information?" Such questions are equivalent to asking, "exactly what best-selling novel in my local library will I enjoy the most?" or, "which newspaper at my local newsstand contains headlines I will find most interesting?"

The answers to such questions depend on the individual who asks. Furthermore, the questions are extremely difficult to answer when they refer to a digital library because the information is dynamic. For example, some Internet discussions last a few minutes, others last for days, and a few archives persist for years. In a digital library, one must rely on automated search tools to find items of interest. One need only supply key words, phrases, or other descriptions to browsing and searching services to find information.

What Is The Internet?

This book begins with the question, "What is the Internet?" We can summarize the answer in a one-paragraph description:

> *The Internet is a wildly-successful, rapidly-growing, global digital library built on a remarkably flexible communication technology. The Internet digital library offers a variety of services used to create, browse, access, search, view, and communicate information on a diverse set of topics ranging from the results of scientific experiments to discussions of recreational activities. Information in the Internet digital library can be recorded in memos, organized into menus, stored as hypermedia documents, or stored in textual documents. In addition, information accessible through the digital library can consist of data, including audio and video, that is gathered, communicated, and delivered instantly without being stored. Furthermore, because the services have been integrated and cross-referenced, a user can move seamlessly from the information on one computer to information on another computer and from one access service to another.*

A Personal Note

At a recent meeting of the network committee at the university where I work, the library staff described how they were enthusiastically installing servers that will allow students, faculty, and outsiders to access the library through the Internet. I was amazed to hear librarians discuss e-mail, Mosaic, gopher, the World Wide Web, and card catalogs on the network.

As I sat there listening to the discussion, I suddenly realized that the world had changed dramatically in a few years, and the change will continue. Librarians understand that in the future, knowledge will be stored in digital form, transmitted over networks, and indexed by computer. They expect that the next generation of students will use computer networks to locate and access information. Librarians are not merely experimenting with new technologies; they are preparing for a digital future. In a few years, libraries as we know them will start to disappear, and information will be found on ''the Net.''

Appendix 1

Example Netnews Newsgroups

Introduction

Chapter *19* discusses the Internet bulletin board service known as Network News. This appendix lists examples of newsgroups that existed in 1994. It does not present an exhaustive catalog because new groups appear frequently. Instead, it gives a sample of the wide range of topics found in network news.

Name Of Newsgroup	Description Of Contents†
alc.alc.bier.pils	Discussion about Pils beer
alc.alc.c2h5oh	General discussion on ethanol
alt.abortion.inequity	Paternal obligations of failing to abort unwanted child
alt.abuse.recovery	Helping victims of abuse to recover
alt.adoption	For those involved with or contemplating adoption
alt.agriculture.misc	All about cultivating the soil and raising animals
alt.alien.visitors	Space Aliens on Earth! Abduction!
alt.angst	Anxiety in the modern world
alt.animation.warner-bros	Discussions of Warner Brothers' cartoons

†Most of the descriptions were written by Professor Gene Spafford of Purdue University; many are intented to be humorous.

alt.appalachian	Appalachian region awareness, events, and culture
alt.aquaria	The aquarium & related as a hobby
alt.astrology	Twinkle, twinkle, little planet
alt.autos.antique	Discussion of all facets of older automobiles
alt.backrubs	Lower...to the right...aaaah!
alt.books.technical	Discussion of technical books
alt.boomerang	The angular throwing club
alt.business.multi-level	Multi-level (network) marketing businesses
alt.celebrities	Discussion of any celebrities, past or present
alt.censorship	Discussion about restricting free speech or free press
alt.child-support	Raising children in a split family
alt.chinchilla	The nature of chinchilla farming in America today
alt.chinese.text	Postings in Chinese; Chinese language software
alt.comedy.british	Discussion of British comedy in a variety of media
alt.comedy.firesgn-thtre	Firesign Theatre in all its flaming glory
alt.comics.superman	No one knows it is also alt.clark.kent
alt.conspiracy.jfk	The Kennedy assassination
alt.cult-movies	Movies with a cult following
alt.culture.internet	The culture(s) of the Internet
alt.current-events.bosnia	The strife of Bosnia-Herzegovina
alt.dads-rights	Rights of fathers trying to win custody in court
alt.discrimination	Quotas, affirmative action, bigotry, persecution
alt.education.disabled	Education for people with physical or mental disabilities
alt.elvis.king	For fans of the King
alt.fan.blues-brothers	Anything you ever wanted to know about the Blues Brothers
alt.fan.dave_barry	Electronic fan club for humorist Dave Barry
alt.fan.holmes	Elementary, my dear Watson - the name of the newsgroup reveals all the clues
alt.fan.howard-stern	Fans of the abrasive radio & TV personality

alt.fan.letterman	One of the top 10 reasons to get the alt groups
alt.fan.monty-python	Electronic fan club for those wacky Brits
alt.fan.ren-and-stimpy	For folks who couldn't find alt.tv.ren-n-stimpy
alt.fan.tolkien	Mortal Men doomed to die
alt.folklore.college	Collegiate humor
alt.folklore.herbs	Discussion of all aspects of herbs and their uses
alt.games.mk	Struggling in Mortal Kombat!
alt.games.sf2	The video game Street Fighter 2
alt.good.news	A place for good news
alt.great-lakes	Discussions of the Great Lakes and the adjacent area
alt.guitar.bass	Bass guitars
alt.hindu	The Hindu religion (Moderated)
alt.hotrod	High speed automobiles (Moderated)
alt.magic	For discussion about stage magic
alt.mothergoose	Nursery rhymes
alt.music.jewish	Jewish music
alt.music.tmbg	They Might Be Giants
alt.org.food-not-bombs	Activism for the homeless
alt.out-of-body	Out-of-body experiences
alt.parents-teens	Parent-teenager relationships
alt.personals.ads	Personals (Geek seeks Dweeb. Object: low-level interfacing)
alt.politics.drinking-age	Regarding age restrictions for alcohol use
alt.politics.libertarian	The libertarian ideology
alt.politics.usa.constitution	U.S. Constitutional politics
alt.politics.usa.republican	Discussions of the USA Republican Party
alt.president.clinton	Will the CIA undermine his efforts?
alt.quotations	Quotations, quips, lines seen in electronic mail, witticisms
alt.rock-n-roll.classic	Classic rock, both the music and its marketing
alt.rock-n-roll.oldies	Discussion of rock and roll music from 1950-1970
alt.rush-limbaugh	Fans of the conservative activist radio talk-show host
alt.satellite.tv.europe	All about European satellite tv
alt.save.the.earth	Environmentalist causes
alt.sex	Postings of a prurient nature
alt.skate-board	Discussion of all aspects of skateboarding

alt.smokers	Puffing on tobacco
alt.society.conservatism	Social, cultural, and political conservatism
alt.society.generation-x	Lifestyles of those born from 1960 through early-1970s
alt.sport.officiating	Problems related to officiating athletic contests
alt.sports.baseball.phila-phillies	Philadelphia Phillies baseball
alt.sports.football.pro.wash-redskins	Washington Redskins football
alt.supermodels	Discussing famous & beautiful models
alt.support	Dealing with emotional situations and experiences
alt.support.arthritis	A support group for arthritis sufferers
alt.support.cancer	Emotional aid for people with cancer
alt.surfing	Riding the ocean waves
alt.tasteless.jokes	Sometimes insulting rather than disgusting or humorous
alt.tv.beavis-n-butthead	Uh huh huh huh uh uh huh uh huh
alt.tv.bh90210	Fans of the TV show "Beverly Hills 90210"
alt.tv.la-law	For the folks out in LA-Law land
alt.tv.mash	Nothing like a good comedy about war and dying
alt.tv.muppets	Miss Piggy on the tube
alt.tv.prisoner	The Prisoner television series from many years ago
alt.tv.seinfeld	A funny guy
alt.tv.simpsons	Don't have a cow, man!
alt.tv.talkshows.late	Discussion of late night talk shows
alt.tv.twin-peaks	Discussion about the popular (and unusual) TV show
alt.usage.english	English grammar, word usages, and related topics
alt.war.civil.usa	Discussion of the U.S. Civil War period (1861-1865)
alt.war.vietnam	Discussion of all aspects of the Vietnam War
aus.books	Australian discussion of books
austin.forsale	Items for sale in Austin, TX
az.general	Items of general interest in Arizona
ba.bicycles	Bicycling issues specific to the San Francisco Bay Area
ba.jobs.offered	Job Postings in the Bay Area
ba.weather	Bay Area National Weather Service updates

bc.general	Items of general interest in British Columbia
bionet.biology.tropical	Discussions about tropical biology
bionet.molbio.hiv	Discussions about the molecular biology of HIV
bit.listserv.blindnws	Blindness Issues and Discussions (Moderated)
bit.listserv.euearn-l	Computers in Eastern Europe
bln.comp.unix	Fragen & Antworten zu Unix-Systemen
bln.general	General discussions in Berlin, Germany
brasil.politica	Discussion of Brazilian and World Politics
ca.driving	California freeways and backroads
ca.earthquakes	What's shakin' in California
can.general	Items of interest to Canadians
can.schoolnet.socsci.jr	SchoolNet Social Sciences for Canadian elementary students
ch.general	Misc. items of interest to Swiss newsgroups reader
chi.eats	Group for discussion of restaurants in or near Chicago
chile.chile-l	Miscellaneous conversations that relate to Chile
clari.biz.commodity	Commodity news and price reports (Moderated)
clari.biz.top	Top business news (Moderated)
clari.feature.mike_royko	Chicago opinion columnist Mike Royko (Moderated)
clari.local.florida.briefs	Local news Briefs (Moderated)
clari.local.nebraska.briefs	Local news Briefs (Moderated)
clari.news.arts	Stage, drama & other fine arts (Moderated)
clari.news.aviation	Aviation industry and mishaps (Moderated)
clari.news.issues.family	Family or child abuse (Moderated)
clari.news.labor.strike	Strikes (Moderated)
clari.news.law.drugs	Drug related crimes & drug stories (Moderated)
clari.news.military	Military equipment, people & issues (Moderated)
clari.news.urgent	Major breaking stories of the day (Moderated)
clari.sports.baseball.games	Baseball games & box scores (Moderated)

clari.sports.football.college	College football coverage (Moderated)
clari.tw.stocks	Regular reports on computer and technology stock prices (Moderated)
comp.apps.spreadsheets	Spreadsheets on various platforms
comp.laser-printers	Laser printers, hardware and software (Moderated)
comp.protocols.kermit	Info about the Kermit package (Moderated)
comp.sys.ibm.pc.games.action	Arcade-style games on PCs
comp.sys.ibm.pc.games.flight-sim	Flight simulators on PCs
comp.sys.laptops	Laptop (portable) computers
comp.sys.mac.hardware	Discussions of Macintosh hardware
courts.usa.federal.supreme	U.S. Supreme Court (Moderated)
dc.smithsonian	Smithsonian related events in the Washington, DC area
de.admin.news.groups	Diskussionen ueber (neue) Newsgruppen
dfw.eats	Dining in Dallas/Fort Worth
dk.jobs	Employment available in Denmark
finet.helsinki.puhe	Keskusteluryhm{ p{{kaupunkiseudun asioille
fl.travel	Travel within Florida
fnet.general	Items of general interest in France
fr.announce.divers	Annonces diverse (pas petites annonces)
ga.atl-braves	Discussions about the Atlanta Braves
houston.singles	Singles for Houston, Texas
k12.chat.junior	Casual conversation for students in grades 6-8
k12.chat.senior	Casual conversation for students in high school
k12.chat.teacher	Casual conversation for teachers of grades K-12
ks.misc	Misc postings in Kansas
ky.motorcycles	Motorcycling in Kentucky
la.wanted	Things wanted in Los Angeles, CA
lon.misc	Miscellaneous news from London, England
misc.consumers	Consumer interests/product reviews
misc.fitness	Physical fitness, exercise, etc
misc.forsale.computers.mac	Apple Macintosh related computer items
misc.invest	Investments and the handling of money
misc.rural	Devoted to issues concerning rural living
misc.taxes	Tax laws and advice

ne.housing	Housing wanted or available in New England
nj.weather	Weather in New Jersey
nlnet.taal	Discussies over de Nederlandse taal
oh.k12	Elementary education in Ohio
ott.events	Seminars and the like near Ottawa, Canada
pdaxs.ads.cars.service	People who work on cars (Pasadena)
pgh.apartments	Rental housing in the Pittsburgh area
phl.dance	Dance events, reviews and discussion for Philadelphia
rec.arts.bonsai	Dwarf trees and shrubbery
rec.arts.comics.marketplace	The exchange of comics and comic related items
rec.arts.comics.xbooks	The Mutant Universe of Marvel Comics
rec.arts.dance	Any aspects of dance not covered in another newsgroup
rec.arts.poems	For the posting of poems
rec.audio.car	Discussions of automobile audio systems
rec.aviation.soaring	All aspects of sailplanes and hanggliders
rec.backcountry	Activities in the Great Outdoors
rec.bicycles.racing	Bicycle racing techniques, rules and results
rec.birds	Hobbyists interested in bird watching
rec.crafts.quilting	All about quilts and other quilted items
rec.food.recipes	Recipes for interesting food and drink (Moderated)
rec.games.chess	Chess & computer chess
rec.games.video.arcade	Discussions about coin-operated video games
rec.gardens	Gardening, methods and results
rec.guns	Discussions about guns and firearms (Moderated)
rec.humor.funny	Funny jokes (in the moderator's opinion) (Moderated)
rec.kites	Talk about kites and kiting
rec.music.beatles	Postings about the Fab Four and their music
rec.music.classical	Discussions about classical music
rec.org.mensa	Talking with members of the high IQ society Mensa
rec.parks.theme	Entertainment theme parks
rec.pets	Pets, pet care, and household animals in general

rec.puzzles.crosswords	Making and playing gridded word puzzles
rec.radio.cb	Citizen-band radio
rec.roller-coaster	Roller coasters and other amusement park rides
rec.running	Running for enjoyment, sport, and exercise
rec.scouting	Scouting youth organizations around the world
rec.sport.football.pro	US-style professional football
rec.sport.olympics	All aspects of the Olympic Games
rec.travel	Traveling all over the world
rec.woodworking	Hobbyists interested in woodworking
sci.archaeology	Studying antiquities of the world
sci.energy.hydrogen	Hydrogen as an alternative fuel
sci.med.nursing	Nursing questions and discussion
sci.space.news	Announcements of space-related news items (Moderated)
seattle.general	Items of general interest in Seattle, Washington
soc.couples	Discussions for couples (cf. soc.singles)
soc.couples.intercultural	Inter-cultural and inter-racial relationships
soc.culture.african.american	Discussions about Afro-American issues
soc.culture.argentina	All about life in Argentina
soc.culture.caribbean	Life in the Caribbean
soc.culture.esperanto	The neutral international language Esperanto
soc.culture.filipino	Group about the Filipino culture
soc.culture.hongkong	Discussions pertaining to Hong Kong
soc.culture.italian	The Italian people and their culture
soc.culture.japan	Everything Japanese, except the Japanese language
soc.culture.jewish	Jewish culture & religion (cf. talk.politics.mideast)
soc.culture.mexican	Discussion of Mexico's society
soc.culture.new-zealand	Discussion of New Zealand
soc.culture.taiwan	Discussion about things Taiwanese
soc.feminism	Discussion of feminism and feminist issues (Moderated)
soc.history	Discussions of things historical
soc.penpals	In search of net.friendships
soc.politics	Political problems, systems, solutions (Moderated)
soc.religion.christian.bible-study	Examining the Holy Bible (Moderated)

soc.religion.eastern	Discussions of Eastern religions (Moderated)
soc.religion.islam	Discussions of the Islamic faith (Moderated)
soc.roots	Discussion of genealogy and genealogical matters
soc.singles	Newsgroup for single people and their activities
soc.veterans	Social issues relating to military veterans
soc.women	Issues related to women, their problems and relationships
srg.tvdrs	Swiss TV related info; sources: ELSA and SRG
stgt.general	Topics of general interest in Stuttgart, Germany
stl.jobs	Job information in St. Louis
su.market.textbooks	Classified ads for textbooks at Stanford University
talk.abortion	All sorts of discussions and arguments about abortion
talk.bizarre	The unusual, bizarre, curious, and often stupid
talk.origins	Evolution versus creationism (sometimes heated)
talk.politics.drugs	The politics of drug issues
talk.rumors	For the posting of rumors
tn.general	Items of general interest in Tennessee
tnn.horoscope	Weekly fortune telling (Moderated)
triangle.talks	Seminars and conferences in North Carolina
tx.forsale	Items for sale in Texas
uk.environment	United Kingdom environmental issues
zer.t-netz.bhp.texte	Interessantes uebers Telefong

Appendix 2

Example Internet Services

Introduction

Several chapters examine individual services available on the Internet, and show how each can be useful. More important, each chapter that focuses on a service explains a basic concept such as hypermedia browsing or automated search that has been used to construct Internet services.

This appendix takes a different approach. Instead of explaining one concept or one service, it describes several Internet services and facilities without giving details. The list is not meant to include all services or to suggest that these services are among the best. Rather, it provides the reader with some intuition about the diversity and variety of services, and shows that they range from trivial to sophisticated.

InterNIC

InterNIC stands for Internet Network Information Center. The InterNIC is a group of people and computers that provide information about the Internet, the software and services available, and the groups who supply services. Currently, the InterNIC is operated by AT&T, and can be reached via telephone:

$$1 - 800 - 444 - 4345$$

or e-mail:

$$\text{mailserv @ ds . internic . net}$$

To receive further information on how to access the InterNIC via e-mail, send an e-mail message that consists of the word "help".

Astra

Another document retrieval service, *astra* consists of servers that accept database queries expressed in a form defined by *astra*. Each *astra* server knows about one or more databases and the specific query language required to access each database. When it receives a request, an *astra* server translates the request into the appropriate query language before sending it to an underlying database. Thus, users can access a variety of database systems without learning multiple query languages.

Finger

The *finger* program contacts a server on a remote machine to obtain information about a specific user or all users on that machine. Usually, when someone invokes *finger*, they supply the identifier of a user:

finger userid@computername

To find out about all users on a given computer, one omits the userid portion:

finger @computername

Although *finger* was originally designed to provide information about users, it has been extended to permit arbitrary programs to answer a request. Thus, using *finger* to locate a given userid at a given computer may produce unexpected results. For example if computer *somewhere.com* has a weather service, the owner may choose to permit Internet users to access the service using:

finger weather@somewhere.com

Internet Relay Chat

The *Internet Relay Chat* (*IRC*) service provides a way for many users to communicate about a given topic. Each communication occurs on a separate "channel." A user who creates a channel chooses a topic and specifies whether the channel is open to anyone or restricted to the set of people specified by the channel creator. A user can request a list of the IRC channels currently in progress, and can choose to join one of the channels. When a user joins an IRC channel, the user enters a nickname that IRC uses to identify the user to others (e.g., *dancer* or *bigshot*). Users often choose nicknames that disguise their identity. For example, a woman might choose *computerman*.

A participant receives each line of text that another participant enters along with the participant's nickname. Thus, a participant who enters a line of text knows that all other participants will receive a copy of the text on their screens.

LISTSERV

The *LISTSERV* service, which originated on BITNET, uses a program to maintain electronic mailing lists. Using LISTSERV, a user can obtain a description of a mailing list, join a mailing list, or leave a mailing list. A user sends an e-mail message to the LISTSERV program, which interprets requests in the message and sends a reply. LIST-SERV can be reached on a variety of computers including:

listserv @ bitnic . bit . net

To obtain more information on how to use LISTSERV, send an e-mail message that consists of the word "help".

Mud

Mud stands for *Multi-User Dungeon*. Mud allows a group of users to establish a game-playing session analogous to the way a group can establish a teleconference. After a user joins a mud game, they explore a large labyrinth, and possibly, encounter other users. Mud uses text, not graphics. The computer describes the scene and waits for the player to enter instructions. Mud may say, for example, *You are standing in a large, dark hall with a door on the left.* The user can direct the computer to open the door, after which the computer describes the scene visible through the doorway.

Netfind

Netfind is a simple service that uses *finger* and e-mail to locate a person. A user enters the name of an individual and information about the organization for which the individual works. *Netfind* consults a list of organizations to obtain the address of a computer at the organization, and then invokes the *finger* service at that computer to obtain information about the individual.

NFS

Although not designed as an Internet service, the *Network File System* (*NFS*) has been used with the Internet. It allows a computer to read or write data into files on remote computers. The major difference between NFS and FTP arises from the way they handle transfers. FTP copies an entire file; NFS accesses pieces of a file as needed. Thus, NFS allows a user to examine the first few lines of a large file without copying the entire file.

Ping

When one makes a telephone call, the phone system plays tones to tell the caller whether the call is proceeding, the remote phone is ringing, or the line is busy. By contrast, the Internet does not inform a sender immediately about the status of communication. If a destination machine cannot be reached, a program may try for several minutes before reporting the problem. Meanwhile, a user can become frustrated. Users run *ping* to test whether a remote computer is alive and reachable via the Internet; *ping* merely reports whether the specified computer is alive†. Computers usually respond to ping instantly, even when they are so heavily loaded that they respond to other requests slowly.

Ph or Cso

The *ph* program originated at the *Computing Services Organization* of the University of Illinois as a way to find the telephone number and e-mail address of a student or faculty member. Several client programs exist. Each requires a user to enter a person's name, and then *ph* looks up that name in the university's database.

Other universities and a few companies have acquired and installed the *ph* software for use at their organization. Sometimes, sites mistakenly refer to the software as the *cso* program (the initials of the organization that designed it) or the *qi* program (the name of the server software).

Prospero

Prospero is the name of a facility that can be used to provide the appearance of a global file system that spans many computers. Using *prospero*, a user can establish folders (sometimes called directories) that contain references to files that reside on several computers. Thus, *prospero* can be used to organize files from many computers.

Talk

Talk provides interaction between a pair of users. After two users agree to communicate, the *talk* service establishes a connection between their computers, and divides their display screens in half. Everything a user types on the keyboard appears in the upper half of the user's screen and in the lower half of the remote screen. When a user types more than half a screen, the talk service moves the cursor back to the first line. Thus, each user appears to control one-half of the screen. Talk sends each keystroke as soon as a user presses the key, so two people can read instantly what the other person types.

---

†Some versions of *ping* also report the number of milliseconds that elapse before a response arrives.

Traceroute

A user who is interested in the structure of the Internet can run the *traceroute* program. Given the name of a remote computer, *traceroute* prints the list of Internet routers along the path from the local computer to the remote computer. Although *traceroute* was intended for use when installing and maintaining Internet connections, it can be interesting to see how many routers separate your computer from a given destination.

Trickle

The *trickle* service provides access to FTP files through e-mail. A user places a request for a file in an electronic mail message and sends the message to:

trickle @ computer

The *trickle* service obtains the file, and sends the results back to the user in an e-mail message.

Whois

The *whois* program contacts a server that has basic information about the networks that comprise the Internet and the names of people who maintain them. For example, the request:

whois harvard

produces a list of all networks at Harvard University and at companies that have *Harvard* in their name.

X Window system

Personal computer users are familiar with conventional window software that divides a computer display into rectangular regions called windows and permits programs to display text or graphics in each window. A user can move windows on the screen, and one window can cover all or parts of others. The *X Window System* provides one additional feature because it allows a remote computer to control a particular region on the user's display. Thus, a user can invoke a service on a remote computer and interact with the service through a window on the local computer.

X.500

X.500 is a service designed by the International Telecommunications Union (formerly CCITT) to allow a user to find information about companies or other users (e.g., an e-mail address or telephone number). Some experimental *X.500* services are available on the Internet.

Appendix 3

Glossary Of Internet Terms

Although learning any new terminology can be difficult, learning the Internet terminology can be daunting. The terms used to describe Internet services, network technologies, and specific computer programs make little or no sense to a beginner. Internet terminology combines terms from computer networking, business, government, and commercial products.

This glossary provides a concise definition of terms used throughout the Internet. It focuses on widely-accepted terminology and avoids terms that have been defined by commercial vendors for their products. Although a brief definition cannot provide a complete explanation of a term, readers who stumble across puzzling terminology will find the definitions sufficient to refresh their memory. The index provides references to pages in the text that provide further explanation.

10Base-T
A particular wiring scheme for an Ethernet LAN. *T* abbreviates *twisted pair*, the type of wire used to connect a computer to the network.

A-to-D converter
Abbreviation for *Analog-to-Digital converter*.

ACK
Abbreviation for *acknowledgement*.

acknowledgement

(ACK) A response sent by a receiver to indicate successful reception of information. In a packet-switching network, an acknowledgement is a packet returned when data arrives. Thus, when two computers exchange information, data packets travel in one direction and acknowledgements travel in the opposite direction.

address

A numeric value assigned to a computer much like a telephone number is assigned to a home. When a packet of data travels from one computer to another, the packet contains the addresses of the two computers.

Advanced Networks and Services

(ANS) A company that owns and operates ANSNET, a major Wide Area Network in the Internet.

Advanced Research Projects Agency

(ARPA) The U.S. government agency that funded the ARPANET and later, the Internet. For several years, ARPA was named *DARPA*.

American Standard Code for Information Interchange

(ASCII) A character code used on the Internet. ASCII assigns each letter, digit, and punctuation symbol a unique sequence of binary digits. When textual data is transferred across the Internet, it is represented in ASCII.

analog

Any representation of information in which the amount of a substance or signal is proportional to the information represented.

Analog-to-Digital converter

(A-to-D converter) An electronic component that converts an analog electrical signal into a sequence of numbers.

anonymous FTP

Use of the special login *anonymous* to obtain access to public files through the FTP service.

ANSNET

A major Wide Area Network that forms part of the Internet. ANSNET is owned by Advanced Networks and Services.

archie

An automated search service available on the Internet that finds all files with a given name. The name *archie* is short for *archive*.

ARPA

Abbreviation for *Advanced Research Projects Agency*.

ARPANET

An early long haul network funded by ARPA. It served from 1969 through 1990 as the basis for early networking research, and as a central backbone network during development of the Internet.

ASCII

Abbreviation for *American Standard Code For Information Interchange*.

Asynchronous Transfer Mode

(ATM) The name of a particular network technology designed to make it easy to build high-speed hardware. ATM is interesting because it can be used as the basis for LANs or WANs.

ATM

Abbreviation for *Asynchronous Transfer Mode*.

audio teleconference

A service that allows a group of users to exchange audio information over the Internet similar to a telephone conference call. Each participant's computer must have a microphone and earphones (or speaker).

automated search service

Any service that locates information without requiring a user to make decisions or select from menus. Automated search services either search titles or complete documents.

backbone network

Used to refer to a central network to which many routers connect. In the Internet, backbone networks use Wide Area Network technology. Individual corporations also refer to their central network as a backbone; such backbones may be LANs.

bandwidth

The capacity of a network, usually measured in bits per second. Network systems need higher bandwidth for audio or video than for e-mail or other services.

baud

Literally, the number of times per second the signal can change on a transmission line. Usually, the baud rate equals the number of bits per second that can be transferred.

best-effort delivery

Used to describe computer networks in which congestion can cause the network to discard packets. TCP/IP software can use best-effort delivery networks because the software detects missing packets and retransmits them.

binary digit

(bit) Either a *0* or *1*. The Internet uses binary digits to represent information, including: audio, video, and text.

binary file

Although all files are encoded in binary, the term is used to refer to nontext files. The distinction is especially pertinent to FTP.

bit

Abbreviation for *binary digit*.

bits per second

(bps) Literally, a measure of the rate of data transmission. Usually, the measure refers to the capacity of a network (see *bandwidth*).

BITNET

(Because It's Time NETwork) A network developed at City University of New York. BITNET permits users to exchange e-mail and files, but does not provide other Internet services.

bookmark

A facility in the gopher service that can record the location of a particular menu, making it possible to return to the menu later. Compare to *hotlist*.

bps

Abbreviation for *bits per second*.

broadcast

A packet delivery mechanism that delivers a copy of a given packet to all computers attached to a network. Compare to *unicast* and *multicast*.

browsing

The act of looking through information by repeatedly scanning and selecting. An Internet browsing service presents a list of menu items or a page of information. After the user reads the information and selects an item, the service follows the reference and retrieves new information.

btw

An abbreviation of of *by the way* used in electronic communication.

bulletin board service

A service that permits one person to post a message for others to read. Each bulletin board contains discussion of a single topic. A bulletin board is sometimes called a *computer conference*.

carrier

A steady electrical signal or tone that is used by a modem to encode information for transmission across a communication line or a telephone connection. A carrier is the tone heard when a computer uses a modem to communicate over a telephone connection.

Cc

(*Carbon Copy*) A line used in e-mail headers to specify additional recipients.

Central Processing Unit

(*CPU*) The electronic component in a computer that performs all arithmetic and logical operations.

checksum

A checksum is a small integer used to detect whether errors occur when transmitting data from one machine to another. Protocol software such as TCP computes a checksum and appends it to a packet when transmitting. Upon reception, the protocol software verifies the contents of the packet by recomputing the checksum and comparing to the value sent.

client

A program that uses the Internet to contact a remote server. Usually, a separate client program is needed for each Internet service.

client-server computing

The interaction between two programs when they communicate across a network. A program at one site sends a request to a program at another site and awaits a response. The requesting program is called a *client*; the program satisfying the request is called the *server*.

collapsed backbone

A single, large router used in place of a backbone Local Area Network and connected routers. The motivation for choosing a collapsed backbone arises because it costs less than the traditional design.

CompuServe

A commercial organization that offers network services primarily through telephone connections. CompuServe subscribers can exchange e-mail with users who have computers attached to the Internet.

computer conference

Communication among a set of individuals that uses the computer. Various computer conference services provide text, audio, or video communication. Also see *bulletin board service.*

computer network

A hardware mechanism that computers use to communicate. A network is classified as a Local Area Network or Wide Area Network, depending on the hardware capabilities.

connection

When two programs communicate using TCP, the TCP software on the two machines forms a connection across the Internet similar to a telephone call.

connectionless

Used to describe any network system that allows the sender to transfer a block of data to a specified address without first establishing a path to the destination. The Internet Protocol, IP, uses connectionless technology.

CPU

Abbreviation for *Central Processing Unit*

CSNET

(*Computer Science NETwork*) An early network that offered e-mail and Internet connections to Computer Science Departments in colleges and universities. Initially funded by the National Science Foundation, CSNET later became self-sufficient.

D-to-A converter

Abbreviation for Digital-to-Analog converter.

DARPA

(*Defense Advanced Research Projects Agency*) Former name of ARPA.

datagram

Synonym for *IP datagram.*

Defense Advanced Research Projects Agency

(*DARPA*) Former name of the *Advanced Research Projects Agency.*

demodulation

The process of extracting information from a modulated signal that arrives over a transmission line or telephone connection. Demodulation usually occurs in a device called a modem. Also see *modulation* and *carrier*.

demodulator

The electronic device in a modem that decodes an incoming signal and extracts data. See *modulator*.

destination address

A numeric value in a packet that specifies the computer to which the packet has been sent. The destination address in a packet traveling across the Internet is the IP address of the destination computer.

digital

Any technology that uses numbers to represent information. A computer is inherently digital because it represents keystrokes, pictures, text, and sounds using numbers.

digital library

A large collection of information that has been stored in digital form. A digital library can include documents, images, sounds, and information gathered from ongoing events (e.g., continuous pictures from a weather satellite).

Digital-to-Analog converter

(*D-to-A converter*) An electronic device that converts a sequence of numbers into an analog electrical signal. A D-to-A-Converter is needed to change the numbers on a compact disc into sounds.

directory

A collection of files and other directories. Some computer systems use the term *folder*.

distributed computing

A term used to characterize computations that involve more than one computer. In the broadest sense of the term, each Internet service uses distributed computing.

DNS

Abbreviation for *Domain Name System*.

domain name

The name assigned to a computer on the Internet. A single computer's name can contain multiple strings separated by periods (e.g., computer1.company.com). Domain names often end in *.com* or *.edu*.

Domain Name System

(DNS) The Internet service used to look up a computer's name and find the computer's IP address.

dotted decimal

A notation used to specify an IP address. Dotted decimal is so named because it represents an address as four small, decimal integers separated by periods. Internally, a computer stores each IP address in binary – dotted decimal notation is used to make addresses easier for humans to enter or read.

e-mail

Abbreviation for *electronic mail*.

e-mail address

Each user is assigned an electronic mailbox address. To send e-mail, a user must enter the e-mail address of the recipient. On the Internet, e-mail addresses usually have the form *person@computer*.

e-mail alias

A shorthand for an e-mail address used to allow a user to send electronic mail without remembering or typing a long e-mail address. Most e-mail software permits a user to define many aliases.

EARN

(European Academic and Research Network) A network using BITNET technology to connect universities and research labs in Europe.

EBONE

(European backBONE) The Wide Area Network facilities that interconnect many European countries to one another and to the Internet.

electronic bulletin board service

Synonym for *bulletin board service*.

electronic mail

(e-mail) A service that permits one to send a memo to another person, a group, or a computer program. Electronic mail software also permits one to reply to a memo.

Ethernet

A popular Local Area Network technology invented at the Xerox Corporation. An Ethernet consists of a cable to which computers attach. Each computer needs hardware known as an interface board to connect the computer to the Ethernet.

exponential growth

A term mathematicians use to describe the growth of the Internet. The Internet has doubled in size approximately each year.

FAQ

(*Frequently Asked Questions*) A document that contains questions and answers regarding a specific topic, technology, or Internet service. Many mailing lists and newsgroups have a FAQ document that helps beginners understand the purpose of the discussion and avoids having the questions appear repeatedly.

FDDI

(*Fiber Distributed Data Interface*) A particular type of local area network that uses fiber optic connections. Although an FDDI LAN runs at higher speed than other LANs, it costs more.

fiber

A thin, flexible glass fiber used to transmit information using pulses of light. A fiber can span longer distances than an electrical cable.

file server

A program running on a computer that provides access to files on that computer. The term is often applied loosely to computers that run file server programs.

File Transfer Protocol

(*FTP*) The Internet service used to transfer a copy of a file from one computer to another. After contacting a remote computer, a user must enter a login name and password; some FTP servers allow access to public files through the special login *anonymous*.

finger

An Internet service used to determine which users are currently logged into a particular computer or to find out more about an individual user.

flame

A slang term used in electronic communication to mean *an emotional or inflammatory note, often written in response to another message.* The word is sometimes used as a verb, meaning *to write an inflammatory message.*

flow control

Control of the rate at which a computer sends data to another computer. On the Internet, TCP software provides flow control, and makes it possible for a fast computer to communicate with a slow computer.

folder

A synonym for *directory*.

Frequently Asked Questions

See FAQ.

FTP

Abbreviation for *File Transfer Protocol*.

FYA

An abbreviation of *For Your Amusement* used in electronic communication.

FYI

An abbreviation of *For Your Information* used in electronic communication.

gopher

The name of an Internet browsing service in which all information is organized into a hierarchy of menus. Gopher displays a menu on the screen and allows the user to select an item. The selection either leads to a file of information or to another menu.

homepage

A page of information accessible through the World Wide Web. The page can contain a mixture of graphics and text, and can include embedded references to other such pages. Usually each user and each organization has a separate homepage.

hop count

A measure of distance in packet switching networks. If a packet must travel through *N* additional routers on its trip from its source to its destination, the destination is said to lie *N* hops away from the source.

host

A synonym for *user's computer*. Technically, each computer connected to the Internet is classified as a host or a router.

hostname

The name assigned to a computer. See *domain name*.

hotlist

A facility used with the Mosaic program that can record the location of a particular page of information, making it possible to return to the page quickly. Compare to *bookmark*.

HTML

(HyperText Markup Language) The computer language used to specify the contents and format of a hypermedia document in World Wide Web (e.g., a homepage). Users are unlikely to encounter HTML; it is an internal detail.

HTTP

(HyperText Transport Protocol) The protocol used to access a World Wide Web document. A user may encounter the term HTTP in a Uniform Resource Locator.

hub

An electronic device that connects to several computers and replaces a LAN, usually an Ethernet. Hubs are used with 10base-T.

hypermedia

An information storage system in which each page of information can contain embedded references to images, sounds, and other pages of information. When a user selects an item, the hypermedia system follows the associated reference. See World Wide Web.

hypertext

A system for storing pages of textual information that each contain embedded references to other pages of information.

IAB

Abbreviation for *Internet Architecture Board*.

IETF

Abbreviation for *Internet Engineering Task Force*.

IMHO

An abbreviation of *In My Humble Opinion* used in electronic communication.

information browsing service

A service that permits a user to browse information by repeatedly scanning and selecting. The service presents a list of menu items or a page of information. After the user reads the information and selects an item, the service follows the reference and retrieves new information.

information superhighway

A term used by the popular press to refer to the emerging national information infrastructure in the United States. The Internet is the first part of the information infrastructure, which is sometimes called the *information highway.*

infrastructure

A service or facility that is fundamental to a society. Examples include systems for delivering food and water, transportation facilities, and telephones.

integrated circuit

A small, complex electronic device that contains many transistors. For example, the central processing unit in a computer is usually built on a single integrated circuit. Informally, an integrated circuit is called a *chip.*

International Telecommunication Union, Telecommunications

(ITUT) An international organization that sets standards for interconnection of telephone equipment. In the past, many organizations responsible for networking in Europe have followed ITUT recommendations. (Formerly, the CCITT.)

Internet

The collection of networks and routers that use the TCP/IP protocol suite and function as a single, large network. The Internet reaches government, commercial, and educational organizations around the world.

Internet address

A number. Each computer attached to the Internet is assigned a unique IP address. Software uses the address to identify the intended recipient when it sends a message. An Internet address is also called an *IP address.*

Internet Architecture Board

(IAB) A group of people who set policy and standards for TCP/IP and the connected Internet.

Internet Engineering Task Force

(IETF) A group of people responsible for designing and testing new technologies for TCP/IP and the Internet. The IETF is part of the IAB organization.

Internet Protocol

See IP.

Internet Multicasting Service

The service that sends audio information across the Internet like a radio station.

internetworking

A term used to refer to planning, building, testing, and using internet systems.

Internet Relay Chat

(*IRC*) A service that allows groups of users to communicate using a keyboard. Each group of users creates a channel and sends messages to it. Each active participant for a given channel receives a copy of each message sent to the channel.

Internet Society

A non-profit organization established to encourage exploration of the Internet.

InterNIC

(*Internet Network Information Center*) An organization that supplies information about the Internet, the organizations that provide Internet connectivity, and other documentation.

IP

(*Internet Protocol*) Literally, a specification for the format of packets computers use when they communicate across the Internet. In practice, the term usually refers to the IP software that a computer must run to communicate on the Internet.

IP address

A synonym for *Internet address*.

IP datagram

A packet of data sent across the Internet. Each IP datagram contains the address of the computer that sent it, the IP address of the computer to which it has been sent, and the data being sent.

IPng

Abbreviation for *Internet Protocol: the Next Generation*. The term is used to refer to the successor of IP being planned by the IETF.

IRC

Abbreviation for *Internet Relay Chat*.

ITUT

Abbreviation for *International Telecommunication Union, Telecommunications*.

jughead

An Internet search service named as a pun on the Archie comic strip. Jughead is not used as frequently as archie and veronica.

kbps

(*Kilo Bits Per Second*) A measure of the rate of data transmission equal to *1000* bps. Also see *bps*, *mbps*, *bandwidth*, and *baud*.

LAN

Abbreviation for *Local Area Network*.

LISTSERV

(*electronic mailing LIST SERVer*) A program that maintains lists of electronic mail addresses. A user can request that LISTSERV add their e-mail address to a list or delete their e-mail address.

Local Area Network

(*LAN*) A computer network technology designed to connect computers across a short distance (e.g., inside a building). Compare to *Wide Area Network (WAN)*.

login

The process of entering an account identifier and password to obtain access to a timesharing computer.

long-haul network

A synonym for Wide Area Network.

mail alias

A synonym for *e-mail alias*.

mailbox

A storage area, usually on disk, that holds incoming e-mail messages until a user reads the mail. Each mailbox has a unique address; a user must have a mailbox to receive electronic mail.

mail exploder

A program that accepts an e-mail message, and sends a copy of the message to each recipient on a list. Mail exploders make it possible to create an electronic mailing list with many users; an e-mail message sent to the list reaches all recipients.

mailbox address

A synonym for *e-mail address*.

mailing list

An electronic mail address that includes a list of recipients. Mailing lists have become popular as a way to disseminate information.

mbps

(*Millions of Bits Per Second*) A measure of the rate of data transmission equal to one million bps. Also see *bps*, *kbps*, *bandwidth*, and *baud*.

menu

A list of items from which a user can select. Some Internet services permit a user to browse information by following a sequence of menus.

MIME

Abbreviation for *Multipurpose Internet Mail Extensions*.

modem

(*modulator – demodulator*) A device used to transmit digital data a long distance across an analog transmission path. The path can consist of a long wire or a connection through the dial-up telephone system. Modems are used in pairs – one modem attaches to each end of the connection. The modem contains a modulator (used to send data) and a demodulator (used to receive data).

moderated newsgroup

A netnews discussion group in which each submission must be sent to a person who checks and edits the contents before making the memo available to the newsgroup.

modulation

The technique a modem uses to encode digital data in an electrical signal for transmission across a wire. Modulation can also be used over telephone connections. Also see *demodulation* and *carrier*.

modulator

The electronic device in a modem that encodes data for transmission. See *demodulator*.

Mosaic

A single, complex computer program that provides a point-and-click interface to the World Wide Web, gopher, and other Internet services. Mosaic contains the code for multiple client programs, and can act like a client for a specific service.

Multipurpose Internet Mail Extensions

(*MIME*) Although Internet e-mail messages can contain only ASCII text, MIME extensions allow an e-mail message to contain a non-ASCII file such as a video image or a sound. To transfer a non-ASCII message, both the sender and receive need special e-mail software that understands MIME.

Multi-User Dungeon

A popular Internet game.

mud

The name of the multi-user dungeon game program.

multicast

The technique used to send a given packet to a selected set of other computers. Internet audio and video services use multicast delivery to send a packet from a single source to many computers on the Internet, or to allow a group of users to interact in an audio or video teleconference. Compare to *unicast* and *broadcast*.

multimedia

A term describing any facility that can display text, graphics, images, and sounds. A computer needs special hardware to handle multimedia output.

National Information Infrastructure

(NII) The emerging information infrastructure in the United States; the Internet forms the first part of the infrastructure. See also *information superhighway*.

navigating the Internet

A phrase used by the popular press that means, "using Internet services to browse information."

Netiquette

A list of suggestions for how to behave when using the Internet. Many are common sense.

netnews

Abbreviation for *network news*.

network news

The name of the Internet bulletin board service.

network of networks

A phrase used to describe the Internet; the characterization is appropriate because the Internet consists of many physical networks interconnected by routers.

network printer

A printer that attaches directly to a network where it can be accessed by any computer on the network. A network printer contains a small microprocessor that handles communication details.

news article

A message that appears on a bulletin board in the network news service. Each news article has the same form as an electronic mail memo.

newsfeed

An agreement by which one site sends copies of network news articles to another. A given site can arrange for multiple newsfeeds to ensure that it receives network news when one of the connections fails.

newsgroup

A single bulletin board in the network news service. A single user can subscribe to multiple newsgroups; each newsgroup contains articles related to one topic.

NFS

(*Network File System*) A service that allows cooperating computers to access each other's file systems as if they were local. The key difference between NFS and FTP is that NFS accesses pieces of a file as needed without copying the entire file.

NII

Abbreviation for *National Information Infrastructure.*

NSF

(*National Science Foundation*) A U.S. government agency that has funded the development of a WAN for the Internet and helped scientists connect to the Internet. NSF has also funded individual researchers working in the network area as well as large projects spanning multiple institutions.

NSFNET

(*National Science Foundation NETwork*) Loosely used to describe the Wide Area Network that forms the backbone of the Internet in the United States.

open system

A non-proprietary technology or system; any vendor can use the specifications of an open system to build products and services. The Internet and its technologies are *open.*

packet

Used informally to describe the unit of data sent across a packet switching network. An Internet packet is called an IP datagram.

packet switching

A technique used on computer networks that requires a computer to divide a message into small packets of data before sending them. Like most computer networks, the Internet uses packet switching.

password

The secret code a user enters to gain access to a timesharing system or to obtain authorization for the FTP service. A computer does not display a password while the user enters it. Anonymous FTP allows a user to enter the password *guest* to obtain access to public files.

peer-to-peer networking

Any network system in which all computers are equal. That is, a program running on one computer can contact a program running on another computer.

ph

The name of the client program used with the *qi* information service. *Ph* provides information about an individual (e.g., the person's electronic mail address).

ping

(Packet InterNet Groper) The name of a program used with TCP/IP internets to test whether a specific computer can be reached. Ping sends the computer a packet and waits for a reply. The term is often used like a verb as in, "please ping computer *hobbes* to see if it is alive."

point-and-click interface

A style of interacting with a computer that uses a mouse instead of a keyboard. The user moves the mouse to position the cursor, and presses a button on the mouse to select the item under the cursor.

Point-to-Point Protocol

(PPP) A protocol used to send TCP/IP traffic across a serial transmission line. Also see *SLIP*, which is used more frequently on personal computers.

postmaster

By convention, an e-mail alias for the person who manages the electronic mail software on a given computer. One can address a request to *postmaster @ computer* to ask questions about the site or the rules for joining or leaving a mailing list.

Post, Telegraph, and Telephone

(PTT) In European countries, the government organization that controls data networking.

PPP

An abbreviation for *Point-to-Point Protocol.*

private e-mail

Electronic mail that has been encrypted using a secret key so that only the sender and receiver can interpret it. Usually, e-mail messages are sent across the Internet with no encryption, which means that a wiretapper who intercepts an e-mail message can read the contents.

prospero

A distributed file system that can be used to access the archie service.

protocol

The rules two or more computers must follow to exchange messages. A protocol describes both the format of messages that can be sent as well as the way a computer should respond to each message.

PTT

Abbreviation for Post, Telegraph, and Telephone.

public files

Files that are available to any Internet user. When using the FTP service, public files can be accessed with login *anonymous.*

public mailing list

An electronic mailing list to which anyone can add themselves, delete themselves, or send a memo. A memo sent to a public mailing list can reach many people.

Request For Comments

(RFC) The name of a series of notes that contain the TCP/IP protocol standards as well as related documents. RFCs are available on the Internet.

qi

The name of the server accessed by the *ph* program.

remote login

A service that allows a user on one computer to connect their keyboard and display to a remote computer and run programs. See *TELNET.*

RFC

Abbreviation for *Request For Comments.*

route

In general, a route is the path that network traffic takes from its source to its destination. In a TCP/IP internet, each IP datagram follows a path through a sequence of networks and routers.

router

A special purpose, dedicated computer that attaches to two or more networks and routes IP datagrams from one to the other. Each router forwards a datagram to another router until the datagram can be delivered to its final destination.

search key

A string of characters that a user provides to a search service. The service searches for titles or documents that contain the string.

search tool

Any program that permits a user to find the location of information. In particular, automated search tools operate without requiring the user to interact during the search.

Serial Line IP

(SLIP) A protocol that permits a computer to use TCP/IP over a serial communication medium (e.g., a telephone line). A personal computer often uses SLIP software to connect to the Internet.

server

A program that offers a service. Many computers on the Internet run servers to offer services. A user invokes a client program on their computer; the client contacts a server on a remote computer.

SLIP

Abbreviation for *Serial Line IP*.

smiley

A sequence of characters, usually found in an e-mail message, that indicates humorous intent. The three-character sequence :-) is especially popular because it resembles a smiling face turned sideways.

source address

The address of the computer sending data. Each packet contains the address of the source computer as well as the address of the destination computer.

stack

A term that refers to all the TCP/IP software on a computer. The term arises from the way software is organized internally.

surfing the Internet

A slang phrase used by the popular press that means, ''using Internet services to browse information.''

talk

A program that allows two users to communicate using keyboards and display screens. Each user's screen is divided in half; one half shows what the user types, while the other half shows what the other person types.

TCP

Abbreviation for *Transmission Control Protocol.*

TCP/IP

Literally, the name of protocols that specify how computers communicate on the Internet. Informally, the name refers to the software that implements the protocols. All computers that use the Internet need TCP/IP software.

The TCP/IP Internet Protocol Suite

The official name of TCP/IP.

TELNET

The Internet remote login service. TELNET allows a user at one site to interact with a remote timesharing system at another site as if the user's terminal connected directly to the remote machine.

text file

Any file that consists of textual characters separated into lines. Text files on the Internet use the ASCII character encoding. Non-text files are often called *binary files.*

textual interface

A style of interacting with a computer that uses a keyboard. A user enters keystrokes to which the computer responds. Compare to *point-and-click interface.*

timesharing computer

A computer system that permits multiple users to run programs at the same time. Unlike personal computers, most large computers are designed as timesharing systems.

token ring

Technically, a type of Local Area Network (LAN) technology in which the network passes from computer to computer in a complete cycle. Informally, the term refers to a specific Local Area Network product sold by IBM Corporation.

traceroute

A program that permits a user to find the path a packet will take as it crosses the Internet to a specific destination. *Traceroute* prints one line for each router along the path.

Transmission Control Protocol

(TCP) One of the two major TCP/IP protocols. TCP handles the difficult task of ensuring that all data arrives at the destination in the correct order. The term often refers to software that implements the TCP standard.

traveling the information superhighway

A phrase used by the popular press that means, "using Internet services to browse information."

trickle

A service that provides electronic mail access to FTP. A user sends an e-mail message to a *trickle* server; the server reads the message, obtains a copy of the file, and transmits an e-mail reply that contains the copy.

unicast

The usual technique for sending a packet through the Internet from a single source to a single destination. Compare to *broadcast* and *multicast*.

Uniform Resource Locator

(URL) A short character string used by Mosaic and other programs to identify a particular page of information. Given a Uniform Resource Locator, Mosaic can fetch and display a page of information quickly.

UNIX

A particular computer operating system developed at AT&T Bell Laboratories.

URL

Abbreviation for *Uniform Resource Locator*.

USENET

The term that applies to the group of computers that exchange network news. Some USENET sites exchange information over the Internet; others use telephone connections.

UUCP

(*Unix to Unix Copy Program*) Software developed in the mid 1970s that allows one computer to copy files to or from another over a (usually dial-up) connection. UUCP was used in the original version of USENET.

veronica

An automated search service available through gopher. Veronica permits one to search through gopher menus for a given string. Because veronica has been integrated with gopher, one can use gopher to access veronica and to display the results of a search.

video teleconference service

A service that allows a group of users to exchange video information over the Internet. Most video teleconferences include an audio teleconference facility. Each participant's computer must have a camera, microphone, and earphones (or speaker).

virtual network

Although the Internet consists of many physical networks interconnected by routers, communication software makes the Internet appear to be a single, large network. The term *virtual network* is used to refer to the appearance of a single, seamless network system.

WAIS

Abbreviation for *Wide Area Information Server*.

WAN

Abbreviation for *Wide Area Network*.

whiteboard service

A service that permits a group of users to establish a session that permits all of them to see and modify the same display. The display can begin blank or can start with a document. Whenever a participant modifies the display by adding text or graphics, all other users see the changes immediately. A whiteboard service is usually combined with an audio teleconference service.

Web

See *World Wide Web*.

whois

An Internet service that looks up information about a user in a database. Originally, information about Internet users was stored in a central database. As the Internet grew, a single database became impractical. Many organizations now run a *whois* server that provides information about users in the organization. Also see *ph*.

Wide Area Information Server

(WAIS) An Internet automated search service that permits one to locate documents that contain key words or phrases.

Wide Area Network

(WAN) Any network technology that can span large geographic distances. Compare to *Local Area network (LAN)*. Also called long-haul networks, WANs usually cost more than LANs.

window

A rectangular area on a screen devoted to one particular application program. Windows can overlap, and a user can move windows on top of other windows. When a computer uses Internet services, a window can connect to a remote computer.

World Wide Web

(WWW) An Internet service that organizes information using hypermedia. Each document can contain embedded references to images, audio, or other documents. A user browses for information by following references.

WWW

Abbreviation for *World Wide Web*.

X Window system

A particular window system that is popular among Internet users. The X window system permits each window to connect to a remote computer.

X.25

An older networking technology popular in Europe.

X.500

A standard for building a directory service. The directory can be used to store individuals' names and e-mail addresses or other information. Some X.500 directories can be reached via the Internet.

Index

-request (in email) 155
10Base-T 283
@ (in e-mail) 148

A

A-to-D converter 21, 283
abort 186, 187
abort key 186
ACK 283
acknowledgement 118, 284
address 92, 284
Advanced Networks and Services 69, 284
Advanced Research Projects Agency 54, 284
American Standard Code for Information Interchange 34, 284
analog 284
analog devices 16
Analog-to-Digital converter 21, 284
anonymous FTP 175, 284
ANS 69
ANSNET 69, 284
archie 225, 261, 284
ARPA 285
ARPANET 54, 285
article 159
ASCII 34, 173, 174, 285
ascii command 174
astra 278
Asynchronous Transfer Mode 285
at sign character 148

ATM 285
audio teleconference 253, 285
authorization 175
automated search service 223, 224, 285

B

backbone 55
backbone network 103, 285
backbone site 103
backup newsfeed 166
bandwidth 252, 285
baseball 160
baud 285
bell 178
Berkeley 62
best-effort delivery 286
bicycle 239
binary 174
binary digit 30, 286
binary file 173, 286
binary transfer 174
bit 30, 286
BITNET 74, 286
bits per second 286
bookmark 204, 221, 286
bps 286
broadcast 286
browsing 224, 286
btw 287
bulletin board service 157, 287
byte 112

C

camera 252
carbon copy 146
card catalog 263
carrier 32, 287
Cc 146, 287
CCITT 74
CD 19
Central Processing Unit 287
channel 90
checksum 287
circuit board 40
clari 160
Clark, David 138
client 124, 147, 287
client-server computing 123, 287
closed system 56
code
    ASCII 35
    Morse 26
collapsed backbone 287
communication protocol 107
comp newsgroup 160
compact disc 19
CompuServe 152, 288
computer conference 158, 288
computer network 31, 288
conference 158
congestion 137
connection 288
connectionless 288
Consultative Committee for International
    Telephone and Telegraph 74
CPU 288
CSNET 64, 288
cso 280

D

D-to-A converter 22, 288
DARPA 54, 288
dash 26
data file 171
datagram 111, 288

Defense Advanced Research Projects
    Agency 54, 288
demodulation 32, 289
demodulator 32, 289
Department of Defense 66
destination address 92, 289
Dewey Decimal System 264
digital 19, 289
digital device 20
digital library 263, 289
Digital-to-Analog converter 22, 289
dir 175
directory 171, 175, 177, 289
directory listing 175
directory of servers 242
directory service 225
discussion group 158
distortion 18
distributed computing 122, 289
DNS 131, 289
DOD 66
domain name 131, 290
Domain Name System 131, 290
dot 26
dotted decimal 290
double-clicking 195

E

e-mail 144, 264, 290
e-mail address 290
e-mail alias 149, 290
EARN 74, 76, 290
EBCDIC 173
EBONE 76, 290
electronic bulletin board service 290
electronic mail 144, 261, 290
escape 186
escape key 186
Ethernet 45, 291
European Academic And Research
    Network 74, 76
exact 227
exponential growth 70, 291

F

FAQ 169, 291
FDDI 291
fiber 99, 291
file 171
file copy 172
file retrieval 173
file server 291
File Transfer Protocol 172, 291
finger 278, 291
flame 291
flow control 292
folder 171, 175, 177, 292
Frequently Asked Questions 169, 292
FTP 172, 190, 261, 264, 292
    client 179
    server 179
FTP authorization 175
FTP command
    ascii 174
    bell 178
    binary 174
    bye 172, 175, 177
    dir 175
    get 172, 173, 175, 177
    hash 178
    ls 175, 176, 177
    open 172, 173, 175, 176
    send 173
FTP example 175
FTP public file 175
FYA 292
FYI 292

G

get 173
global Internet 73
golden gophers 191
gopher 191, 261, 292
gopher client 192
gopher server 192
guest 175

H

hash 178
header 92
homepage 221, 292
hop count 292
host 129, 292
hostname 129, 292
hotlist 221, 293
HTML 293
HTTP 293
hub 293
hypermedia 212, 293
hypertext 210, 293

I

IAB 65, 293
IBM 68
IEN 57
IETF 66, 293
IMHO 293
information browsing service 189, 293
information superhighway 294
infrastructure 81, 294
integrated circuit 19, 294
International Telecommunication Union,
    Telecommunications 74, 294
Internet 54, 294
internet 54
Internet Activities Board 65
Internet address 112, 294
Internet Architect 65
Internet Architecture Board 66, 294
Internet Engineering Note 57
Internet Engineering Task Force 66, 294
Internet Multicasting Service 253, 294
Internet Protocol 55, 108, 294
Internet Relay Chat 278, 295
Internet Society 65, 295
internetwork 54
    see internet
internetworking 295
InterNIC 177, 277, 295
interstate highway system 82

IP 55, 108, 136, 295
IP address 112, 295
IP datagram 108, 295
IPng 295
IRC 278, 295
ITUT 74, 295

J

JANET 76
Joint Academic NETwork 76
jughead 236, 295

K

kbps 296

L

LAN 39, 42, 49, 296
LISTSERV 279, 296
Local Area Network 39, 296
logging out 183
login 182, 296
login identifier 182
long-haul network 51, 296
ls 175

M

mail alias 149, 296
mail exploder 152, 296
mailbox 144, 296
mailbox address 144, 296
mailing list 151, 296
master-slave 121
mbps 297
MCI 68
menu 191, 297
MERIT 68
MIME 297
minicomputer 39, 49
misc newsgroup 160
modem 32, 297
moderated newsgroup 164, 297
modulation 32, 297

modulator 32, 297
Morse code 26
Morse, Samuel 26
Mosaic 214, 297
mud 279, 298
Multi-User Dungeon 279, 298
multicast 298
multicasting 253
multimedia 211, 298
multiple media 211
Multipurpose Internet Mail
    Extensions 297

N

name 127, 159
National Aeronautics And Space
    Administration (NASA) 66
National Information Infrastructure 298
National Science Foundation 64
navigating 223
navigating the Internet 298
netfind 279
Netiquette 168, 298
netnews 159, 298
network 31
network news 157, 159, 261, 298
network of networks 105, 298
network packet 111
network printer 94, 298
news 157
news article 159, 299
news newsgroup 160
news reader 162
newsfeed 160, 299
newsgroup 159, 299
NFS 279, 299
NII 299
nocase 228
non-selfreferential 310
NSF 64, 299
NSF Mid-Level Networks 68
NSF Regional Networks 68
NSFNET 67, 68, 299
NSFNET backbone 68

O

open 173, 175
open system 56, 299
optical fiber 99

P

packet 91, 111, 299
packet switching 91, 300
page down 163
parity bit 36
password 182, 300
peer-to-peer networking 122, 300
ph 280, 300
ping 280, 300
point-and-click interface 193, 230, 300
Point-to-Point Protocol 300
Post, Telegraph, and Telephone 74, 300
postmaster 155, 300
PPP 301
printer 94
private e-mail 301
prospero 280, 301
protocol 107, 301
PTT 74, 301
public files 175, 301
public mailing list 151, 301

Q

qi 280, 301

R

rec 160
rec newsgroup 160
reliability 137
remote login 301
Request For Comments 57, 301
retransmission 119
RFC 57, 301
RFC Editor 65
rn 162
route 302
router 102, 302

routing 102

S

Samuel Morse 26
sci newsgroup 160
search key 302
search tool 224, 302
searching 224
send 173
Serial Line IP 302
server 124, 147, 302
signal loss 18
SLIP 302
smiley 146, 169, 302
soc newsgroup 160
source 241
source address 92, 302
space bar 163
speaker 252
stack 303
standards 136
subscribe 164
supercomputer 67
surfing the Internet 303

T

talk 280, 303
talk newsgroup 160
task force 65
TCP 55, 117, 137, 303
TCP/IP 55, 57, 58, 59, 86, 117, 123,
    135, 137, 138, 179
TCP/IP software 120
TCP/IP standards 136
TCP/IP 303
telegraph 25
TELNET 186, 227, 303
text file 173, 303
textual interface 303
The TCP/IP Internet Protocol Suite 55,
    303
timesharing computer 303
timesharing system 181

token ring   304
traceroute   281, 304
transistor   19
Transmission Control Protocol   55, 117,
    304
traveling the information
    superhighway   304
trickle   281, 304

U

U. C. Berkeley   62
unicast   304
Uniform Resource Locator   216, 304
universal delivery   82
universal service   9
UNIX   62, 304
Unix to Unix Copy Program   74
unsubscribe   164
URL   216, 304
USENET   159, 304
UUCP   74, 305

V

veronica   198, 233, 261, 305
video teleconference service   305
video teleconferencing   257
virtual network   109, 305

W

WAIS   198, 240, 261, 305
WAN   51, 305
Web   305
whiteboard service   255, 305
whois   281, 305
Wide Area Information Server   240, 306
Wide Area Network   51, 306
window   186, 306
working groups   66
World Wide Web   213, 261, 306
WWW   306

X

X Window system   281, 306
X.25   75, 306
X.500   282, 306

The Series Of Internetworking Books
from Douglas Comer and Prentice Hall

Internetworking With TCP/IP Volume I: Principles, Protocols, and Architecture   2nd ed., 1991, ISBN 0-13-468505-9

The classic reference in the field for anyone who wants to understand Internet technology, Volume I surveys the TCP/IP and describes each component. The highly accessible text presents the scientific principles used in the construction of TCP/IP, and shows how the components were designed to work together. It covers details of each protocol, including ARP, RARP, IP, TCP, UDP, RIP, OSPF and others.

Internetworking With TCP/IP Volume II: Design, Implementation, and Internals (with D. Stevens)   2nd ed: 1994, ISBN 0-13-125527-4

Ideal for implementors, Volume II continues the discussion of Volume I by using code from a running implementation of TCP/IP to illustrate all the details. The text shows, for example, how TCP's slow start algorithm interacts with the Partridge-Karn exponential retransmission backoff, and how routing updates interact with datagram forwarding.

Internetworking With TCP/IP Volume III: Client-Server Programming and Applications (with D. Stevens)
BSD Socket Version: 1992, ISBN 0-13-474222-2
AT&T TLI Version: 1993, ISBN 0-13-474230-3

Volume III describes the fundamental concept of client-server computing used to build all distributed computing systems. The text discusses various server designs as well as the tools and techniques used to build clients and servers, including Remote Procedure Call (RPC). It contains examples of running programs that illustrate each of the designs and tools. Two versions of volume III are available for the widely used BSD socket and AT&T TLI interfaces.

The Internet Book: Everything you need to know about computer networking and how the Internet works
Paperback: 1994, ISBN 0-13-151565-9
Study Guide: 1994, ISBN 0-13-188012-8
Book plus Study Guide: 1994, ISBN 0-13-400029-3

A gentle introduction to networking and the Internet, *The Internet Book* does not assume the reader has a technical background. It explains the Internet, how it works, and services available in general terms, without focusing on a particular computer or a particular brand of software. Ideal for someone who wants to become Internet and computer networking literate, *The Internet Book* explains the terminology as well as the concepts; an extensive glossary of terms and abbreviations is included. A separate *Study Guide* provides suggestions for readers, review questions, and exercises).

To order from North America, contact your local bookstore, call 1-515-284-6761 or send a FAX 1-515-284-2607 Outside North America, contact your Prentice Hall representative